Stephen Leacock

Humour and Humanity

GERALD LYNCH

McGill-Queen's University Press
Kingston and Montreal

© McGill-Queen's University Press 1988
ISBN 0-7735-0652-7

Legal deposit third quarter 1988
Bibliothèque nationale du Québec

Printed in Canada on acid-free paper

This book has been published with the help of a grant from the Canadian Federation for the Humanities, using funds provided by the Social Sciences and Humanities Research Council of Canada.

Canadian Cataloguing in Publication Data

Lynch, Gerald, 1953–
    Rounded with a smile: Stephen Leacock's tory-humanist humour
    Includes bibliographical references and index.
    ISBN 0-7735-0652-7
    1. Leacock, Stephen, 1869–1944 – Criticism and interpretation. I. Title.
    PS8523.E15Z76 1988   C818'.5209   C88-090143-8
    PR9199.3.L367Z78 1988

This book is dedicated to Mary Jo.

Contents

Preface

Stephen Leacock is still often regarded as a writer of lightweight amusements and unchallenging satire, as an author without an imaginative centre who lacked a vision of sufficient power and clarity to sustain a lifetime of serious writing. According to this view, which has been too easily accepted, Leacock squandered an early, promising talent (though he was, in fact, middle-aged when in 1912 he published *Sunshine Sketches of a Little Town*), and consequently his writings, like his legendary Lord Ronald, "rode madly off in all directions." After years of chasing down Leacock's numerous literary mounts, I can assert that none of this is true. Leacock's writings emerge from a centre that is the confluence of the two traditions of humanism and toryism, traditions that found in Leacock fertile ground for the propagation of such qualities as a tolerance of human fallibility and an acceptance of social responsibility. What is remarkable with respect to Leacock's literary output is that even his furthest-flung, seemingly inconsequential humorous pieces move in relation to this tory-humanist centre. Without an understanding of Leacock's humanism and toryism, the understanding that he made readily accessible in *The Unsolved Riddle of Social Justice* (1920) and *Our Heritage of Liberty* (1942), even his theory of humour will seem, especially in view of his otherwise firmly stated opinions, somehow curiously limp, if not insipid, in its insistence on the need for "kindliness." And without the context of Leacock's tory humanism and theory of humour, his two most accomplished works of fiction, *Sunshine Sketches* and *Arcadian Adventures With the Idle Rich* (1914), will continue to be misread or to be less than fully appreciated, or they will mistakenly be considered exceptionally indicative of Leacock's "unfulfilled literary promise."

In this study I first present and discuss Leacock's tory-humanist philosophy and ground his theory of kindly humour in that tory humanism. I then examine *Sunshine Sketches* and *Arcadian Adventures* in light of that tory-humanist philosophy and theory of humour. Considered together, the *Sketches* and the *Adventures* ultimately reveal what was for Leacock a real difference between the United States and Canada: the ascent to dominance in the former of liberal individualism (Plutoria) and the presence for imaginative retrieval in the latter of an interdependent community (Mariposa). Of equal importance in a general sense, my study of Leacock shows him to be a thinker, a humorist, and a literary artist of an order not usually accorded him.

The late Desmond Pacey observed in *Creative Writing in Canada* that Leacock was the "only one" of his fiction-writing Canadian contemporaries in the early twentieth century who challenged, satirized, and attempted to order the crassly commercial, chaotic age in which he lived.[1] But in the cult of personality that understandably has gathered around Leacock, criticism of his writings has lagged far behind the biographies, reminiscences, and oral histories. I hope this book helps to make up the difference.

Acknowledgments

The present study owes much to the advice and encouragement of D.M.R. Bentley of the University of Western Ontario. Without his generous contribution this book would not have been written. I am grateful to J.M. Zezulka, also of Western, who read the manuscript with a keen objectivity that expanded its range at a number of points, and to Joan Irving and Joan McGilvray, my editors at McGill-Queen's University Press. Thank you to Mary Jo Lynch for diligent proofreading and unstinting encouragement. To Marie McKinnon of the University of Ottawa, many thanks for her proficiency at the computer keyboard. And thank you to my colleagues in the Department of English at the University of Ottawa for their advice and encouragement, especially Glenn Clever, Seymour Mayne, David Rampton, David Staines, and Frank Tierney.

Portions of this study have been published previously, though with substantial differences, in the following: *Studies in Canadian Literature* 9, no. 2 (1984); *Saturday Night*, September 1985; *Stephen Leacock: A Reappraisal*, ed. David Staines (Ottawa: University of Ottawa Press 1986); *Canadian Notes and Queries* no. 34 (Winter 1985); and *Canadian Literature* no. 107 (Winter 1985).

This book has been published with the help of a grant from the Canadian Federation for the Humanities, using funds provided by the Social Sciences and Humanities Research Council of Canada. Final work on the manuscript was completed while I held a Canada

Research Fellowship at the University of Ottawa. I am grateful to SSHRC for its generous support.

Abbreviations

BOOKS BY STEPHEN LEACOCK

AA   *Arcadian Adventures With the Idle Rich*.
     Toronto: Bell & Cockburn; London: John
     Lane 1914.

CD   *Charles Dickens: His Life and Work*. Garden
     City, N.Y.: Doubleday 1934.

ELS *Essays and Literary Studies*. London: John
     Lane 1916.

HH   *Humour and Humanity: An Introduction to
     the Study of Humour*. London: Thornton
     Butterworth 1937.

HL   *Our Heritage of Liberty: Its Origin, Its
     Achievement, Its Crisis; A Book for War Time*.
     London: John Lane 1942.

HTT *Humour, Its Theory and Technique: With
     Examples and Samples; a Book of Discovery*.
     London: John Lane 1935.

HTW *How To Write*. New York: Dodd, Mead
     1943.

LL *Last Leaves*. New York: Dodd, Mead 1945.

RU *My Remarkable Uncle and Other Sketches*. New York: Dodd, Mead 1942.

SS *Sunshine Sketches of a Little Town*. Toronto: Bell & Cockburn; New York: John Lane 1912.

UR *The Unsolved Riddle of Social Justice*. New York: John Lane; Toronto: S.B. Gundy 1920.

Stephen Leacock: Humour and Humanity

CHAPTER ONE

The Middle Way: An Introduction to Leacock's Tory-Humanist Norm

> As man is ever the prime object to man, already it was my favourite employment to read character in speculation, and from the Writing to construe the Writer.
>
> Carlyle, *Sartor Resartus*

The critic who would present a comprehensive study of Stephen Leacock's writings soon encounters a seemingly insurmountable obstacle: how to provide a context for his sixty-odd books and pamphlets and his virtually uncountable essays and newspaper articles. Peter McArthur first noted the problem in his *Stephen Leacock* (1923): "A careful reading of Mr. Leacock's works with a view to discovering the man back of them," McArthur writes, "is an exhilarating, but somewhat bewildering task."[1] McArthur's anthology and appreciation, which was published when Leacock had twenty-one years of a prolific writing career remaining, suggests the approach that will be taken in this chapter to the initial problem confronting the ambitious Leacock critic: establish the views of the man, then go "back of the fiction."

Leacock was a tory – a democratic, not an aristocratic or especially elitist tory. Nor should Leacock's toryism be associated with the present-day Conservatism (or "neo-Conservatism") that is often aligned with big business. As Charles Taylor writes in his *Radical Tories*, "Unlike the caricatured capitalist, Canadian conservatives believe in an organic society and the mutual obligations among all classes. Which is why ... they embrace the principle of social justice and even the welfare state."[2] Taylor begins his exploration of the Canadian tory tradition with Leacock, and his penultimate definition of a Canadian toryism is especially applicable to him: toryism, he writes, is "based on a sense of community and order, a feeling for the land, a respect for human diversity and human rights, a concern for social justice, and a non-ideological approach to the problems of political and economic organization."[3] Taylor ultimately defines toryism as follows: "Above all ... tories have a sense of reverence. Defending human dignity, they also recognize human fallibility ... They know that we are part of some larger order, which we can only dimly comprehend, and which must command our allegiance. This is the ultimate source of their optimism."[4] Taylor's use of such words as "reverence," "dignity," "fallibility," and "allegiance" suggests that he may have been aware of Erwin Panofsky's earlier succinct definition of humanism, a definition which is also especially pertinent to a study of Leacock. "Humanism," Panofsky writes, is "an attitude which can be defined as the conviction of the dignity of man, based on both the insistence of human values (rationality and freedom) and the acceptance of human limitations (fallibility and frailty); from these two postulates results – responsibility and tolerance."[5] The similarity between Taylor's definition of toryism and Panofsky's of humanism suggests how nineteenth-century toryism grew out of the eighteenth-century humanism that originated in the Renaissance and, indeed, why these two concepts are ideally suited to describe Leacock's social-political philosophy.

Two of Leacock's titles, *The Garden of Folly* and *Our Heritage of Liberty* – the first describing a work of fiction, the second an historical analysis of liberty – aptly illustrate his tory-humanist's view of mankind's inherent weaknesses (fallibility) and traditional strengths (responsibility)[6]. Desmond Pacey was the first to remark the unifying toryism in Leacock's work, observing that it "was the Toryism of Burke and Goldsmith."[7] Ralph Curry was the first to suggest that Leacock's work is unified also by its humanism.[8] It is to such views of Leacock's humour and non-fiction, as unified by his tory humanism, that the present study subscribes and owes a debt of gratitude. But these observations require what is frequently lacking in the many general studies of Leacock's writings – illustration and analysis.

Leacock, though not a religious man in the conventional sense, adhered to a secular version of the Anglican *via media*. His voluminous writings are consistent with the thoughts and feelings of a writer who expounded a tory-humanist "middle way."[9] With few exceptions, his non-fiction reveals a belief in a mediating approach to all problems. His views on many subjects, particularly social justice and liberty, represent an attempt to balance the rights of the individual and the needs of the social organism, to temper the extremes of liberalism and socialism. Believing that society was a developing organic whole, Leacock was wary of any capitalist scheme or any plan that ignored man's responsibility to mankind or was intolerant of human fallibility. In Leacock's view, the social organism should be neither radically altered nor left untended: the way of the extreme left would lead to the destruction of the social organism; the course of the extreme right would encourage a plutocratic law of the jungle, the sacrificing of social justice to individual liberty. It was not by chance that Harold Macmillan, one of the last true tories in British politics, found a typically pithy Leacock line congenial to his own view of socialism. In his book, appropriately entitled *The Middle Way*, Macmillan observes, "A wit once said that Socialism is workable only in Heaven where it is not needed, and in hell where they already have it."[10] It is both revealing of Leacock's place in the tradition of toryism and a testimony to the manner in which those values he championed have remained the values of modern tory thought that Macmillan did not seem to know whom he was paraphrasing in support of his "middle-way" view.[11]

G.G. Sedgewick perceived in 1945 what most subsequent critics have failed to observe, namely, that "no schism existed … between Leacock the serious critic of affairs and Leacock the humorist." "Great humour," continued Sedgewick, "is the product of a whole creative effort."[12] Robertson Davies also recognized that humour was "in the grain of [Leacock's] intelligence." "A humorist is a humorist," remarked Davies, "for the same reason that a poet is a poet; he has a disposition of mind, a bias of sensibility."[13] The appearance of inconsistency in Leacock's work stemmed from an orientation towards life and literature that was eclectic and far-ranging. His moderating approach to problems does, on occasion, reveal an unwillingness to commit himself; his middle-way methods sometimes convey the impression that compromise – the reputed bane of his beloved nineteenth century – was his truest art. And yet, his willingness to compromise in social-political questions also reveals the Leacock who admired Charles II because the king saw "things as they are" and knew "that no opinion is altogether right, no purpose altogether laudable, and no calamity altogether deplorable" (*ELS*, 225). Charles Taylor, in defence of such non-ideological conservatism, quotes the Canadian historian W.L. Morton: "Conservatism, unlike liberalism or socialism, [is] not constrained by dogma: 'Conservatives are the party of tradition, not the party of ideology. So they can keep going. They can pick up anything, including traditional liberalism. There's no countervailing ideology.'"[14] Although Leacock's position was non-ideological, this does not mean that he had no centre; on the contrary, his centre was an insistence on balance and equipoise in all matters, through the middle way of tory humanism.

Donald Cameron also seems to have recognized the middle way as the method behind what he calls Leacock's "little pieces": "Any loss of decorum or the sense of proportion invites Leacock's scalpel."[15] But in his chapter entitled "Who Was Stephen Leacock?" Cameron supports his perception with examples drawn mainly from Leacock's topical satires. For the most part, he overlooks Leacock's many affectionately humorous essays and quasi-fictions that deal positively with – in the hope of recovering – various aspects of a vanished or vanishing past. The essays in *My Remarkable Uncle* and the posthumously published *Last Leaves*, for example, reveal that Leacock valued continuity in human affairs and advocated, in his approach to the past, the use of imagination in the service of informed memory, and remembrance as opposed to simple, nostalgic recollection. Time and again Leacock turns to the leisurely and colourfully heightened past – to the tolerant and variegated, to the reasonable as opposed to the merely rational, and to the organic as opposed to the mechanistic – to provide the norm necessary to correct what he often perceived to be a disintegrating and somewhat decadent twentieth-century society.

At the end of the academic year Leacock always left Montreal's McGill University as soon as he could, and often before he rightfully should have. He departed from an environment not unlike the "Plutoria University" of *Arcadian Adventures* to summer in Orillia, Ontario, the small Canadian town that is generally acknowledged to have provided the model for *Sunshine Sketches'* Mariposa. The biographical information is remarked here to suggest that Leacock's fictional persona resembles, with reference to "the middle way," Maynard Mack's description of Alexander Pope's dramatic personality: "A personality who is at once the historical Alexander Pope and the fictive hero of a highly traditional confrontation between virtuous simplicity and sophisticated corruption." And as Mack further observes, touching upon the critic's chief difficulty with the many seemingly contradictory aspects of Leacock, that persona's "effectiveness is precisely in its seamlessness."[16]

Nonetheless, this loosely defined (and purposely so) tory-humanist mind informs Leacock's conception of humour. Humour is for Leacock the literary manifestation of humanism. It is the literary vehicle of the middle way. Humour exists midway between caustic satire and sentimentality, softening satire with pathos. Humour can be of service in the moral melioration of mankind, though it should not be satirically reformist, and it can offer a reprieve from disillusioning reality. Such a tory-humanist mind also controls the imagination behind Leacock's most accomplished works of fiction, *Sunshine Sketches of a Little Town* and *Arcadian Adventures with the Idle Rich*. In general terms, "Mariposa" is the past, the qualified ideal community of the Canadian tory humanist, the community eulogized for its diversity in unity yet viewed with an acknowledgment of human fault. "Plutoria," the main avenue of *Arcadian Adventures'* city, is the present (*c.* 1914), a negative exemplar of the twentieth-century tendencies of liberal individualism and materialism. Quotation marks have been placed around "Mariposa" and "Plutoria" to suggest that they are the key concepts in Leacock's work. What is worthwhile in "Mariposa" must be remembered and "remembered forward" if the extremes of mechanistic capitalism – "Plutoria" – are to be, if not defeated or avoided, at least countered. In this way, "Mariposan" (that is, imaginatively evocative of the tory-humanist's qualified ideal) and the majority being more "Plutorian" (that is, satirically directed at the follies of liberal materialism). It would be "Mariposan" (that is, imaginatively evocative of the tory-humanist's qualified ideal) and the majority being more "Plutorian" (that is, satirically directed at the follies of liberal materialism). It would be mistaken, however, simply to designate *Sunshine Sketches* the work of a kindly tory ironist and *Arcadian Adventures* the work of a kindly tory satirist. Leacock's vision of "Mariposa" and "Plutoria" is not so easily categorized. Irony and satire are present in both books in significant amounts and with varying degrees of kindliness. In both books, as in all of Leacock's fiction, there are characters who exist fully in either "Mariposa" or "Plutoria," and there are metaphorical movements of characters between the two. For example, Josh Smith of the *Sketches* is, in a metaphorical sense, on his way to "Plutoria," and the Tomlinson family of the *Adventures* sojourns in Plutoria and returns to "Mariposa."

But rather than attempt to define satire and to discuss Leacock's work in terms of his Horatian (gentle) and Juvenalian (virulent) propensities, I will follow Matthew Hodgart's sensible advice and consider further "the satirist's attitude to life."[17]

The *Literary History of Canada* enunciates the problem of Leacock's authorial disposition that is the focus of this first chapter: "Leacock has been regarded as a displaced eighteenth-century squire viewing the maddening scene of modern science and industrial organization with a benign eye from his country estate outside Orillia. He also has been seen as an irascible, embittered, witty satirist with many double-edged axes to grind. Both views have some truth in them; there are, perhaps, two Leacocks."[18] Although this statement succinctly presents the problem of unity versus dissipation in Leacock's vision, there are a couple of difficulties with the statement itself. The writers – Gordon Roper, Rupert Schieder, and S. Ross Beharriell – appear to have uncritically accepted the two opposing, and at the time (1965) prevailing, views of Leacock which were first set forth by Desmond Pacey ("eighteenth-century squire") and Robertson Davies ("irascible ... satirist").[19] As well, in leaping from the eighteenth to the twentieth century, they have overlooked the seminal influence that nineteenth-century writers had on Leacock's theory and practice of humour. Leacock believed that the nineteenth century represented the zenith of literature, especially humorous literature. He considered the unkind sort of Juvenalian satire that Davies ascribes to him to be the nadir of humorous literature. In Leacock's view, virulent satire is atavistic and regressive: he called it "grouch writing" (*HTT*, 225). He might not have resented being described as a "gentle ironist" or as an eighteenth-century squire, but he would surely have thought the descriptions to be unfairly limiting. Although it is not the purpose of this chapter systematically to trace the influence of the nineteenth century in Leacock's thought and writing, it may be noted that his non-fiction and fiction owe a debt of influence to such nineteenth-century writers as Coleridge, Hazlitt, Carlyle, Matthew Arnold, George Meredith, Dickens and Twain, W.M. Thackeray, Alphonse Daudet and Henri Bergson, as well as to a whole host of nineteenth-century American humorists whom he anthologized, and to the numerous contributors to the later *Punch*.

Over the past two decades, a few critics have attempted to restore to Leacock criticism a recognition of the importance of the nineteenth-century, or "Victorian," influence. Unfortunately, though, too much is often covered under a blanket application of the term "Victorian." For example, Leacock's first biographer, Ralph Curry, explains the important matter of Leacock's toryism as but "another of the Victorian touches in his life."[20] And David M. Legate, Leacock's next biographer, employs "Victorian" to account for far too many facets of his subject's beliefs and attitudes.[21] As Jerome H. Buckley has argued, such uses of "Victorian" are uninformed; they represent a critically naïve acceptance of what was in fact a reactionary Edwardian fiction.[22] Donald Cameron more accurately indicates the basis of the tensions that inform Leacock's writings when he points to "the gulf between [Leacock's] Victorianism and his modernism" and labels Leacock a "late and troubled Victorian."[23]

Certainly two of the most revealing of Leacock's few personal statements occur in the first paragraph of his unfinished autobiography, *The Boy I Left Behind Me*: "I was born in Victorian England, on December thirtieth in 1869, which is exactly the middle year of Queen Victoria's reign ... I am certain that I have never got over it."[24] Even a cursory reading of Leacock's work leaves the distinct impression of a writer who was never quite comfortable or, in Leacock's understanding of the phrase, "at home" in the twentieth century.

Leacock's fiction and non-fiction are most rewardingly viewed as a belated grappling with the many seemingly insoluble problems that engaged British writers of the nineteenth century. How instigate social justice? What should be the limitations of individual liberties? What function should the Anglican Church fulfill? What should be the purpose of literature? What should be the purpose of a university? What is to become of "the Empire"? Like the century itself, Leacock can appear a mixture of idealism and pragmatism, of hope and resignation, of fervency, seeming paradox, and, inevitably, of compromise. But to the questions of his day Leacock always brought what Cameron has termed "a coherent conservative view of man's nature and history." Cameron's view of Leacock's social-political orientation deserves quotation at length:

Man is selfish, deeply imperfect and imperfectible; society is in part an attempt to control these imperfections; utopian societies, however, are inevitably over-simplifications, and a society which has grown organically, whose institutions represent a gradual accretion of experience, is to be preferred even in its irrational archaisms, to a planned and regulated society. He considered the law a formal and regulated recognition of society's desire to act in certain ways. It was not a dynamic principle but a formulation after the fact.[25]

Although Cameron correctly observed that Leacock was "conservative – and Conservative,"[26] it should be kept in mind that Leacock described his political orientation as follows: "To avoid all error as to the point of view, let me say in commencing that I am a Liberal Conservative, or, if you will, a Conservative Liberal with a strong dash of sympathy with the Socialist idea, a friend of Labour, and a believer in Progressive Radicalism. I do not desire office but would take a seat in the Canadian Senate at five minutes notice."[27] And although Leacock states flatly in the preface to *Sunshine Sketches*, "In Canada I belong to the Conservative party," he immediately clarifies his involvement in practical politics, ironically regretting that he has received no political patronage and is, therefore, a "failure" (*SS*, x).

Leacock was, nonetheless, often involved in Canadian politics on the side of the Conservatives. In the 1911 general election, he helped defeat the Laurier Liberals on the issue of trade reciprocity with the United States. (This campaign is treated ironically, and somewhat cynically, in the tenth and eleventh sketches of *Sunshine Sketches*.) He disliked Mackenzie King for his narrow nationalism and his anti-imperialist views, and he publicly supported his friend, Prime Minister R.B. Bennett, who in 1935 asked Leacock to seek a seat in parliament. This said, it can be maintained that Leacock remained philosophically opposed to petty partisan politics, a view which he expressed fictionally in "Mariposa Moves On."[28] Prior to that, in 1907 he wrote disparagingly of what still remains the perennial Canadian political problem – federal and provincial self-interests:

The mud-bespattered politicians of the trade, the party men and party managers, give us in place of patriotic statecraft the sordid traffic of a tolerated jobbery. For bread, a stone. Harsh is the cackle of the little turkey-cocks of Ottawa, fighting the while as they feather their mean nests of sticks and mud, high on their river bluff. Loud sings the Little Man of the Province, crying his petty Gospel of Provincial Rights, grudging the gift of power, till the cry spreads and town hates town and every hamlet of the country side shouts for its share of plunder and pelf.[29]

No wonder that the author of these words refused Bennett's invitation to run for political office (which was just as well, because the Conservatives were routed in the 1935 campaign).

The designation "Conservative" does not do justice to the political beliefs of the mature Leacock. In *My Discovery of the West* (1937), the most Canadian of his social-political books, Leacock embraced a politically pluralistic vision of government: "I wish for our welfare we could combine those elements which have chiefly distinguished each of our political parties: the empire patriotism of the Conservative, the stubborn honesty of the Liberal, the optimism of the Socialist, the driving power of the Social Creditor, and the unsullied enthusiasm of all who write on their banner the name and the inspiration of youth."[30] As was suggested earlier, Leacock's toryism allowed him to select from various philosophies – conservatism, liberalism, socialism – the best which each had to offer for the hope of a free and compassionate society. As with his conception of the function of humour, which utilizes pathos to keep satire from degenerating into sarcasm, Leacock relied on his conservatism and socialist sympathies to point up the more alarming tendencies of the widespread liberal ideology of his time. His efforts to correct these tendencies – the materialistic-mechanistic conception of progress, the exaltation of the rights of the individual over the welfare of the community, the appreciation of the merely rational over "right reason," and the lack of respect for traditional institutions – often resulted in what Cameron has described as "eruptions of narrow-mindedness and peevishness" – "the crotchets of a tired Tory."[31] Thus Leacock's readers were treated annually to his satires on automobiles, modern education, moving pictures, trade unionism, electrical appliances, formula writing, men's and women's fashions, and so forth.

But Leacock also believed in progress, that panacea of the nineteenth century. He believed that mankind had developed morally, contended that literature had evolved from primitive beginnings to fulfilment in the nineteenth century, and considered democracy to represent considerable advancement in the political sphere. Cameron has written that "if such a Tory also genuinely believes in progress, ... he is probably going to have points of confusion."[32] This comment ignores, however, the tenacious humanism of Leacock's idea of progress. Leacock's writings frequently evince a distrust of change, and of those who view change as an advancement over traditional proven institutions. Of the decline of feudalism (to take an extreme example), he writes, "The consequences were not all good. Change seldom is" (HL, 26–7). Feudalism had saved "Europe from anarchy, and sustained it for nearly a thousand years. The essential point is that it offered a fixed setting for social life" (HL, 22–3). Yet when Leacock perceived that change was necessary, as it was with regard to the social injustice that he saw about him, or in the matter of Canada's failure to assume what he considered to be a responsible role in the British Empire (increased military spending, for example), he reprimanded those who relied passively on a philosophy of social Darwinism and thought it "best to leave well enough alone, to wait for the slow growth, the evolution of things. For herein lies the darling thought of the wisdom of the nineteenth century, in this same Evolution."[33] Like T.H. Huxley, Leacock did not dispute the Darwinian view of evolution in the material sphere, but he distinguished between this and the moral progress of mankind.[34] For Leacock, as for Huxley, man is the ethical animal; man has a responsibility to intervene in the social process when the humane and the ethical are threatened by the mechanical and the amoral. Leacock valued those institutions and traditions that had proven their usefulness, but he stressed that men must continually revitalize the mechanical form. He concluded his "apology" for the British Empire with the observation, "the point of it all is that it works" (LL, 60). But his frequent pragmatic recourse to efficacy should not be confused with an acceptance of the dehumanizing efficiency of (liberal) technological advancements. Nor should Leacock's reasonable recourse to "what works" be seen as simple political expediency: his practical suggestions, like his furthest flung humorous pieces, arise from his tory-humanist centre. Although Leacock espoused no rigid social-political dogma, he did possess a humanistic philosophy and a view of society that are deeply rooted in the tradition of toryism, that is, democratic, or Disraelian, toryism.[35]

Moreover, Leacock by no means believed that progress was assured. Progress will ensue only if those institutions that have proven worthwhile are allowed to continue developing slowly and accumulating collective experience. The true progress of mankind is endangered by such false notions of progress as technological advancement and self-development to the exclusion of a communal consciousness, as well as by liberation movements (women's suffrage) that threaten the value of human labour, the pre-eminence of the social organism, and such institutions as the home and the family. Leacock held that in the twentieth century true progress was actually poised on the brink of "retrogression" (HL, 57). His apprehension of the possibility of retrogression was not a "point of confusion" in Leacock's thought. It was a clearly defined possibility. In "The Devil and the Deep Sea: A Discussion of Modern Morality," the possibility of moral retrogression is contained in the image of the "deep sea." The Devil "with his twin incentives of pain and pleasure coaxed and prodded humanity on its path, till it reached the point where it repudiated him, called itself a Superman, and headed straight for the cliff over which is the deep sea. Quo vadimus?" (ELS, 52). Although the suggestion here is of an impending general moral catastrophe, earlier in the essay Leacock makes clear that the basis of the "new morality" is the "cult of self-development," which is retrogressive: "It arrogates to itself the title of New Thought, but contains in reality nothing but the Old Selfishness" (ELS, 45). In Humour, Its Theory and Technique, Leacock asks concerning contemporary humour (c. 1935), "Is it progressing – moving forward or backward or sideways? There is no doubt, sideways" (HTT, 255). But previous to this ambiguous assessment, he doubts that humorous literature in an age of electrical babel can ever again attain the heights it reached in the nineteenth century: "One wonders whether, in our age of flickering shadows and raucous voices, it can ever be done again. Perhaps the time is past" (HTT, 135). Leacock readily acknowledged the positive achievements of technological progress in alleviating the social squalor of the nineteenth century, but he wrote more revealingly that with the invention of the printing press "the machine began its mock servitude to man" (HL, 27; see also *UR*, 38). He was scarcely hopeful in his assessment of civilization's technological achievements: "Very few of us recognize this great truth. We have a mean little vanity over our civilisation. We are touchy about it. We do not realize that so far we have done little but increase the burden of work and multiply the means of death. But for the hope of better things to come, our civilisation would not seem worth while" (*ELS*, 146–7).

"The hope of better things to come" expresses his sincere belief. Better things will be attained, though, only by moderate means through painstaking progress, only by remembering and carrying forward the worthwhile from the past. Retrogression is ever a possibility that must be met with "constant vigilance" (*HL*, 57): post-World War One social agitation "represents a vast social transformation in which there is at stake, and may be lost, all that has been gained in the slow centuries of material progress" (*UR*, 13). The fascist tyrannies of mid-century Europe show that "Liberty is here derided, there trampled under foot, and everywhere in danger. Human kindliness is replaced by cruelties unknown for centuries" (*HL*, 8). "The Plague is still ready to leap again out of the filth of Asia, if we carry destruction far enough and cast down humanity low enough" (*HL*, 26). Leacock's suggestions for bringing about "better things" – for attempting modestly to solve the riddle of social justice, for preserving the social order and liberty – can be gleaned from any number of his essays and books. His first book, the *Elements of Political Science* (1906), a workmanlike treatment of its subject, contains passages in which Leacock's opinions surmount the requisites of a textbook. His second book, *Baldwin, Lafontaine, Hincks: Responsible Government* (1907), displays what were to be the hallmarks of Leacock's approach to social-political questions: an abiding respect for traditional institutions and the British connection mingled with a dislike of unearned privilege and a sympathy for the victims of injustice.[36] His social-political attitudes are, however, most accessible and fully developed in two or his later books, *The Unsolved Riddle of Social Justice* (1920) and *Our Heritage of Liberty* (1942). Leacock rejects out of hand any radical solution to the riddle of social justice such as revolutionary socialism, though he sympathizes with its inspiration and shares many of its objectives: "We must do this [reform the economic system] or perish. If we do not mend the machine, there are forces moving in the world that will break it. The blind Samson of labor will seize upon the pillars of society and bring them down in a common destruction" (*UR*, 13–14).

Prior to the publication of *The Unsolved Riddle of Social Justice*, Leacock had observed that "the general abolition of poverty ... is to prove the great question of the century before us" (*ELS*, 129).[37] As its title suggests, the book offers tentative answers to this "great question," though the riddle of social justice remains, in practical terms, unsolved. "The details are indistinct," writes Leacock in his conclusion. "But the outline at least in which it is framed is clear enough" (*UR*, 151). Emphasizing the correct approach to the problem of social justice, Leacock desires to infuse the discussion with the proper *spirit*. His writings on social, political, and economic questions are always predicated upon this principle. As he was to write emphatically in his poignantly succinct "To Every Child," "The fault with economics was the assumption that what *can only be done by the Spirit* could be done by material interest" (*LL*, 106).

There is much in Leacock's *Unsolved Riddle* that recalls Thomas Carlyle's *Past And Present*.[38] The *Riddle* in Leacock's title distantly echoes the question that Carlyle's "Sphinx" addresses to England – "Knowest thou the meaning of this Day? What thou canst do Today; wisely attempt to do?"[39] In Carlyle's view, the pressing problem of mid-nineteenth-century England is that "England is full of wealth, of multifarious produce, supply for human want in every kind; yet England is dying of inanition." He proceeds to elaborate the paradox: "We have more riches than any Nation ever had before; we have less good of them than any Nation ever had before. Our successful industry is hitherto unsuccessful." Leacock's presentation of the "unsolved riddle" is strikingly similar to Carlyle's:

The record of the age of machinery is known to all. But the strange mystery, the secret that lies concealed within its organization, is realized by but the few. It offers, to those who see it aright, the most perplexing industrial paradox every presented in the history of mankind. *With all our wealth we are still poor.* After a century and a half of labor-saving machinery, we work about as hard as ever. With a power over nature multiplied a hundred fold, nature still conquers us. And more than this. There are many senses in which the machine age seems to leave the great bulk of civilized humanity, the working part of it, worse off instead of better. (*UR*, 22–3, emphasis added)

In both Carlyle and Leacock there is an underlying fear of a workers' insurrection – of revolution for Carlyle, of socialism and bolshevism for Leacock. In both writers fear is mixed with compassion for those workers who constitute the potential for drastic, destructive change. Leacock is as unwilling to proffer a "Morrison's Pill" – a placebo of sorts for the "maladies of Society" – as is Carlyle.[40] "I am not one of those," writes Leacock, "who are able to see a short and simple remedy" (*UR*, 32). Carlyle's alternative to a "Morrison's Pill" is the romantic hope for the spiritual regeneration of the individual.[41] Leacock perceives, too, that "the path of human progress is arduous and its forward movement slow and that no mere form of government can aid unless it is inspired by a higher public spirit of the individual citizen than we have yet managed to achieve" (*UR*, 114). In "Casting Out Animosity," the World War Two equivalent of the *Unsolved Riddle*, Leacock is more forthrightly Carlylean in his advice for reconstruction: "I propose, my dear friend, that as a first need for a post-war world you reconstruct yourself a little; shovel up a lot of yourself and throw it away; knock yourself down and start over. And, in particular, cast away a whole lot of minor grievances and mimic animosities that the fierce light of war has brought down to their true pettiness" (*LL*, 88). As Alice Chandler has observed, the first three chapters of *Past and Present* show that for Carlyle "reform must be spiritual."[42] Such is also Leacock's contention. As was remarked earlier, he believed that the science of economics had failed mankind because economists failed to recognize the role of the spirit. His British Imperialism was not, as he argued, a "truckling subservience to English people and English ideas."[43] It was, as Cameron has observed, "a sort of limited internationalism."[44] Leacock's imperialism was simply an appeal for a "greater Canada," a call for a broader spirit of patriotism as an antidote for self-serving, narrow nationalism.[45] As he concludes *Our Heritage of Liberty*, "For all things in the world the spirit comes first. Liberty can only serve and survive among people worthy of having it. The soul alone can animate the body (*HL*, 75).

Leacock's *Unsolved Riddle* recalls Carlyle's *Past and Present* in a number of important ways: both consider the riddle of social justice as a paradox of plenty and poverty; both eschew the "Morrison-Pill" solution; both insist that meaningful, lasting reform can only be realized by the spiritual reform of the individual citizen; and both recognize that there is a "noble Conservatism" and an "ignoble," reactionary, and passive conservatism.[46] And yet, Leacock's debt to *Past and Present* is but one noteworthy instance of his debts to writers of the Victorian period. Leacock's thought in social-political and social-religious issues is suffused with echoes of the nineteenth century. Desmond Bowen has shown that, beginning with Coleridge's writings in the 1830s, a major thrust of the Church of England was to alleviate the discrepancy between rich and poor.[47] The critic of Leacock's thought in the realm of religion (particularly as that thought is expressed fictionally in the sketches on the churches in *Sunshine Sketches* and *Arcadian Adventures*) could find many nineteenth-century antecedents and possible influences for his ideas. But as has been observed, the influences on and sources of Leacock's thought are not limited to the nineteenth century. Ralph Curry observed that Leacock "had a phenomenal memory, seeming never to forget anything he had ever read, and there seemed to be nothing one could ask him that he did not know something about."[48] The critic who aspires to discover the sources of Leacock's thought in particular writers will find, as Leacock did when he attempted to follow the implications of Mill's idea of individual liberty, "how hard it is to follow consistently the thread of a single principle in a maze of circumstance" (HL, 50).[49]

The few practical reforms that Leacock recommends in the *Unsolved Riddle* and *Our Heritage of Liberty* – recommendations that distinguish his work from Carlyle's – can be briefly presented. His primary concern in both books is that the "upward path of social progress" is contingent upon "every child of the nation [having] the right to be clothed and fed and trained irrespective of its parents' lot" (UR, 138; see also HL, 67). He argues for a redirection of the machinery of production towards the necessities of life, for a government-paid minimum wage in line with what the private sector pays, and, somewhat suprisingly, for the shortening of work hours to four or five per day (UR, 144–9). Leacock holds that work is an "absolute necessity for human character" (UR, 148), but he wryly concedes, with respect to drudgery, that "many of us, as applied to ourselves, at least, would take a chance on character at two" hours per day (UR, 149). He best summarizes the essentials of his proposals for reform as follows: "Put into the plainest prose, then, we are saying that the government of every country ought to supply work and pay for the unemployed, maintenance for the infirm and aged, and education and opportunity for the children" (UR, 140). In *Liberty*, Leacock advocates the need for government censorship in time of war, and in peacetime to protect the liberty of those who can be slandered (HL, 61). He perceives that democratic governments must regulate the business practices of "monopoly" and "unfair competition" (HL, 64); and he recognizes the need for government intervention to protect tenants, for what has come to be called "rental controls" (HL, 63). He concludes the book with a relatively lengthy plan for a system of government housing. Of the existence of "slums" he writes, "Strange that civilized humanity, for generations past, was too absorbed in needless hates and vain ambitions to have time to burn with indignation at such a sin" (HL, 69). In charming detail, he then concludes his plan for a government-subsidized "Tudor style" house: "Set it back ten feet from the street – a little ten-foot garden all ablaze with flowers – have you any notion of the magic of it?" (*HL*, 70). Such is Leacock's closing advice in *Our Heritage of Liberty* – improved row-housing for Canada, England, and the United States. The "magic of it" resides in the fact that *homes*, not merely houses, would be provided for those who otherwise could not afford them. Home and family are central to Leacock's vision of society and to his fiction. For Leacock, the preservation of our heritage of liberty begins, like charity and much else, in the home. His niece, Elizabeth Kimball, writes pointedly in her reminiscence of her uncle: "Family. Home. Country. The first realities."[50] "Home" is of course the key concept in *Sunshine Sketches'* concluding "L'Envoi: The Train to Mariposa," and the "slums" provide a pointed contrast to *Arcadian Adventures'* sinful Plutoria.

Though Leacock's practical suggestions for solving the riddle of social justice and preserving liberty do reveal his socialist sympathies, they are not as pertinent here as is the general attitude that he brings to the problem of social reform. Leacock favoured the path-of-progress trope to convey his image of social development. To the right of this "narrow path" (*UR*, 124), this "upward path of social progress" (*UR*, 138), squats a stubbornly guarded liberal individualism; to the left flits the dream of socialism. Of the proponents of revolutionary socialism and extreme individualism, Leacock writes, "There are others, of whom the present writer is one, who see in socialism nothing but disaster: yet who consider that the individualist principle of 'every man for himself' ... favours overmuch the few at the expense of the many" (*UR*, 37). "Somewhere between the two," suggests Leacock, "lies such narrow safety as may be found" (*UR*, 124).

Leacock always gave the idea of socialism its due (*HL*, 56) – it is a "beautiful picture" (*HL*, 54) – but he flatly rejected socialism for the simple reason "that it won't work" (*UR*, 94; see also *HL*, 54, 56). Regardless of its gradations of militancy, socialism can never succeed as a system of government because it ignores "the most nearly true of all the broad generalizations that can be attempted in regard to mankind" – "a general selfishness or self-seeking as the principal motive of the individual in the economic sphere" (*UR*, 40). It is ultimately the humanist's recognition of human fallibility that leads Leacock to reject the socialist plan. Socialism as a form of government is dangerous, enticing with its "beautiful dream" (*UR*, 32) but offering "chaos" if pursued (*UR*, 123). The socialist "loses sight of the possibility of our falling into social chaos. He sees no longer the brink of the abyss beside which the path of progress picks its painful way. He leaps with a shout of exultation over the cliff" (*UR*, 98), and he lands in his imagination where "it is sunshine all the time in the lotus land of the loafer" (*UR*, 120). That is, he lands in such a socialist utopia as Edward Bellamy depicted in *Looking Backward* (1888).

Leacock recognized that modern socialism was inspired by "the writings of Marx and Engels and Louis Blanc" (*UR*, 91; see also *HL*, 54); he viewed their work as a justifiable response to the squalor of the masses in the nineteenth century. But he takes issue with Bellamy's utopian fiction because it is "the most attractive and the most consistent outline of a socialist state that has, within the knowledge of the present writer, ever been put forward" (*UR*, 101–2). The choice of Bellamy's socialist fiction as a focus for attack is consistent with Leacock's views. In an appendix to *Hellements of Hickonomics*, he writes that "we are moved and stimulated to understanding far more by our imagination than by our intellect: more even than by our self-interest."[51] In essence, he rejects Bellamy's utopian dream, and socialism in general, because the socialist "loses sight of the supreme fact that after all, in its own poor, clumsy fashion, the machine [modern industrial society] does work" (*UR*, 98). Leacock's progressively conservative plan is to "mend the machine" (*UR*, 13–14), not to destroy it "in the fierce attempt to do in a day what can only be done in a generation" (*UR*, 87).

When he turns to the extreme of liberal individualism, Leacock is as dismissive as he is of socialism, though he is not philosophically opposed to the premises of liberalism. As has been seen, he agreed with Thomas Hobbes that self-interest is the one reliable motive in economic affairs (*UR*, 40). In *The Unsolved Riddle* he argues that the rise of beliefs in individual liberty resulted in the economic theory of Adam Smith and the *laissez-faire* economics which is the product of liberal individualism. With characteristic irony and disingenuity, Leacock writes of the rise of *laissez-faire* economics that "St. Paul's puzzling admonition that every man should pursue every other man's wealth took on a new meaning" (*HL*, 11). Leacock values the concept of individual liberty, of course, and he recognizes with Matthew Arnold that "the passion to be left alone, if only to one's own foolishness, lies deep rooted in the British character" (*HL*, 29).[52] Yet he asserts that "individualism of the extreme type is ... long since out of date" (*UR*, 36). Because of the increasing complexity of modern industrial society, Leacock regards the "maxim of *laissez-faire*" to be no longer applicable (*UR*, 41). Although he endorses "this doctrine of liberty" (*HL*, 40), he contends that to base a conception of society predominantly upon individual rights, as did Rousseau, is to condone social injustice (*HL*, 34). For Leacock, finally, the "insistence on individual rights ... is worth keeping if only as a metaphor" (*HL*, 37). But "unrestrained individualism" must be checked if social injustice is not to incite socialism or, worse, "the unspeakable savagery of bolshevism" (*UR*, 93): "It is restriction of individualism by the force of organization and by legislation that has brought to the world whatever social advance has been achieved by the great mass of the people" (*UR*, 86).

Leacock rejects socialism, then, because it will not work in a world of imperfect and imperfectible citizens: "If the day ever comes when we are good enough for such a system, then we shall need no system at all" (*HL*, 56). He also apprehends the danger and injustice of continuing under a system of unrestrained liberal individualism. And somewhat in anticipation of George Grant's *Technology And Empire* (1969), he associates liberal individualism with faith in technological progress: "There is no great hope for universal betterment of society by the mere advance of industrial technical progress and by the unaided play of the motive of every man for himself" (*UR*, 85).[53] He dismisses the extremes of, on the one hand, a conservative passiveness with respect to change and, on the other, a liberal propensity to interfere overmuch, implying that he is not the "'little Liberal or ... little Conservative'" of the Gilbert and Sullivan opera (*HL*, 36). Yet when Leacock considers the history of the progress of liberty in England and France, his tory bias is evident: "In the one case liberty came by evolution, in the other by catastrophe; in England by growing up, in France by smashing down" (*HL*, 30). He commends Edmund Burke, the father of modern toryism, for his *Reflections on the Revolution in France* (1790) because Burke possessed a "longer vision" than the young Robert Southey or Charles Fox (*HL*, 38). Only Burke, with his "soberer or sourer thought," perceived the danger when "the world seemed full ahead for liberty" (*HL*, 38). In short, Leacock's toryism, his disposition towards the literally "progressive conservative" and the middle way, dictates that individual liberty be allowed restricted play within "a sane, orderly and continuous social reform" (*UR*, 87).

Leacock's social-political thinking can be understood as typical of British pragmatism. He respects the ideals of liberal individualism, socialism, and even anarchism (*HL*, 51–3), but he stresses again and again that such ideals become "meaningless when taken from the arm-chair of the philosopher and applied to large groups" (*HL*, 53). He views anarchists and socialists as Coleridge viewed "democrats" and "infidels": such extremists contemplate the ideals of "truth and justice in the nakedness of abstraction, condemn constitutions and dispensations without having sufficiently examined the natures, circumstances, and capacities of their recipients."[54] Leacock believes, as did Carlyle, that "alas, the Ideal always has to grow in the Real."[55]

For Leacock the politically "Real" is "modern democracy, – not as its founders dreamed of it," but democracy as "the best system of government as yet operative in this world of sin." He knows democracy "too well to idealize its merits"; indeed he recognizes its "peculiar defects": "'cliques' and 'interests' and 'bosses'" (UR, 111–4). Democracy is, nonetheless, malleable and amenable to reform. Socialism, Leacock feels, would not be so; nor will liberal democracies remain so if allowed to continue mechanically towards an unjust tyranny of capitalists – a plutocracy. As will be shown in the next chapter, he held that the rise of a tolerant democracy made possible the further progress and ultimate fulfilment of humorous literature in the nineteenth century. In one sense of the word "humour," democracy humours, tolerates, the individuality that is essential to the inspiration of comic characters. The democratic system, warts and all, allows for the kind of reform that preoccupied the moderate Leacock: "In any social movement, then, change and alteration in a new direction must be balanced against the demands of social stability" (UR, 85).

The preceding passages, and especially the final quotation above, should suggest that Leacock's vision of social order is, like Coleridge's, one of "equipoise and interdependency."[56] In Leacock's view, World War One should have made especially clear to the unenlightened "that our fortunes are not in our individual keeping" (UR, 130). From this derives his central proposal to shift the burden of individual misfortune "from the shoulders of the individual to those of society at large" (UR, 130–1). His simple logic in so proposing is as follows: if society can conscript an individual to die for it, it must be prepared to provide that individual with a secure living (UR, 127–8). The ideal of individual liberty must be sacrificed to the reality of an ever-increasing interdependency, for "more and more things have to be done by associated effort and each man's rights against his fellows become more and more limited by the demands of the general welfare" (HL, 41). The doctrine of individual rights – however admirable, "worth keeping if only as a metaphor" – must be sacrificed to the general welfare. "What we give thus, we do not lose, or if it is lost for ourselves, it is given to humanity" (HL, 24). The extent to which Leacock was prepared to realize this ideal can be seen in his reaction to one of the greatest disappointments of his life – his forced retirement from McGill University. Although Leacock never forgave his beloved McGill for retiring him in 1936, he wrote only one year later of the reasoning of the school's trustees:

"They add that the application of a general rule is better than endless disputes over individual cases; and that, when you come to think of it, is a pretty sensible argument."[57]

Leacock esteemed "liberty of conscience," an "immortal dictum" that he learned apparently from Mill's *Political Economy* (*HL*, 50). The fact is, however, that "liberty of conscience" is the only liberty Leacock truly condoned. In the modern industrial world, liberty could have free play only in the conscience of the individual; liberty of conscience that approached liberty of action must be restrained lest such liberty manifest itself in the social-economic sphere as "unrestrained individualism." However, Leacock was not arguing for a system of government suppression or collectivist regulation. He stipulated that he would not "extend the régime of compulsion over the whole field": "The vast mass of human industrial effort must still lie outside of the immediate control of the government. Every man will still earn his own living and that of his family as best he can, relying first and foremost upon his own efforts" (*UR*, 142). He did not desire a socialist "land of the loafer," nor did he wish to see a continuation of the social injustice that is engendered "by the unaided play of the motive of every man for himself." Cautiously benevolent, he realized that "success in life and capacity to live we cannot give. But opportunity we can" (*UR*, 138). His conclusion to the *Unsolved Riddle* succinctly illustrates the social-political attitude of a man who saunters along the tory-humanist's middle way, "never hurrying and never pausing."[58] "The safety of the future lies in a progressive movement of social control alleviating the misery which it cannot obliterate and based upon the broad general principle of equality of opportunity" (*UR*, 151–2). The conclusion of *Liberty* shows that Leacock's faith in progress did not derive from a belief in the efficacy of government regulation, but from reliance on "the spirit" (*HL*, 75). Earlier in *Liberty* he calls this Bergsonian spirit "good will, the only force in the long run that makes anything politically" (*HL*, 59).

It may be reiterated in concluding that the vigilant spirit of good will that Leacock recommended for the alleviation of social injustice and the preservation of liberty is best described as his tory humanism. He tolerantly acknowledged human fallibility and promoted man's responsibility in the cause of preserving the traditions of democracy. He rejected the radical solutions of anarchism, revolutionary socialism, and bolshevism; he perceived the dangers of unrestrained liberal individualism and the limitations of technological progress. He apprehended the threat to true social progress of continuing under an unjust system and he wished to preserve those traditional institutions which had, over the course of generations, proven their worth to mankind. He sought social safety along the path of progress somewhere between socialism and liberalism. He was by turns a "radical" tory, a reactionary conservative, "a friend of Labor."

Finally, it is revealing to observe that when Leacock wished to alter the industrial system, when he wished to appear as a social engineer and so to appease hot-headed reformers and apprehensive plutocrats, the industrial system was imaged as a machine: "The danger is that the attempt to alter things too rapidly may dislocate the industrial machine. We ought to attempt such ... as will strain the machine to a breaking point, but never break it" (UR, 149). But when he wished to constrain those who would "break it" (socialists) or strain it beyond its limits (plutocrats), the industrial system was imaged as a natural growth: "The industrial system is too complex, its roots are too deeply struck and its whole organism of too delicate a growth to permit us to tear it from the soil" (UR, 126). Indeed, the image of a growing organism better conveys Leacock's view of industrial society. Knowledge of how the social organism has grown – of its history – will best direct those who desire to guide it wisely into the future. "For all wise thinking," he wrote, "for all careful social control, it is necessary to see things as they have grown, to look on our institutions in the light of their past. Such dim vision as we can have of the future depends absolutely on this. Cut off the human race from the knowledge and comprehension of its history, and its government will just turn into a monkey cage. We need the guidance of history."[59] It is such "wise thinking" or "right reasoning" – reasoning informed by a sense of history and humanity – which informs Sunshine Sketches of a Little Town and Arcadian Adventures With the Idle Rich. The Sketches portrays a community as it has grown and is growing; the Adventures depicts a "Plutoria" of liberal individualists "cut off ... from the knowledge and comprehension of its history." Mariposa represents fictionally the "guidance of history"; Plutoria, without memory, is the regressively atavistic "monkey cage."

Leacock's tory-humanist attitudes resemble those of any number of "noble conservatives," from Edmund Burke and Oliver Goldsmith, through Benjamin Disraeli to (in Leacock's opinion) R.B. Bennett.[60] Leacock espouses a kind of secular via media over any deviation to left or right. Such a tory-humanist philosophy values moderate, painstaking progress over radical alterations and balances the needs of the interdependent community against the rights of the individual. Leacock understood "kindly humour" to contain the spirit of good will which he untiringly recommended as the proper approach to social-political riddles.. Humour, the literary vehicle of the middle way, mediates between satire and sentimentality, which are, in Leacock's thought, roughly the literary equivalents of extreme liberalism and socialism.

CHAPTER TWO

Between Satire and Sentimentality: Leacock's Theory of Humour

"Use him as though you loved him, that is, harm
him as little as you may possibly, that he may live
the longer." The implication of a slow death behind
the apparently kindly words is one that might make
the coldest-bloodest frog boil with indignation.

But the point is that Izaak Walton was out to get the
fish.

Leacock, "What Can Izaak Walton Teach Us?"

It was suggested in the preceding chapter that Leacock was not a conventionally religious man. That statement can be qualified with what may appear at this point to be a laughable claim: that humanism served for Leacock's religion and that humour was its literary manifestation. It may also be asserted that humanism and humour are, in a consideration of Leacock's writings, virtually interchangeable concepts. If Christianity offers opportunity for faith in something that transcends the individual, hope for the moral improvement of mankind, and encouragement towards a charitable – a *kindly* – disposition, then humour can indeed be said to be Stephen Leacock's religion. His understanding of "humour" ranged from a knowledge of the etymological history of the word to a sense of its being synonymous with the world's best literature, regardless of whether that literature possesses what are conventionally considered humorous qualities. For Leacock, humour "runs thus a gamut which passes all the way from the ridiculous to the sublime (*HTT*, 99). Humorous literature does not occupy a position at "the lower level of literature, but lies around the summits of its highest range" (*HH*, 247; see also *HTW*, 224). Humour is ultimately "the highest product of our civilization."[1] In his unpaginated prefatory note to *Humour and Humanity*, Leacock prescribes what he believed to be in the prime ingredient of humour, the one essential element of the truly humorous to which he invariably returns: "The essence of humour is human kindliness." He adds, lest his readers presume that his book deals merely with comic diversions, that it is humour's "kindliness" which lends it "the character of a leading factor in human progress, and which is destined still further to enhance its utility to mankind." Leacock asked of humorous literature no less than what Matthew Arnold asked of true culture, that it offer the alternative to philistine, liberal materialism. And he would perhaps have said with Arnold in answer to opposing views, "Whoever calls anything else culture [humour], may indeed, call it so if he likes, but then he talks of something quite different from what I talked of."[2]

Leacock's debt to such nineteenth-century theorists as George Meredith and W.M. Thackeray is revealed by his contention that humour "in its highest form, no longer excites our laughter, no longer appeals to our comic sense, no longer depends upon the aid of wit" (HTT, 280). Humour "in its highest form" was no longer necessarily funny, no longer a laughing matter. With an uncharacteristic, though characteristically late-Victorian, appreciation for gentler amusement, he writes, "With all the exquisite development of our humour from primitive fun to refined reflection, the power to laugh at it grows less" (HH, 24). In Humour and Humanity, he calls this refined humour the "humour of sublimity" (HH, 237). Whereas in Leacock's day "humour" had come to be associated with laughter, he reverted to the word's etymological history and employed it in the medieval sense to describe temperament; specifically, he understood humour to describe an authorial disposition towards kindliness and humanism.

As repetitive as the above quotations may appear, similar statements could readily be repeated twenty-fold from Leacock's writings on humour (and frequently word-for-word; he was a relentless self-plagiarist). They are not isolated or casual remarks, nor are they instances of his confessed preference for half-truths.[3] They illustrate concerns central to his understanding of the correct, and necessary, conception of humour. His theory of humour is intricately involved with his understanding of the function of imaginative literature in relation to life. Besides its utility to mankind as meliorating, Leacock held that humorous literature serves a more private purpose: it provides temporary, illusory respite from a life that is fundamentally disillusioning. By providing temporary escape from disillusionment, humour functions as a kind of enchanting spell to charm hard reality. In this way, Leacock's theory of humour can be seen to share something with those theories that find in the origins of satire the magical properties once attributed to incantory invective.[4]

Leacock's definition of sublime humour, first articulated in his essay, "Amerian Humour," and reiterated like a flourishing drum-roll at the conclusion to his many writings on humour, deserves full transcription:

The final stage of the development of humour is reached when amusement no longer arises from a single "funny" idea, meaningless contrast, or odd play upon words, but rests upon a prolonged and sustained conception of the incongruities of human life itself. The shortcomings of our existence, the sad contrast of our aims and our achievements, the little fretting aspiration of the day that fades into the nothingness of to-morrow, kindle in the mellowed mind a sense of gentle amusement from which all selfish exultation has been chastened by the realization of our common lot of sorrow. On this higher plane humour and pathos mingle and become one. To the Creator perhaps in retrospect the little story of man's creation and his fall seems sadly droll. (ELS, 92–3)

The conception of humour as based on incongruity is a conventional view; broadened to include "the incongruities of human life itself," which "kindle in the mellowed mind a sense of gentle amusement," the vision is uniquely Leacock's. The association of the sublimely humorous point of view with "the Creator" suggests the cosmically ironic perspective that should be assumed by the creator of humorous fiction. Referring to Charles Dickens and Mark Twain (his two favourite writers), Leacock describes the humorous perspective as "that 'divine retrospect' upon life which is the culmination of humour" (HTT, 109). Ideally, the humorist should view his characters' affectations, and perhaps even their sins, in "retrospect" as "sadly droll."

Leacock's descriptions of the ultimate reach and purpose of humour seem to have arisen from the context of late-Victorian disillusionment with the hopes of the mid-nineteenth century. In Leacock's view, disillusionment is the truth about "human life" which is perceived by the humorous vision and which humour makes bearable. In one of his finest autobiographical essays, "Three Score and Ten: The Business of Growing Old," he writes of life as a movement "from the eyes of wonder to those of disillusionment – or is it to those of truth?" (RU, 296). Because life is an inevitable maturation through incongruity to disillusionment, true humour is tolerant and sympathetic – "the kindly contemplation of the incongruities of life, and the artistic expression thereof" (HH, 11). That, Leacock's concise definition of humour, has given some of his critics ample room to belittle his theoretical work.[5]

Critical disparagement of Leacock's insistence upon the need for humour to be kindly usually seeks justification on the grounds of a seeming discrepancy between his theory and practice. On the one hand, critics point out that, although Leacock demanded humour be "kindly," he is in his fiction frequently unkind, or apparently so. (Certainly he could never be thought unkind in comparison with Rabelais, Dryden, or Swift.) On the other hand, critical emphasis on the kindliness of Leacock's work – the gentle irony – makes Leacock appear not so incisive a satirist, not as keen an analyst of mankind's historical shortcomings as he was. Leacock deplored satire that tends towards the overly intellectual and the rationalistically intolerant. Humour must humour – that is, tolerate – deviation and shared folly. And he was not, in the bulk of his work, what he did not want to be. At the conclusions of those few humorous satires that are unkind, he often takes pains to cast a backward-glancing, kindly remark.[6]

But Leacock's "kindly contemplation" did not disallow incisive satire. Nor should "kindly" be taken as synonymous with or confused with "gentle." For Leacock, "kindly" described primarily the attitude of the author of the work and the vision of humanity the work offers. Such an understanding does not, for example, preclude satire on the prim and plutocratic inhabitants of Plutoria. Because such characters live narrowly in denial of their humanity, they are prime targets. "Kindly" also carried recognition of shared humanity, of "kin." In the conclusion of his essay "Fun as an Aid to Business," Leacock's narrator plays on the associations between kindliness and kin, calling "kindliness the 'touch of nature that makes the whole world kin.'"[7] In literary terms, "kindly" is intended to encourage a perspective and response above and beyond those particularized faults shared by all mankind. There is succinct perception in Malcolm Ross Ross's observation that Leacock is not a satirist "because *he loves what he hates* ... To attack and defend, to love and hate in one breath, is not the genius of satire but the genius of irony ... The satirist must always hate better than he loves. The ironist cannot. Leacock never could."[8] However, virulent satire often suggests by negation an alternate, equally humanitarian vision of life; like Ross, Leacock failed to perceive that the satirist need only appear to "hate better than he loves."

It is in terms of satiric intent that Leacock's view of humour differs most from that of the majority of writers who have analyzed various aspects of the comic. Although he refers glancingly to many of the major theorists of the comic, these references are dismissive, anti-intellectual, and anti-analytical. Dismissing the "deep" approaches of other theorists, Leacock asserts that the "surface is the best thing to see" (*HH*, 12). Yet his analysis of the surface of humour, of technique, is neither as rewarding nor as revealing as are his proposals concerning the sublime reach of humour. Although he pretends generally to the Aristotelian method of categorization in his analysis of technique, he persistently groups all aspects of the comic under the heading of *humour*. For example, he considers wit "not as something contrasted with the humorous, but offering merely a special and, relatively speaking, unimportant subdivision of a general mode of intellectual operation: it presents a humorous idea by means of the happy juxtaposition of verbal forms" (*ELS*, 92). He laments the lack of "proper terms" for discussing the art of humour (*HH*, 65), yet he dismisses other theorists who painstakingly distinguish such elements of the comic as the ludicrous, the ridiculous, and the absurd. He considers such analyses to be exercises in futility and "out of place" in their attempts to emulate the methodology of science (*HH*, 15–6). The ostensible cause of such contradiction is Leacock's desire to present his studies as a fresh approach to the subject, a study that will be accessible to the student of humour. The truer cause is Leacock's desire to skirt the baser elements of the comic impulse, to illustrate at length some important aspects of technique, and thus to proceed quickly to a discussion of his conception of humour as sublimely elevating. Whereas the comic impulse had most frequently been analyzed in terms of a closed fist, Leacock intends to present humour as an open hand, a hand which is weaponless and ready to clasp. Whereas laughter had come to be discussed in terms of bared fangs, Leacock understands it in terms of the compassionate smile of acknowledged folly and of humanity.

Aristotle's remark in the *Poetics*, that the ludicrous "consists in some defect or ugliness which is not painful or destructive,"[9] is the one authoritative statement Leacock considers supportive of his own central thesis. Although Leacock mistakenly assumes that Aristotle was remarking on the laughable, he contends that Aristotle's qualification "contains the essential element which the word kindly" in his own definition of humour "is meant to convey" (*HH*, 11). In *Humour and Humanity*, Leacock indicts Thomas Hobbes as representative of those who consider laughter to be an expression of triumphant superiority (*HH*, 21–2). And the negativism with respect to humour which Leacock felt himself to be countering can best be illustrated by Hobbes's definition of laughter: "*Sudden Glory*, is the passion which maketh those *Grimaces* called LAUGHTER; and is caused either by some sudden act of their own, that pleaseth them; or by apprehension of some deformed thing in another, by comparison whereof they suddenly applaud themselves."[10] This is as far from Leacock's understanding of sublime humour as it is possible to go. He believed that such conceptions of laughter as Hobbes's serve only to carry "us all the way from the exulting laugh of the triumphant savage to the 'mocking laugh' of the melodrama" (HH, 22). It is not until the eighteenth century, with its conception of a sympathetic humour of sensibility, that Leacock finds a congenial general understanding of humour.

Most commentators and writers on the comic, from Aristotle to Arthur Koestler, have assumed that some form of incongruity is the technical and affective basis of comedy.[11] Leacock also perceives that "the basis of the humorous, the amusing, the ludicrous, lies in the incongruity, the unfittingness, the want of harmony among things" (ELS, 86). In the first of his Lectures on the English Comic Writers (1819), William Hazlitt expressed the centrality of incongruity to the comic: "The essence of the laughable then is the incongruous, the disconnecting one idea from another, or the jostling of one feeling against another."[12] Hazlitt's determination of why man is the only animal that laughs and weeps – "for he is the only animal that is struck with the difference between what things are, and what they ought to be" – is expressed by Leacock as "a contrast between the thing as it is, or ought to be" (HTT, 12), and "as between things as they are supposed to be ... and things as they are" (HH, 239). Hazlitt understands one of the functions of the comic to be a "healing influence to many a hurt mind."[13] Similarly, Leacock perceives that "laughter is the last refuge of sorrow" (RU, 159), and that humour is "a relief from pain, ... a consolation against the shortcomings of life itself" (HH, 72). Hazlitt stipulates, as did Aristotle, that the discomfort or suffering evident in the comic must be "momentary, or overwhelming only to the imagination of the sufferer."[14] As Leacock observes, "It becomes a condition of amusement that no serious harm or injury shall be inflicted, but that only the appearance or simulation of it shall appear" (ELS, 90). Such stipulations reveal Hazlitt's and Leacock's recognition that comedy and humour forever flirt with tragedy. In Sunshine Sketches there is a possibility that Jeff Thorpe's illusory financial fortune could result, as a similar fortune results for Young Fizzlechip, in suicide (SS, 45); and in Arcadian Adventures the potential happy ending of a love story actually resolves into a pathetic tragedy (AA, 196).

There are other noteworthy instances in which Leacock's statements on aspects of the humorous echo those of Hazlitt on the comic.

Leacock's discussion of the "humour of personal discomfiture," "of reversed egotism" (*HTT*, 129), recalls Hazlitt's original designation of such an attitude as "an irony directed against oneself."[15] Leacock's evaluation of Molière as "the unsurpassed genius of comedy" (*HH*, 135) is reminiscent of Hazlitt's early praise of Molière as "one of the greatest comic geniuses that ever lived."[16] And, in a lighter vein, Leacock's frequently repeated condemnation of the competitive practices of unskilled after-dinner *raconteurs* seems to remember Hazlitt's complaint against persistent jesting: "There is no answer to a jest, but another, and even where the ball can be kept up in this way without ceasing, it tires the patience of the by-standers, and runs the speakers out of breath. Wit is the salt of conversation, not the food."[17]

Some of the previous comparisons may appear inconsequential or, at best, coincidental (Leacock's and Hazlitt's shared opinions of Molière's genius, for instance, however similar the expressions of admiration). It is difficult, however, to dispute Leacock's debt to Hazlitt's study of the comic, particularly to Hazlitt's definition of comedy as based on incongruity and on the nature of that incongruity – "the difference between what things are, and what they ought to be." These perceptions inform Leacock's discussions of humour from its primitive origins to its sublime heights. In the brief bibliography which he appended to *Humour and Humanity*, Hazlitt's *Lectures on the English Comic Writers* is the earliest listed work (*HH*, 249). It would thus appear that Leacock considered Hazlitt's contribution as the first serious study of the subject. Interestingly, Hazlitt's appreciation of the comic is best illustrated by his remark, "I would rather have been the author of Aesop's Fables, than of Euclid's Elements!"[18] Leacock conveys his high esteem for humour in a syntactical borrowing from Hazlitt: "Personally, I would sooner have written *Alice in Wonderland* than the whole Encyclopaedia Britannica" (*SS*, xi).[19]

There are, however, important differences between Hazlitt's and Leacock's treatment of the comic and humour. For all his apparent debt to Hazlitt, Leacock felt himself to be justified in noting dismissively, and unfairly, that previous studies of the comic, "from Aristotle to Hazlitt, turn rather on what is laughter than on what is humour" (*HH*, 20). For Leacock, who insisted that humour be sympathetic and kindly, Hazlitt's study retains too much respect for caustic satiric wit, discomfittingly assuming that aggressive superiority is innate in the comic impulse. Hazlitt also appreciates that sexual intrigue is especially necessary to comedy, a view that was anathema to Leacock (*HTT*, 266–7). It is only with George Meredith's

An Essay on Comedy (1877) that an articulate theory of comedy appears which begins to view the subject in a manner that anticipates Leacock's idiosyncratic theory of kindly humour.

(It is worth opening a lengthy parenthesis to note that Leacock's conception of humour is also anticipated somewhat by W.M. Thackeray's studies of humour in the mid-nineteenth century, particularly his "Charity and Humour." Thackeray's opinion of humour is certainly congenial to Leacock's when he states that "the best humour is that which contains most humanity, that which is flavoured throughout with tenderness and kindness."[20] And in his appreciation of Dickens, Thackeray overreaches Leacock in his use of derivations from "kind." He writes of Dickens' "multiplied kindnesses"; he calls Dickens "this kind friend, who soothed and charmed so many hours"; he designates Dickens "the kind satirist"; and he doubles up on "kind" when discussing Dickens' characters, remarking on "the names of kind folk with whom this kind genius has made us familiar." But Thackeray is, finally, too sentimental in "Charity and Humour" for a sound comparison with Leacock. Leacock may share Thackeray's view of kindly humour, but he hardly resembles the gushing Thackeray who writes, "Humour! humour is the mistress of tears; she knows the way to the *fons lachrymarum*, strikes in dry and rugged places with her enchanting wand, and bids the fountain gush and sparkle." Such lachrymose sentimentalism is the one aspect of his beloved Dickens' work that Leacock regrets.)

George Meredith, like Leacock, believed comedy to be a civilizing influence. Leacock's claim that humour plays a leading role in the progress of civilization recalls Meredith's assertion that "there never will be civilization where comedy is not possible."[21] But Meredith's taste for a "thoughtful laughter" of "unrivalled politeness" is perhaps (like Thackeray's sentimentalism) a touch too gentle for Leacock, though his distaste for caustic satire is certainly not too gentle. Employing the key Leacockian word, "kindliness," Meredith admonishes, "If you detect the ridicule, and your kindliness is chilled by it, you are slipping into the grasp of satire." In a kindred vein that also anticipates Leacock, Meredith considers that the true comic spirit must be, in its relation to all manner of affectation and hypocrisy, "humanely malign." Like Leacock, Meredith values a tempered satire, regarding the kindly satirist as a "moral agent" in whose works "irony is the humour of satire" – an aphorism that bears comparison to Northrop Frye's definition of satire as "militant irony."[22] For both Leacock and Meredith, non-militant irony saves humour from caustic satire. Meredith believes, as does Leacock, that "the humorist ... has an embrace of contrasts beyond the scope of the comic poet."[23] Nonetheless, it is still the satiric element in comedy that Meredith ultimately praises as the best defence and attack against folly, unreason, sentimentalism, and boredom. And it is in this respect that his views, like Hazlitt's, diverge from Leacock's.

Unlike Leacock, who wishes to present humour as an agent of spiritual elevation and ethical humanism, Meredith values the comedy of manners for its service as a social check. Whereas Leacock understands humour as actively offering a perspective from which to view and comprehend the incongruities of life, Meredith believes that comic examples teach the reader (or viewer) to avoid similar vanities and hypocrisies. His faith in the practical efficacy of comedy is somewhat in contradiction of Jonathan Swift's belief that satire is "a sort of Glass, wherein Beholders do generally discover every body's Face but their Own."[24] But with Swift's disillusioned comment in mind for purposes of contrast, it can be seen that the differences among Thackeray, Meredith, and Leacock are ones of degree, not of kind. Just as Hazlitt's study provides an initial perception, similar to Leacock's, that incongruity is the technical basis of humour, so Meredith's study can be seen to offer a theoretical basis similar to Leacock's conception of the function of humour. But Leacock does not stress the practical purpose of comedy as argued by Meredith. (It is Henry Bergson's Le Rire [1900] which considers "laughter" in a light most reminiscent of Meredith's An Essay On Comedy.) Leacock's general opinion of Meredith's writings can be seen in "Who Canonizes the Classics?" when he remarks that "every one thought, forty years ago, that George Meredith's books would prove to be 'classics': and they haven't" (RU, 86).

Leacock's theory of humour appears in its most "Victorian" light when considered in comparison to those of his contemporaries, Bergson and Sigmund Freud. The three writers are products of the late nineteenth century, and all lived well into the twentieth. Their theories of humour seem to highlight critical facets of the Victorian era: Bergson's definition of the comic as "something mechanical encrusted upon the living" can now be seen to have partaken of the attack against dehumanizing industrialization;[25] Freud's understanding of wit as pleasure-seeking and anti-social can now be perceived to have arisen from Victorian prudery and social-sexual repressiveness; and Leacock's insistence on humour's kindliness and potential sublimity can be viewed to have grown from the sentimentalism and idealism of the era.

Bergson understands laughter as "a sort of social gesture" directed against the "mechanical encrusted upon the living."[26] Laughter functions in service to Bergson's notion of the élan vital; that is, it serves as a corrective to whatever in man and society tends towards the mechanical or absent-mindedly inhuman. From arguments made in the first chapter, it should be clear that Leacock, the humanist, would applaud Bergson's conception of the role that laughter plays. As a tool of social conformity, however, Bergson's laughter has a darker side. "In laughter," he writes, "we always find an unavowed intention to humiliate, and consequently to correct our neighbour, if not in his will, at least in his deed." In effect, Bergson is taking Meredith's notion of comedy's exemplary function to its logical conclusion. For all laughter's service in defence of the "elastically" human, for all its use of "evil with a view to good," Bergson finds in it something base and coercive, something manipulative and egotistic, and "behind this latter, something ... more bitter, the beginnings of a curious pessimism which becomes the more pronounced as the laugher more closely analyses his laughter." Aware of Bergson's dissection of laughter, Leacock understandably wanted to dissociate his sublime humour from its taint.[27] It is perhaps for this reason that he dismissively assesses Bergson's definition of the comic as one that "would leave some readers unsatisfied" (HH, 11).

In a concluding metaphor that uses the image of society as a sea, Bergson posits laughter as the "fringe of snow-white foam, feathery and frolicsome," dancing on the waves. But, as his analysis has intimated throughout, appearances are deceiving, for this feathery and frolicsome foam is also "a froth with a saline base. Like froth, it sparkles. It is gaiety itself. But the philosopher who gathers a handful to taste may find that the substance is scanty, and the aftertaste bitter."[28] No wonder Leacock cautions that "if the study of humour is ever taken seriously we must handle it carefully, lest it work its own undoing"(HH, 113).[29] As will be shown, Leacock was cognizant of this "saline base" to humour. But where he chose not to dwell analytically – with excessive liberal rationality – on humour's base and bitter, supposedly scanty substance, Freud plunged in.

Within the workings of the witticism that solicits laughter, Freud discovers the unconscious at work, indefatigably bent on gratification. Wit serves as the agent of the unconscious, which unconscious is irrational and without a "reality principle" (that which socializes or civilizes the individual). Wit can serve the unconscious only by assuming a semblance of rationality in order to circumvent internal and external censorship and repression. And to do so, it must contain what Freud designates "sense in nonsense."[30] The pleasure wit affords the unconscious is either subversively sexual or irrationally childish. By definition, therefore, wit tends to be anti-social, serving as it does the most hedonistic master conceivable, the unconscious pleasure principle, the ignoble "id." Freud understands the chief characteristic of wit to be "condensation" – compression, brevity, doubling for the purpose of disguising the unacceptable, unconscious purpose. In this and other respects, he draws a parallel between what he terms "wit-work" and "dream-work," noting that the two share a "similar psychic process" and function, namely, the gratifying release of psychic energy which is suppressed by society or repressed by the rational individual.

For Freud, wit is most often either obscene or hostile, and it is frequently both. "Any libidinal impulse confronted by a hindrance," he theorizes, "becomes distinctly hostile and cruel, and utilizes the sadistical components of the sexual instinct against the hindrance." Wit, whether obscene or hostile, is aggressive. To realize its self-gratifying ends, wit requires a third party whose laughter signals the wit's victory, and consequent pleasure, with regard to a second party. Or, to put the matter differently, a joke requires a "butt."[31] Laughter becomes a discharge of the inhibiting psychic energy which the assumed taboo subject of the witticism brought into play. For these reasons, Freud considers the laughter evoked by wit to be indicative of a "pleasurably perceived superiority which we adjudge to ourselves in comparison with others."

Not surprisingly, Freud's conclusion about wit strongly echoes Hobbes's concise definition of laughter. Freud's description of the unconscious presents that formation in as solitary, poor, nasty, and brutish a condition as that in which Hobbes depicted life in the state of nature. Both theorists begin with the body and end with the body; philosophically materialists, they inductively view all mental phenomena as expressions *of* the body. Leacock begins deductively with a conception of sublime humour, proceeds to the need for a kindly disposition, and concludes with his theory that humour works through pathos to elevate the human spirit. Hobbes and Freud possess a mechanistic vision, one which is ultimately, in its materialistic assumptions, no less predicated on deduction; Leacock adheres to a humanistic, organic view of man's and society's development. Surprisingly, though, Leacock and Freud do share some perceptions.

A frequently overlooked aspect of Freud's *Wit and Its Relation to the Unconscious* is its distinction between wit and humour. In the conclusion of his treatise, Freud discusses humour in terms that can be viewed as parallel to Leacock's. Whereas wit and the comic arouse repressive energies on account of their taboo subject matter, humour arouses sympathy as a further defensive "affect." For Freud, the psychic process involved in humour results "in that humour which *smiles under its tears*. It withdraws from the affect [the aggressive emotion] a part of its energy and gives it instead the additional humoristic ring" (emphasis added). Apparently humour is not as aggressive as are wit and the comic. In Freud's view, humour is distinguished from wit because it turns pain to sympathetic, as well as pleasurable, purpose. He concludes of humour, relative to wit and the comic: "Humour can now be conceived as the loftiest of these defense functions [the psychoneuroses]. It disdains to withdraw from conscious attention the ideas which are connected with the painful affect, as repression does." From his first essay on humour until his last, Leacock defines the highest reach of humour to be where "tears and smiles" mingle.[32] But Leacock could never accept only the limiting assumptions about human nature upon which Freud bases his conclusions. Leacock deliberately opposes his conception of the "super-self" (to be discussed presently) to "the subconscious self, that evil, inward thing" (RU, 206). Such a conception of human nature is evil because it seems characterized, like liberalism (in the nineteenth-century sense), by competitiveness, individualism, "cold reason," and a conception of happiness as physical pleasure which is reminiscent of Benthamite utilitarianism.

This is not to say, however, that Leacock denies the existence of an aggressive, pleasure-seeking basis to the comic impulse. As will be recalled from chapter one, he recognizes that self-interest is "the most nearly true of all the broad generalizations that can be attempted in regard to mankind" (UR, 40). But he does not consider the literary manifestations of selfishness – virulent satire, sarcasm, tendentiously caustic wit – to be true humour. With reference to Hobbes, Leacock laments, "It seems but a sad commentary upon the history of humanity to think that the original basis of amusement should appear in the form which is called demoniacal merriment. But there is much to support the view" (ELS, 87).[33] Similar to Freud's perception of the need for self-gratifying wit to contain "sense in nonsense" is Leacock's understanding that the pun requires "a sort of intellectual merit" to gain acceptance (HTT, 23). He realizes, too, that humorous verbal effects work through "our sub-conscious connection of words and sounds" (HTT, 155). He understands that witty puns enable "one to say with delicacy things which would never do if said outright" (HH, 40), and that epigrammatic verse serves as a vehicle "to convey in a merry and inoffensive fashion what would otherwise sound either very dull or very offensive" (HH, 168). In short, Leacock takes account of, and gives full value for, the more satiric forms of literary expression, but he maintains firmly that such aggressive tendencies are atavistic, a persistence of the triumphant shout of the victorious savage – "the very origin and fountain source of laughter" (*ELS*, 87). Metaphorically, he likens virulent satire to a rank stream forking away from the true, progressive stream of humane humour. He concedes, though, that both streams of "humour" arose from the same source: "One is tempted to think that perhaps the original source parted into two streams. In one direction flowed, clear and undefiled, the humour of human kindliness. In the other, the polluted waters of mockery and sarcasm, the "humour" that turned to ... infliction of pain as a perverted source of pleasure" (*HH*, 30). In "American Humour," he considers this defilement of the original source to represent the "anti-social character" of primitive humour, a character which persists tenaciously in the more caustic forms of satire. But true humour, "once started on the upward path of development," is not "antagonistic to the social feelings, but contributory to them" (*ELS*, 92).

The conflict between Leacock's and Freud's theories of humour and wit can perhaps best be understood as one between the Victorian ethical view of comedy (as typified by Meredith's study) and a Darwinian conception of wit as red in tooth and claw. Leacock, like the Huxley of *Evolution And Ethics*, distinguishes between the "Cosmic" process and the ethical: "The evolutionary explanation of morals is meaningless, and presupposes the existence of the very thing it ought to prove. It starts from a misconception of the biological doctrine. Biology has nothing to say as to what ought to survive and what ought not to survive" (*ELS*, 49–50).[34] And like Huxley who perceives that "ethical man" is the product of the human virtue of "sympathy," Leacock repeatedly insists upon the need for "kindliness" in humour – that is, for a sympathetic recognition of kinship. It is a failure of many twentieth-century views of human nature – albeit a failure rendered understandable by the carnage of two world wars – that the valid insights of psychoanalysis are accepted uncritically and applied indiscriminately to all branches of human endeavour. Such presumption leads Donald Cameron to dismiss Leacock's theory of humour as characterized by a "failure of psychological insight."[35] Of course, Cameron, who is apparently uncomfortable with Leacock's *spiritual* insights and hopes for mankind, means *psychoanalytical* insight. Unfortunately, in this regard Cameron's view is typical of the unfavourable criticisms of Leacock's humanistic approach to humour.

Leacock believed, then, that the truly humorous is civilizing, humane, cosmically ironic in its perspective on human affairs, and sublime at its highest reach. His general rule that incongruity is the basis of humour had been recognized by writers on the comic from Aristotle to Henry Fielding and had been articulated by William

Hazlitt in terms remarkably similar to Leacock's. Furthermore, Leacock's belief that humour has a civilizing function is reminiscent of George Meredith's and Henri Bergson's conceptions of the function of comedy and *le rire*. Yet, in discussing any of its aspects and expressions, no writer on the comic, from Aristotle to Arthur Koestler, had so *appropriated* the subject; no writer but Leacock felt compelled to apoiogize for humour's "primitive" features: its persistent childish savagery and prurient pleasures. Humour is, however, the one hope that Leacock could offer to a world that was, in his view, religiously and philosophically decimated and bankrupt: "Humour in a world of waning beliefs remains like Hope still left at the bottom of Pandora's box when all the evils of the Gods flew out from it upon the world" (*HTT*, 15). Humour offers "Hope," the second of the Christian cardinal virtues. Towards the end of *Humour and Humanity*, Leacock describes "sublime humour" as follows: "The kind of humour that is here described seems to me to reflect the humour of the highest culture, the humour of the future. Its distinction is its kindliness. It does not belong to the literature of effort, of strong convictions and animating purpose. It is rather that of disillusionment, of loss of faith, and the wide charity of mind that has come with the shattering of narrower ideals, not yet replaced." Here, without recourse to a diverting context, Leacock associates humour with all three Christian cardinal virtues: "the humour of the future" again suggests Hope, though not eschatological Hope; humour may substitute humanely for the "loss of faith"; and humour, distinguished in Leacock's theory by its "kindliness," inculcates a "wide charity of mind" (*HH*, 205-7). All of which is to repeat, humanism served for Stephen Leacock's religion, and humour was its literary manifestation.

There is, understandably, some discrepancy between theory and practice in the vast, disjointed, and uneven body of Leacock's work. There are a few "unkind" sketches. For example, there are the scathing remarks on the "average man," and worse on the "average woman," in the preface to *Winnowed Wisdom*;[36] there are mean-spirited attacks on the aristocracy of the defeated Germans of World War One in *The Hohenzollerns In America*;[37] and there are many snide ripostes for plutocrats, politicians, and progressives. Yet even such patently satiric pieces serve Leacock's tory-humanist purposes, and he is never virulently unkind or extremely Juvenalian. The attack on the average man is, more truly, satire against the tendency to reduce people to statistical information. The attack against the Hohenzollerns, partially excusable as the product of anti-German feeling engendered by World War One, also serves as satire against the rapacity of business practices in the United States. It would be a mistake, though, to attempt to excuse or rationalize Leacock's few unkind satires. They, too, are a small component of the kindly tory humorist and humanist. As Charles Taylor discovered, "Asperity, passion and quarrelsomeness *were* common to a lot of conservatives."[38]

Even so, Leacock is seldom a satirist in terms of Northrop Frye's useful definition of satire as "militant irony." For Frye, satire's "moral norms are relatively clear, and it assumes standards against which the grotesque and absurd are measured."[39] This is only sometimes the case in Leacock's fiction. The moral norms of *Sunshine Sketches* are not "relatively clear," and even such tendentious satire as *Arcadian Adventures* presents difficulties. To view Leacock's best work in isolation from his tory-humanist norm and his theory of humour is to require much presumption on the part of the reader who would extrapolate and apply standards of judgment. For instance, readers of the *Sketches* have had difficulty in determining Leacock's opinion of so central a figure as Josh Smith, or in determining Leacock's attitude towards the "enchanted" resolution of Peter Pupkin's and Zena Pepperleigh's charming romance. Excluding the immediate response of smiles or laughter, Leacock's best work invites an ambivalent response, the contours of which Frye begins to suggest: "Whenever a reader is not sure what the author's attitude is or what his own is supposed to be, we have irony with relatively little satire."[40] With respect to the author of a work, an apparently non-judgmental attitude implies an emphasis on irony. When that author is Stephen Leacock at his best, this is indeed the case. Dean Drone embezzles church funds partially to pay for his daughter's *de rigueur* French lessons, yet Drone is an ineffectual old man, a kindly, pathetic soul, if an incompetent pastor. The members of Plutoria's Mausoleum Club are brazenly hypocritical and opportunistic, yet Leacock softens his satire when he goes after the money-getters with a broad broom. His humorous vision, which is essentially ironic and often touches on the pathetic, contains pointed satire, though "relatively little satire" as satire was written, say, by Swift. The confusion between theory and practice dissipates somewhat when Leacock's tory-humanist orientation is recalled and he is understood to be viewing the vanities and hypocrisies of his characters – and intends the reader to view the same – from a "sublimely humorous" height. Or, as Leacock writes in a different context, "To express the situation in Irish, the more you think of its future, the less you think of it" (*HTT*, 256).

His "analysis" of the history of humour provides further evidence regarding Leacock's satiric norm.

Leacock views the development of humour with a Victorian interest in historical analysis and a Victorian belief in progress. That is, he applies no true methodology to his analysis but finds in the historical development of humour what his tory-humanist vision selectively seeks: confirmation of a progression towards greater kindliness and humanity. In all his writings on humour, he begins by briefly and selectively sketching the upward path of humour's progress from an imagined scene of the primitive savage's triumphant shout. From literally "savage laughter," humour progresses until the *appearance* of physical triumph replaces the actuality; this appearance constitutes the genesis of incongruity. With the development of language, incongruity comes to reside in the triumph over words themselves, in witticisms and puns, "a contrast or incongruity ... between the apparent and the real significance of the sounds and characters" (*HTT*, 14). Humour next manifests itself in the "brutal" humour of classical Greek literature and develops little in its progress towards the "rawness" of Chaucer. Leacock detects a rise in true humour in the Renaissance (with Shakespeare's Falstaff, for example), but it is only with the eighteenth century that he perceives the beginnings of a tolerant and kindly humour. This progress and development of the humorous sensibility from savagery to kindliness is the result of a concomitant maturity in man's humanity: "From the earliest stages of human development malice had to take account of the contrary principle of sympathy" (*HH*, 26). As was suggested earlier, Leacock's view of progress is informed, as was Huxley's, by a differentiation between the ethical, which is based on sympathy, and the natural or "cosmic." Sympathy gave rise to kindly humour, malice to virulent satire.

In the nineteenth century, humour "reaches its real ground," where "it becomes the humour of situation and character: and, at its highest reach, laughter fades into a smile, that verges closely upon tears, when humour reflects the incongruity of life itself, our human lot" (*HTT*, 99). This is humour as practiced by Dickens, to whom Leacock frequently refers as "the Master" (*ELS*, 172), Twain, and Daudet. Leacock's admiration for the humorous literature of the nineteenth century was circumscribed only by his qualified criticism of its indulgence in sentimentality (*HTT*, 72). With reference to the progress of humour through the ages, he writes, "It was the nineteenth century that brought the full effulgence of the day. The Victorian Age represents an epoch in the history of letters greater than any that preceded it; greater, in pure letters, it may well be than any about to follow it" (*HTT*, 16).

Although humour developed progressively, in Leacock's view its progress peaked then stalled in the nineteenth century, subsequently losing its direction in the twentieth. As chapter one has shown, Leacock feared the possibility of "retrogression" in the social-political sphere. Similarly, he believed that in his own time humour was moving neither forwards nor backwards, but "sideways" (*HTT*, 255). His reasons for such a conclusion reveal the basis of his concern for humour's future (*HTT*, 257–76). As might be expected, his apprehensions focus on the fracturing of the requisite popular sensibility for humorous literature by technology (radio, movies), an analysis which distantly anticipates the work of Harold Innis and Marshall McLuhan, and the social liberation of women, which, in Leacock's prudish view, made necessary the inclusion of "sex stuff" in all popular fiction. Leaving in well-earned rest his tirades against modernity and briefly sketching his opinions of writers whom he considered typical of the various stages of humour's progress will, however, reveal more of Leacock's theory of kindly humour.[41]

As a writer educated in the classical tradition, who specialized in languages (Greek, Latin, Italian, French, and German) before completing graduate work in political economy at the University of Chicago (Ph.D. 1903), Leacock was remarkably unremitting in his disparagement of classical literature.[42] But if humour – or literature itself – is to be viewed as progressive, it follows that ancient literatures have to be presented as crude. His essay "Homer and Humbug" is but the opening volley in a lifelong war against the scholarly opinion that classical literature is superior to the literature of the nineteenth century. Homer's catalogue of ships "has that same majesty of style that has been brought to an even loftier pitch in the New York Business Directory."[43] Leacock concludes "Homer and Humbug" with a message that he would like to inscribe on a "large stone" to be thrown through the window of a university: "The classics are only primitive literature. They belong to the same class as primitive machinery." While Homer is too brutal (*HTT*, 236), Herodotus' "efforts deserve all the credit attached to a praiseworthy beginning" (*ELS*, 104). This is faint praise from Leacock, but his comment that Aristophanes is "so witty that it takes half a page to explain one of his jokes" sounds trenchantly anti-scholarly (*HTT*, 15). Conceding that humour loses much in translation, Leacock nonetheless insists on concluding that the "standard of humour" of the classical writers was "pretty primitive and clumsy" (*HTT*, 241). It was such Leacockian baiting that spurred Douglas Bush to write that Leacock was "guilty, if not of ignorance, then of almost incredibly crass philistinism."[44] Leacock was of course innocent of the first charge; in his determination to appear "just plain folks," he often implicated himself in the second cultural crime. But the true cause of his anti-classicism is to be found in the limitations of his rigorously applied, selective historical perspective. In his contortions to prove his thesis that humour is historically progressive, he will write, "And then there were also Dante and Milton and John Bunyan and a lot other fun-makers who keep their readers in a roar" (*HTT*, 15).[45] Yet, as the opening of this chapter has shown, keeping readers in a roar is neither central to Leacock's vision of the humorist's function nor a component of his definition of the truly humorous. His thesis that "the sense of humour and the expression of it undergo in the course of history an upward and continuous progress" (*HH*, 27) led him to assume critical positions that were, to put it kindly, untenable. He contends, for example, that Irvin Cobb, the nineteenth-century American humorist, is "a far funnier man than Shakespeare"; and "if the 'funny' sounds too comic," Leacock argues, "I will put it as a far more 'humorous' man than Shakespeare" (*HTT*, 276). Here, there is no disclaimer about preferring half-truths to whole (though such an admission should always be kept in mind), only the following anti-intellectual dismissal: "Scholars will say this marks me as an ignoramus. Very good, in that case so I am: and so is Cobb: and so is Shakespeare" (*HTT*, 276). This Leacockian piece of bombast can be called a two-thirds truth.

It is not until the eighteenth century that true humour, in Leacock's view, begins to appear general in literature. The century is distinguished from preceding ages because "the age carried with it an increasing kindliness" (*HTT*, 251). Leacock writes approvingly of the "geniality" of eighteenth-century literature "that finds voice in the humour of the Steeles, the Addisons and the Goldsmiths" (*HH*, 29); which is to say, in the humour of those eighteenth-century writers who may safely be termed the humanist essayists. While reflecting on the true beginnings of kindly humour in the eighteenth century, Leacock makes a revealing statement: "The new indifference called religious tolerance was spreading rapidly. Without this broad and kindly outlook humour is not possible" (*HTT*, 251). The "broad and kindly outlook" of religious tolerance is suggestively belittled as "the new indifference." Yet, in characteristic fashion, Leacock holds in balance the good and the bad of this indifference which is tolerance. As the above passage further demonstrates, sympathetic tolerance is the soil wherein flourish the incongruities perceived by the humorist's vision. The humorous vision then functions as a temporary charm or enchantment to alleviate the uncertainties of living in an anxiety-ridden, relativistic universe. And it is the eighteenth-century conception of a humour that is sympathetic in regard to the shared range and depths of human nature that comes closest initially to

Leacock's understanding of humour – genial humour as practiced in his view by Shaftesbury, Goldsmith, and Sterne.

Leacock viewed humour in a tempering role, as occupying a mediatory position between satire and sentimentality. He believed that humour is saved from indifference or cruelty by union with pathos, and that this union "keeps humour from breaking into guffaws [unsympathetic satire] as humour keeps pathos from subsiding into sobs" (HH, 233). It was the beginnings of just such a synthetic humour which he welcomed in "the charm that envelops The Vicar of Wakefield" (HTT, 251) or appreciated, perhaps, in the way the humour of Tristram Shandy mitigates the pretentious scientism of Walter Shandy and the sentimentality of Uncle Toby. Leacock remained adamant, however, in his dislike of the Juvenalian form of satire which is typified by Swift's work and the productions of the highly politicized Tory Satirists (Dryden, Pope, Gay, Arbuthnot, Congreve, and Fielding). He preferred the humour of Charles II, which he describes as "exquisite, ... of that tolerant gentle character that bespeaks a lofty mind," and he approvingly quotes the king: "'Good jests,' he said, 'ought to bite like lambs, not dogs: they should cut, not wound'" (ELS, 226–7).

Leacock calls Juvenalian satire "vitriolic satire," a term which he applied to the "humour" of post-World War One Germany – "as far from humour as blasphemy from blessing" (RU, 171). Such satire he understood to be synonymous with sarcasm, which "scrapes the flesh of human feeling with a hoe," and it is featured in the "sneer of the scoffer ... as opposed to the kindly tolerance of the humorist" (HH, 30). It is certain, though, that Leacock did understand the power and methods of caustic satire: "Satire may be of a dozen kinds and used for a dozen purposes. It may be personal, malicious, diabolical, or political and colourless, just a stick to beat a dog. But humour is the very life of it" (HH, 188). For many theorists (Bergson and Freud, for example), satire in this sense "is the very life" of laughter and wit. But Leacock's distinction no longer needs belabouring. Humour as "the very life" was for him an especially felicitous cliché. Humour is a spirit. Humour as the very life of satire is characteristic of and essential to Leacock's vision of humour. Humour should uplift mankind in a morally meliorating manner. Humour should also provide temporary relief from the disillusionments of life. Humour should make life's incongruities bearable. Humour at its best is charm, enchantment, the literary expression of Leacock's tory-humanist "high dream." Rabelais, Ben Jonson, Dryden, Swift, Pope – in Leacock's view these writers were not central to the hu-

morous tradition. He stipulates that "malice has no place" in humour, "nor the degradation of things sacred to others" (*HH*, 198).
He would even go so far as to claim that *anything* that bites or wounds
"is not humour. That is satire and as it gets more and more satirical
the humour dries out of it, leaving only the rasp of sarcasm" (*HTW*,
214).

It remains difficult, still, to understand the absence of praise for
the eighteenth-century novelists Henry Fielding (especially) and
Smollett (*HH*, 29) in Leacock's limited view of the history of humour.
Perhaps Fielding is virtually ignored for the malice of his allegorical
satires against Walpole (*Tom Thumb* and *Jonathan Wild*) and for the
sexual raciness of his novels. Smollett may have been slighted because of the earthiness of his characters, which is best illustrated by
the misanthropic diatribes of Humphrey Clinker. But as Walter Allen
has shown, Smollett was "Dickens' favourite novelist as a boy, and
Dickens took over and carried further his practice of rendering character in terms of its externals, of reducing it to caricature."[46] The
presentation of character-as-caricature is partially what Leacock so
admires in Dickens' work (especially the characters of Pickwick and
Micawber), and such comic characterization is the reason why Falstaff is the one piece of evidence Leacock offers as to Shakespeare's
comic genius. But surely this tradition of characterization in prose
fiction includes Fielding, the first English comic novelist. Moreover,
Fielding's definition of the "comic romance" is the first articulation
of a mode/genre that will include such works as *Sunshine Sketches*
and *Arcadian Adventures*, as does Fielding's elaboration of what constitutes the subject matter of a comic romance anticipate Hazlitt's,
and subsequently Leacock's, belief that incongruity is the basis of
the comic.

In his preface to *Joseph Andrews*, Fielding asserts that "the only
source of the true ridiculous ... is affectation," which "proceeds from
one of these causes: vanity or hypocrisy." He considers vanity the
less offensive affectation because "it hath not that violent repug-
nancy of nature to struggle with which that of the hypocrite hath,"
and because a vain man may possess to some degree "those qualities
which are affected."[47] In one important sense, the difference between the degree of kindliness in the humour of *Sunshine Sketches*
and *Arcadian Adventures* can be understood as an effect of the former
dealing kindly with vanity and the latter depicting less kindly the
more offensive hypocrisy. Although Fielding does not use the word
"incongruity," the incongruous is the probable source of his "true
ridiculous." Revealed affectation points up the discrepancy between

what a character pretends to be and what he is. (It may be noted, incidentally, that Fielding's affectionate and affected Parson Adams offers one probable literary ancestor for Leacock's Dean Drone.)

The fact remains, however, that Leacock overlooks Fielding's fiction and theory. As has been shown, Leacock believed that Juvenalian satire too readily degenerates into sarcasm at one end of the comic spectrum and that humour saves pathos from bathos at the other end. Fielding and Smollett, like Swift, belonged to the age of satire. For Leacock, satire evinces the primitive impulse to vanquish rather than to sympathize overtly, which propensity is a corruption of the true humorous impulse. He preferred the eighteenth century for its rising vogue of sentimentalism and viewed it as a budding before the full flowering of humour in the nineteenth century. Or, to borrow Leacock's solar metaphor, "The eighteenth century with its Addison, its Sterne, its Goldsmith, shows the rising sun" (HTT, 15), the rising sun which was to attain its zenith in the nineteenth century. There, in the reflected soft light which he selectively filters from Dickens' work, Leacock is wont to bask.

The "broad and kindly outlook" which was fostered by increasing "religious tolerance," and which Leacock understood to be essential to the progress of humour, was to increase into and throughout the nineteenth century: "It was only in quite modern times, pre-eminently in the nineteenth century, that [humour] received its highest development ... Only with the modern world and only in proportion as it loses its primitive credulity and the intense earnestness of its beliefs and superstitions does humour enter largely into literature" (HTT, 14–15). Leacock writes of the nineteenth century that "the very wistfulness of its new ignorance – contrasted with the brazen certainty of bygone dogma – lends it something pathetic" (HTT, 17). The progress of humorous literature was also contingent upon increasing democratization in the nineteenth century, which allowed for, or humoured, the individuality that inspires the popular characters of humorous literature. Specifically, democracy bred the opportunistic politician as *the* comedy type – "the master genius of democracy" (RU, 170). And, of course, the progress of Josh Smith and of the plutorians towards political victory is central to *Sunshine Sketches* and *Arcadian Adventures*.

While the nineteenth century's "new ignorance" eroded faith in a stable universe (Leacock does not illustrate this new ignorance, but he may have been thinking of the Higher Criticism and the evolutionary theory that challenged people's steady faith in biblical authority and a providential God), many Victorians did subscribe to a belief in progress. It is this primarily mid-Victorian faith in material progress which Leacock adapted to his theory of a meliorating humour that serves, ironically, to counter the dispiriting products of rationalism and progress. In the conclusion of *Humour and Humanity* he writes, "The underlying thesis is that humanity has as a whole grown better, and its literature has grown also from simpler forms to higher meaning and complexity" (*HH*, 233). It is precisely the "pathetic" nature of this "world of waning beliefs" that makes the truly humorous possible and necessary. The humorist must be tolerant and sympathetic because "humour in its highest reach mingles with pathos: it voices sorrow for our human lot and reconciliation with it" (*HH*, 232). For Leacock, this highest reach of humour was attained in the nineteenth century. But his affinity for humour and pathos as the reconciling agents in satire does not prevent him from seeing, with the vision of the ironist, that the overly sentimental is as deplorable as the harshly satiric.

Leacock points out that the nineteenth century's "righteous anger and its copious tears helped to smite to pieces and to wash away the older cruelty of the law, the inhumanity of the prison, the bitter isolation of the work house." But he adds,

Just because [nineteenth-century literature] was great, it had the defects of its noble qualities. It ran easily to prudery and overdone morality, and the hypocrisy that apes the moral attitude. It dissolved feeling into sentiment and sat in a flood of tears. It became namby-pamby and self-righteous: and while it kept for the most part its class system and its regime of status and privilege and the snobbery and subservience that dispersed it, it sought to hide it all under a make-believe of noblemindedness and false equality. (*HTT*, 71–2)

Leacock admires Dickens' use of pathetic scenes to elicit the reader's sympathies, but he does criticize overwrought sentiment in his favourite author's works. He feels that "all through" Dickens' novels, the humour "is disfigured by the sentiment and sentimentality so often linked with it. At times the flood of tears turns his page into a very morass of sentimentality" (*HTT*, 102). Nonetheless, Leacock values sentiment in literature and considers its inculcation a prerequisite for the development of the kindly humour he prescribes. What he dislikes is the literature of bathos. He prizes parody especially for its usefulness in countering the tendency of sentiment to run to sentimentality or the bathetic. (A parallel can be drawn here to Leacock's social-political views: extreme pathos – bathos – occupies in Leacock's theory of humour the place which the "dream" of the overly-sympathetic socialist occupies in his political thought;

just as socialism is tempered by Leacock's moderate tory humanism and assimilated to his social-political vision, so the bathetic is tempered by parody and becomes, as pathos, a crucial component of humour.) "The Victorians," Leacock writes, "needed parody. Without it their literature would have been a rank and weedy growth, over-watered with tears. A lot of their writing called aloud for parody" (*HH*, 71). Employing further the organic analogy, he calls parodic literature "parasitic humour" and argues that, "just as the parasite may bring to the parent-plant elements of life and sustenance and purify it from disease, so the parasitic forms of literature may serve to invigorate and purify the whole body of letters" (*HTT*, 46–7). Leacock considered parodies of a "class" of literature to occupy a "higher level" than parodies of a particular author, the former conforming to his definition of "parody," the latter to his definition of "burlesque." His preference for general parodies over particular burlesques is consistent with his disposition toward kindly humour. He dislikes the hypercritical implications of the specifically directed burlesque, preferring to "invigorate and purify" a body of literature rather than to attach himself to the corpus of a single author.

Although he employed "Humour" as an all-encompassing term, Leacock did not like literary productions of a crusading bent. In *How To Write* he offers his opinion of the reason why the nineteenth-century magazine *Punch* mellowed: "As *Punch* grew wiser, being unable to set all the world right, it replaced biting satire with mellow humour" (*HTW*, 218). The "all the world" is typical of the generalizing tendencies to which Leacock often succumbed. With his habit of using the broadest generalizations (or half-truths) and his sweeping views of human progress, he seldom considered that virulent satire can set *some*, if not all, wrongs right.[48] For instance, he writes of Thomas Hood's *The Song of the Shirt* that "deadlier earnestness was never penned. More scathing denunciation of social injustice was never written. Nor ever was greater effect produced on public opinion by private words." It might seem from this that Leacock could be induced to praise Swift's *A Modest Proposal*, until he adds, "But the effect is heightened, the satire goes deeper, the pathos is more intense ... because the cry of distress is voiced to the happy lilt of merriment" (*HH*, 191). Leacock liked only that kind of reform-intentioned satire containing obvious elements of sympathetic humour. He argues for the effectiveness of Dickens' works on similar grounds: "He did as much as, or more than, all the Benthams and the Romillys and the Shaftesburys to sweep away the removable hardships, the cruelties and injustices of the England of his day. He led where legislation followed. The pen was mightier than the parliament ... But he did it with laughter and the smiles that mingled even with anger as April sunshine glimmers through the rain" (*HTT*, 118–9). There may seem to be some contradiction between belittling "biting satire" (relative to "mellow humour") for its inability to reform "all the world" and praising Hood and Dickens for sweeping away the "removable hardships." One of the reasons for this seeming contradiction is Leacock's ingrained distaste for the evident anger and the means employed by virulent, tendentious satire. He believed that kindly humorous literature will prove finally to be more efficacious because it arouses the sympathies of its readers. Humour, to be true humour, must never attack people; it should direct its energies at the responsible institutions, and it should do so in a humanitarian fashion. Although the ends of reformist satire and kindly humour may sometimes coincide, Leacock did not believe that the unkind, regressive means justify the commendable, progressive ends. Appropriately, in his critical biography of Dickens, Leacock singles out *Hard Times* for denunciation. *Hard Times* is "mistaken and unsuccessful" (*CD*, 153), of "no other interest in the history of letters than that of its failure ... A large part of the book is mere trash" (*CD*, 169). And what is the reason behind Leacock's vehement criticism of one of his favourite author's most reform-intentioned works? "Dickens confused the faults of men with the faults of things" (*CD*, 171). *Hard Times* is too obviously angry for Leacock's tastes. It may be that Leacock felt, with Samuel Taylor Coleridge, that "intolerance, even in the gentlest temper, will frequently generate sensations of an unkindly order."[49] Satire must be guided by sympathetic humour, not by a regressive passion which betokens self-interest. For Leacock, caustic satire is not humour, though humour can be an aspect of satire. Of a satiric poem by G.K. Chesterton, "Antichrist, or the Reunion of Christendom: An Ode," Leacock observes, "He could prick the bubble of windy invective with the sharp point of humour" (*HH*, 190).[50] Is not satire, then, "the sharp point of humour"? Leacock is reluctant to concede so; rather than admit the importance of the satiric impulse *per se*, he writes instead of the "effectiveness of humour in satire" (*HH*, 189). In view of his insistent humanism and dislike of the rationalistic extremes of liberal individualism, this is a consistent distinction.

In Leacock's "gamut" of humour "which passes all the way from the ridiculous to the sublime," all aspects and expressions of the comic have their place and relative worth, from the primitive savage's triumphant shout to Prospero's decision to be "kindlier moved" (*Tempest*. IV.i.24). To a marked degree, Leacock's theory of humour is a hierarchical schema. Although he can appreciate the efficaciousness of satire, reform-intentioned works that employ caustic satire simply do not partake of the humour of sublimity. If Leacock remained ambivalent about the value to mankind of reform-intentioned satiric literature, it was because in his final analysis even when successful it mattered little. His praise of Charles ii is most revealing of Leacock himself: "He had grasped as but few men have done the great truth that nothing really matters very much" (*ELS*, 225). A more striking instance of this other possible motive behind Leacock's scepticism with respect to the value of reformist satire is his assessment of purposeful action: "In retrospect all our little activities are but as nothing, all that we do has in it a touch of the pathetic, and even our sins and wickedness and crime are easily pardoned in the realization of their futility" (*HTT*, 134). The import and cadences of Prospero's speech, "our little life / Is rounded with a sleep," can be heard in "our little activities are but as nothing." Whether or not the similarity is granted, the comparison is suggested to argue that it is the transforming, as opposed to the reforming, capacity of humorous literature that in Leacock's view distinguishes it and offers the hope of briefly alleviating "our human lot" (*HTT*, 99).

Leacock was of course a man much in and of the world; his ample writings on social-political issues testify to his compassionate involvement. Yet the concerns of his social-political writings do not figure largely in his conception of the true value and ultimate purpose of humour. Or, to put the matter differently, practical concerns figure in a negative manner in Leacock's theory as those things that make humour possible and necessary. Proof of these assertions involves an examination of Leacock's belief in the transforming, or magical, properties of humorous literature, and of the basis of his support for romance in the literary controversy over romance and realism that arose during the mid- to latter-nineteenth century. The most fruitful path to Leacock's thoughts lies through his writings on Dickens. Leacock's studies of Dickens are, like his essay on Charles ii, most valuable for what they reveal about Leacock.

Although a frequent satirist of myticism and what he described as an age "addicted to thaumaturgy" (*ELS*, 43), Leacock himself frequently employed diction that suggested the magical. The following are but a few of many examples. Dickens' characters were "created as from a magician's hand" (*HTT*, 113). In *The Pickwick Papers*, he created "an enchanted world," whose characters are a "great company of immortals, more real than life itself" (*ELS*, 161). Of Alfred Jingles, Leacock remarks on "the extraordinary magic by which

[Dickens] turns a cheat and a crook into a charming character" (*CD*, 32). *Martin Chuzzlewit* "shares with all Dickens' best work that strange alchemy of transformation whereby even sin and wickedness are softened" (*CD*, 108). And "the magic words transpose the scene" of David Copperfield's falling in love with Dora (*CD*, 145). Leacock considered Dickens a kind of literary wizard, a practitioner of white magic, of "necromancy" (*ELS*, 164). He viewed Dickens as a wizard not only for his "master's" powers of fictive creativity but also for what Dickens could effect in Leacock as reader. Dickens' fiction could take Leacock "out of himself" (the cliché partially explains Leacock's reticence in regard to reform-intentioned satire that would take him "into" a sordid world).

The word "necromancy" and the phrase "company of immortals more real than life itself" occur in an essay/story which rewards attention because it dramatically conveys Leacock's belief in the magical properties of humorous literature. The piece is appropriately entitled "Fiction and Reality: A Study in the Art of Charles Dickens" (*ELS*, 159–88). It is a defence of Dickens' method of characterization against the charge that his characters are "merely caricatures" (*ELS*, 159).[51] In this story the Leacock persona falls into a dream-state and experiences a "cherished vision" (*ELS*, 188) which, like the influence of the punch mixed by the apparition of Micawber, "must have been brewed from the very lemons of reminiscence, mixed by a strange alchemy of affection that is wafted to us still from the pages of *The Unforgotten Master*" (*ELS*, 164). The dream-vision concerns the proceedings of a court trial in which a gallery of Dickens' characters defend themselves against the charge (as read by Pickwick) "*that we are not real, that we are caricatures,* ... that we are mere monstrous exaggerations, each of us drawn in a crude and comic fashion from a few imaginary characteristics" (*ELS*, 169).

The gist of Leacock's fictionalized argument is that exaggeration is intrinsic to literary art and that exaggeration best achieves the purposes of universality and idealism. But no paraphrase can capture the proceedings as summarized by the sketch's apparent spokesman for Leacock's views, Dr. Blimber: "From the time of the Romans onward Art had of necessity proceeded by the method of selected particulars and conspicuous qualities: that this was the nature and meaning of art itself: that exaggeration (meaning the heightening of the colour to be conveyed) was the very life of it: that herein lay the difference between the photographer (we believe the doctor said the daguerreotype) and the portrait: that by this means and by this means alone could the real truth – the reality greater than life be conveyed" (*ELS*, 187–8). "Selected particulars and conspicuous qualities," the telling details, suggest that Leacock recognized and condoned the narrative technique of selective, or metonymous, realism in fiction. But it is Dickens' combination of the narrative strategies of realism and romanticism that Leacock ultimately champions.[52] Leacock did not care, however, for what he considered overdone realism, or for the "naturalism" that seeks novelty in the occupations of social classes not treated in traditional fiction. Writing in 1943 on what he considered "the besetting sin of the fiction of the present hour," he concludes with characteristic testiness and humour: "Life in odd places may be peculiar but I can do without it. I've read enough. If there are any other kind of farmers, sharecroppers, hillbillies, mine workers and such, I'll do without them. I don't care how hard they swear" (HTW, 87). It may be, therefore, that Leacock objected particularly to the tenets of *naturalisme* as formulated by French writers, especially Émile Zola, in the 1870s and 1880s, that he objected to the conveyance of minute detail, the complete fidelity to reality, and the portrayal of contemporary scenes of ordinary life.[53] Leacock considered documentary realism "not interesting in a literary sense unless made so by art" (HTW, 88). And the purpose of literary art is, in his view, to convey "the reality greater than life."

Yet Leacock was also concerned that the romantic, if left unchecked by the realistic, would tend toward sentimentality. "The valid basis for realism," he observes, "is its protest against the exaggerated sentiment" (HTW, 103). In this respect, realism shares with parody (and with humour itself) the function of keeping "pathos from subsiding into sobs" (HH, 233). Ever the conservative moralist, Leacock was more concerned with the threat that relentless realism presents to the humane feelings: "A realist is becoming the new name for the man who used to be called an 'unprincipled scoundrel'" (HTW, 104). For Leacock, considerations of the romantic and realistic are "not merely a question of art, but a question of reality, and of the relation between the two" (ELS, 172). Operative in his discussions of literary art is what Jerome Buckley has termed the "moral-aesthetic" of Victorian literature. Leacock believed, though to a lesser extent than did the "High Victorians" (Carlyle, Arnold, Ruskin), that art should be moral, that it should speak up-lifting truth in terms of universal emotion, and that it should instruct as well as amuse, in accordance with the Horatian dictum.[54] As he interjects in an essay on the twentieth-century fascination with violent crime, "But the moralist – that's me."[55] However, the moral aspect of Leacock's aesthetic is balanced by the belief that humour can serve, in a way that is curiously parallel to the late-Victorian decadent aesthetic, as an escape from disillusioning reality, as a humour for humour's sake.

The moral danger of the romantic attitude is its tendency towards self-indulgent sentimentality and consequent self-satisfaction. Although the following quotation refers specifically to the relationship between the romantic and sentimentality, it is essentially the same criticism that Leacock directed at the melodramatic in Dickens' work: "One is apt to suspect that the Victorians felt as if their flood of generous tears washed them free from obligations" (*HTW*, 104). Sentimental romanticism, like overdone realism, tends to produce, if not "unprincipled scoundrels," then literary voyeurs who feel absolved after a good cry. Nonetheless, when Leacock appraises the ultimate purpose of humorous literature, he leaves no doubt of his idealistic, romantic bias. Insistent realism is incapable of conveying the truth that he considered to be "truer" than factual truth. As was the case with "extreme individualism" and caustic satire, extreme realism is, for the tory humanist, too liberally intellectual; such an aesthetic implies that the intellect alone, accumulating facts and more Gradgrindian facts, can come to the truth which, for Leacock, transcends hard fact. Extreme realism denies the existence of unfactual, spiritual truth and is, therefore, incapable of eliciting the reader's "super-self" (*RU*, 206).

Leacock acknowledged that the heroes and heroines of traditional romances (Walter Scott's, for example) were portrayed too ideally. He insisted, though, that this idealism is inherent in mankind. "After all," he propounds, "heroism will out, tears will flow. ... The stock in trade of the romanticist is part of human nature itself" (*HTW*, 103). More to the point, the insistent realist is incapable of depicting the experience of romantic love, an ideal central to Leacock's humorous vision: "You cannot depict love inside a frame of fact. It needs a mist to dissolve in. You cannot tell a love story just as it is – because it isn't. There is something else there, something higher than our common selves and perhaps truer. When a young man sees in his girl an angel, and a young girl sees in her lover a hero, perhaps they are seeing what is really there – the self we each might have but which we grasp only in our higher moments and too late" (*HTW*, 106). This "something higher than our common selves and perhaps truer," which in literature cannot be intimated by realistic techniques, Leacock termed the "super-self."

For Leacock, the "super-self" is discerned only in the state of "enchantment" which he depicted as typified in the spirit of Christmas (*RU*, 203–8) – itself a conventionally sentimental subject which

Leacock exploited for his own humane purposes. In his study of Dickens, he praises "the sheer beautiful idealism" of *A Christmas Carol* and concludes, "It is of no consequence whether *A Christmas Carol* is true to life. It is better than life" (*CD*, 110–11). He writes in the dream-vision defence of Dickens that Dingley Dell's house is "the kind of house that might be found by those who had the eyes to see it, especially at Christmas time" (*ELS*, 185). Leacock considered the enchanted atmosphere of Christmas "a part of that super-self, that higher self that is in each of us" (*RU*, 206). He deliberately opposed his conception of the super-self to "the subconscious self, that evil, inward thing, ... that hideous stuff, ... the new hideous brood of the new Black Art" (*RU*, 206). The opposition is between conceptions of man as driven by the equivalent of the Freudian subconscious (or the mechanistic/individualistic) and man as aspiring to an unselfconcious ideal that includes good will.

Leacock's concept of a super-self that "lifts the individual life above itself" (*RU*, 206) may owe something to Matthew Arnold's idea of the "best self" which blossoms only in the "light" of true culture.[56] But where Arnold's purpose in conceiving the "best self" is primarily pragmatic (the "best self" as a reliable basis for "the State"), Leacock's "super-self" is more a spiritual construct. Both writers hoped, however, to counter the mundane obsession with "doing as one likes," and both imagined an ideal that "lifts the individual life above itself": the philistine, liberally material self. For Arnold's "sweetness and light" – the means out of individualism to the "best self" – Leacock offered the edification of true humorous literature, his "sweetness and light." But whereas Arnold's "best self" was to provide the reliable basis for a supposedly classless State, Leacock's "super-self" is glimpsed but momentarily during periods of literal enchantment. In Leacock's tory-humanist scheme, the super-self is fleetingly evoked by enchanting romantic love, by the patriotic spirit called forth by a just war, by adversity related to family and community, and by the charms of sublime humour. Leacock's use of the term "sublime" with respect to humour is reminiscent of the Longinian definition: "The effect of elevated language upon an audience is not persuasion but transport."[57] There is in Leacock, the tory humanist, a decided strain of, to borrow D.M.R. Bentley's coinage, "Tory transcendentalism."[58]

In his essay on the enchantments of Christmas, Leacock illustrates analogically, with reference to romantic love, the nature of Yuletide charm: "All lovers – silly lovers in their silly stage – attain for a moment this super-self ... – till the light passes and is gone" (*RU*, 206–7). The words "attain" and "super-self" connote the sort of thaumaturgy for which the initiates of Mrs. Rasselyer-Brown's Yahi-Bahi Oriental Society are so roundly satirized in *Arcadian Adventures*. Yet here Leacock is serious. Humour, "the highest product of our civilization," can lift man above the self-contained and the mundane to offer him the experience of his super-self "till the light passes and is gone." Although Leacock viewed sublimely humorous literature in such a light, this quasi-mystical vision of humour is one he seldom advanced, and it was not his central concern. Substantiation of Leacock's "Tory transcendentalism" relies on his connotative use of diction which is suggestive of the magical; substantiation depends also on the associations which he establishes between humour and enchantment, enchantment and love, and love and the super-self. His use of transcendental rhetoric is clarified when it is understood that he viewed humorous literature and the sublimely humorous perspective as the best strategy by which the incongruities at the core of a disillusioning life can be made momentarily bearable. When toleration has been attained, when the individual has apprehended a higher order, then a kind of transcendence becomes possible.

Leacock describes the experience of reading Dickens as momentarily slipping off "the dead weight of your own individuality" (*HH*, 115). He considers Pickwick "the greatest humorous character ever known" because Pickwick provides "the unsullied laughter of self-forgetfulness" (*HH*, 139). Self-forgetfulness and transportation into a world transformed in humorous literature – an enchanted or charmed world – is what Leacock invariably praises in the work of writers he most admires. Self-forgetfulness is needed because the individual and the world of *temporalia* are ultimately unsatisfactory. As always with Leacock, the individual finds true freedom by forgetting his sorry self in something greater, be it the community, just causes, or humorous literature. "What we give thus, we do not lose," he writes in a social-political context, "or, if it is lost for ourselves, it is given to humanity" (*HL*, 24). Leacock was, philosophically, not only a skeptical man, but, temperamentally, a man of a deep-seated "humorous sadness" (*As You Like It*, IV.i.18). In his writings he often retells an anecdote concerning the incongruity between the humorist as a man who makes others laugh and who is in himself predisposed to melancholy. In "Laughing Off Our History," he suggests that "a humorous person ... would be apt to be cut more nearly to the heart by unkindness, more deeply depressed by adversity ... than a person with but little of that quick sense of contrast and incongruity which is the focus of the humorous point of view" (*RU*, 151).[59] In his books on humour, as well as in the many essays and chapters, Leacock moves unwaveringly towards the consideration that humour's greatest utility is in providing respite from a life rife with disillusionment. The central position of "kindliness" in Leacock's theory of humour can be fully appreciated only when his perspective on life as fundamentally disillusioning begins and ends that assessment.

Perspective is in fact the key to understanding Leacock's theory of humour. His humorous vision focuses on the middle ground between satire and sentimentality, between reality and illusion. The humorist indeed requires the powers of a magician to fabricate illusions of sufficient charm to counter the "reality" of Leacock's appraisal. At the conclusion of *Humour, Its Theory and Technique*, he writes that the "highest humour ... represents an outlook upon life, a retrospect as it were, in which is contrasted the fever and fret of our earthly lot with its shortcomings, its lost illusions and its inevitable end" (*HTT*, 280). The humorous perspective depends, therefore, on temporal distance, on what Leacock calls "the refracting prism of past distance" (*HTT*, 281), and it is analogous to the way in which past disappointments are forgivingly perceived. At the conclusion of *Humour and Humanity*, he repeats that "the humour of sublimity ... views life, *even life now*, in as soft a light as we view the past" (*HH*, 237, emphasis added). The emotional impulse is a nostalgic humanitarianism which attempts to transcend the harsher realities of past and present. Leacock does not ignore fault, of course, but he strives at all times to tolerate it in a manner which he understands to be innate to human nature at its best. In *How To Write*, he contrasts this humorous perspective with the perspective of Juvenalian satire, again employing the image of a prism. He berates the writer who would present a conventionally sentimental event – in this instance, a class reunion – in a satiric light as one who is looking at the world "through glasses all split into distorting prisms, showing everything in false perspective." Realizing perhaps that he has, with regard to class reunions, pushed his kindly dictum a touch too far, Leacock concludes, "Humour, it cannot be too often said, must be kind" (*HTW*, 252–3).

There is no avoiding the conclusion that Leacock's theoretical understanding of the purpose of humorous literature contains a qualified endorsement of humour as providing a temporary escape: "Each of us in life is a prisoner. The past offers us, as it were a door of escape. We are set and bound in our confined lot. Outside, somewhere, is eternity; outside, somewhere, is infinity. We seek to reach into it and the pictured past seems to afford to us an outlet of escape" (*HTT*, 281). "The pictured past" is humorous literature, and the "seems to afford" acknowledges the illusory quality of humorous literature itself. In the chapter dealing with historical novels in *How*

To Write, Leacock ponders that "perhaps we can create a dream world of the past if we cannot make a real one … make something which is better than reality … since actual life is poor stuff anyway" (*HTW*, 158, Leacock's ellipses). "Perhaps we can." Leacock feels compelled to hedge because he knows, of course, that abdication from reality is not desirable on a permanent basis. That would be insanity of a decadent sort. In one of his typically short sentences, he concludes, "Escape is barred" (*HTT*, 283).

Leacock's conception of the highest form of humour, the humour that treats of the "incongruous contrast between the eager fret of our life and its final nothingness" (*HH*, 241), is a humour that offers an impermanent reconciliation with disillusioning life and a temporary illusion of escape. Humorous literature also provides a perspective that contains glimmerings of the greater, or transcendent, reality. Of equal importance, though, "humour is saved from [indifference, cruelty, and self-indulgence] by having made first acquaintance and then union with pathos, meaning here, pity for human suffering" (*HH*, 232–3). It thus appears that Leacock's theory of humour owes something to both the "moral-aesthetic" concerns of the mid-Victorians and the purely aesthetic concerns of the late Victorians. Although the premises of the "Aesthetic Movement" were first articulated by Walter Pater in the conclusion of his *Studies in the History of the Renaissance*, Jerome Buckley has shown that the ideal of an art for art's sake was never completely condoned by Pater. What Buckley concludes of Pater's moral-aesthetic applies equally to Leacock's: "There could be for him no full experience in a world of artifice beyond humanity. Great art 'set the spirit free' by lifting it above itself – not by admitting the individual to some esoteric enjoyment, but rather by carrying him to a vantage point from which he might see the essential pattern of all life."[60]

To illustrate further his view that the humorous vision depends upon heightened perspective, at the conclusion of *Humour and Humanity* Leacock quotes from Prospero's famous speech in *The Tempest*: "We are such stuff as dreams are made of [sic] and our little life is rounded with a sleep." He concedes that these lines are not, strictly speaking, humour, yet he contends that they "convey the point of view from which the greatest humour seems to start" (*HH*, 232). Earlier in the book, he describes the "highest stage" of humour as being a literature wherein "tears and laughter are joined, and our little life, incongruous and vain, is rounded with a smile" (*HH*, 31). This is the divinely, sublimely humorous perspective – "rounded with a smile" instead of a sleep. It may or may not be fortuitous, but the reference conjures up images of Shakespeare's magnanimous magician, of Prospero's transformative expression of the belief that "the rarer action is / In Virtue than in vengeance" (V.i.27–8). For Leacock, as for Prospero, it is a perspective – a wisdom – that has little room for virulence. When Leacock views the world from such a cosmically ironic height, he can think only in "kindly" terms. When he descends fictionally into the incongruous brave new world, he frequently finds himself portraying characters who ground his kindly flights. Leacock makes this point in his own inimitable way: "Yet somehow just when I am reflecting on my own kindliness I find myself getting furious with a waiter for forgetting the Worcester sauce" (RU, 301).

The last paragraph of Humour, Its Theory and Technique begins, "Thus does life, if we look at it from sufficient distance, dissolve itself into 'humour'" (HTT, 287). Here, in the ultimate fate of the material world, Leacock finds a kind of humour of creation. The scientific basis of the following passage appears to be the nineteenth-century astronomical theory of entropy, the implications of which point to a universal "cancellation of forces": "With it goes out in extinction all that was thought of as matter, and with that all the framework of time and space that held it, and the conscious life that matched it. All ends with a cancellation of forces and comes to nothing; and our Universe ends thus with one vast, silent unappreciated joke" (HTT, 288). Such is Leacock's elegiac vision of the end of creation: a universal negation of the forces that hold the incongruous universe in tension. The world ends, in Leacock's vision, not with a revelatory or satiric bang, but with a humorous whimper of a kind because the cosmically ironic joke is unappreciated. No human remains to appreciate the humour.

Humanism served for Leacock's religion and humour was indeed its literary manifestation, its spirit made word. Such a humorous vision embraces the incongruities of life itself, presenting life's disillusionments in a bearable form. It is meliorating in its hope to inculcate greater kindliness in mankind, illusory in its purpose to provide temporary escape, and ideal in its dream to proffer the possibility of temporary transcendence. Leacock sees the world romantically and steadily – in a word, humorously. His all-encompassing humorous vision readily perceived and took full measure of the Smiths and Drones and Fyshes and Boulders of his fictional landscapes. In Sunshine Sketches of a Little Town, the subject of Leacock's humorous vision is "Mariposa". The Sketches enacts all that Leacock hoped for from humour.

CHAPTER THREE

Sunshine Sketches: *Mariposa Versus Mr Smith*

One of the principal concerns of *Sunshine Sketches of a Little Town* is perception, and the primary subject of the book's perception is "Mariposa." Mariposa is the typical Canadian town between city and hinterland. Populated with colourful individuals, it is Leacock's ironically portrayed ideal of an interdependent community. Mariposa is the place from which many affluent city dwellers migrated, the community which they have partly forgotten, and the "home" towards which they nostalgically yearn. Mariposa is the Canadian past, at once individual and collective. And most importantly for present purposes, Mariposa is the temporary location of JOS. SMITH, PROP.

Before I proceed to an analysis of the opposition between Mariposa and Josh Smith, a few words must be said on the important matter of perspective, the organization of *Sunshine Sketches*, and the narrator(s). Leacock's "Preface" to the *Sketches*, the narrator of the sketches, and the narrator of the closing sketch, "L'Envoi: The Train to Mariposa" (hereafter called the Envoi narrator), persistently reveal an interest bordering on obsession with the reader's perspective on and knowledge of "Mariposa." This interest arises before the reader is permitted to enter fully into "the present work" (*SS*, xi), and it persists until the auditor of "L'Envoi" is allowed figuratively to leave "such a book as the present one" (*SS*, 255). A parallel concern with the reader's response to *Sunshine Sketches* as literature is announced when the prefacer disdainfully disclaims that he is "trying to do anything so ridiculously easy as writing about a real place and real people" (*SS*, xi). Thus, the prefacer not only forestalls legal suits for libel but also implicitly opposes the relative merits of an imaginative, romantic literature to those of a more documentary realism. Taking over from the prefacer, the narrator of the sketches begins his first story with the doubly doubting remark, "I don't know whether you know Mariposa" (*SS*, 1), and thereby reveals his intention of introducing "you" to Mariposa by showing you around (almost as if he were a tour guide). Finally, the Envoi narrator begins his second sentence, "Strange that you did not know it" (*SS*, 255). Five times within the space of the following five short paragraphs, the Envoi narrator presumes upon what his auditor either "knows" or "knew." The Envoi narrator's closing remarks, the last words of *Sunshine Sketches*, refer to "the little Town in the Sunshine that once we knew" (*SS*, 264), thus emphasizing that his main concern, evident throughout "L'Envoi," is with memory and imagination in so far as these contribute to self-knowledge. As an imaginative work of fiction, *Sunshine Sketches* enacts that which so concerns its "narrators": a correct perception of "Mariposa" which is to be achieved by means of sight, knowledge, memory, and imagination.

As a book dealing so insistently with perspective on and knowledge of Mariposa, *Sunshine Sketches* is best approached on its own terms as a treatment of the incongruities between appearances (or illusion) and reality. More precisely, the book is a humorous treatment of characters, actions, and themes that illustrate the incongruity between appearances and reality, aspiration and achievement, intention and realization. The humour of the *Sketches* is in most instances self-evident, and it is not the purpose of this chapter to analyze the book's humour in the sense of what is funny. Because Leacock treats his subjects humorously, ironically, and satirically, many of the questions that arise from the incongruity between appearances and reality remain unresolved. In *Sunshine Sketches* Leacock's irony does not simply suggest the truth of the opposite to what is stated (the irony of *Arcadian Adventures* is nearer to this handbook definition of dramatic irony). Leacock accepts the possibility of truth in both appearances and reality. His insistently ironic attitude implies, in essence, the impossibility of discovering simple truth. There are in the *Sketches* repeated movements of appearances towards reality, followed by a falling back or collapsing. Moreover, there is repeated manipulation of appearances by the prefacer, by the narrator of the sketches, by the Envoi narrator, and by characters in the sketches. In "L'Envoi," Mariposa and *Sunshine Sketches* themselves recede into the realms of illusion, the illusions of memory and literature. When appearances are manipulated by Leacock or his narrators, the result is an ironic truth or insight of the equivocal sort touched upon above. When appearances are exploited by Josh Smith, the product is self-advancement at the expense of, and frequently to the diminution of, Mariposans. When, on the other hand, the manipulator is an indigenous Mariposan such as Judge Pepperleigh, the result is communally beneficial. In short, *Sunshine Sketches* is a tory humanist's humorous anatomy of the useful illusions by which Mariposans live, whereas the later *Arcadian Adventures With the Idle Rich* is a dissection of the illusory nature of dehumanizing reality in "the City." Despite Douglas Spettigue's compelling argument to the contrary, the difference between Mariposa and Plutoria is not quantitative; it *is* qualitative.[1] Broadly stated, the illusions of Mariposa sustain the community, whereas the accepted realities of Plutoria "weigh on the other side of the scale" (*ELS*, 50).[2] In both books, illusions can be used for either good or evil purposes; in both books, images of transformation and tansmutation suggest that magic can be either white or black.

This final point concerns the utilization of the past, of memory, and of imagination. "L'Envoi: The Train to Mariposa" finally and firmly underscores the importance of maintaining an enlightened response to "Mariposa" in order properly to incorporate its values into the present. *Sunshine Sketches* demonstrates that Leacock, the tory humanist, believed that such an appreciation of the past is necessary to a full life, a life that develops organically rather than one which is radically cut off from its roots. By means of its imaginative humorous vision, *Sunshine Sketches* enacts that which the Envoi narrator leads his auditor to attempt: a return to Mariposa, a distillation and embodiment of its virtues with an honest appraisal of its faults.

revisions   —   ⚹

Leacock made three major structural revisions to *Sunshine Sketches of a Little Town* between its serial publication in the *Montreal Star* from 17 Feb. 1912 to 22 June 1912 and its publication in book form later the same year. He added the preface and re-organized the sketches as follows: the first two installments for the *Star*, "Mariposa and its People" and "The Glorious Victory of Mr. Smith," were combined to form the book's opening sketch, "The Hostelry of Mr. Smith"; and the sixth installment for the *Star*, "Mariposa's Whirlwind Campaign," was divided to become the fifth and sixth sketches of the published book, "The Whirlwind Campaign in Mariposa" and "The Beacon on the Hill." The addition of the preface is significant because it, with "L'Envoi: The Train to Mariposa," provides a kind of framing device for the sketches proper. That is, Leacock's preface and "L'Envoi" present the reader with different, though complementary, perspectives on *Sunshine Sketches* and Mariposa, perspectives that differ not only from one another but also from the point of view of the narrator of the sketches proper (sketches one through eleven). All three perspectives – those of the authorial prefacer, the ironically involved narrator, and the distanced reflective narrator of "L'Envoi" – are necessary to a rounded view of the town and the book. By re-organizing the opening and middle sketches, Leacock gave prominence to the character of Josh Smith and created in the interior sketches – sketches four through nine – two, three-sketch sections, of which the first is concerned with Mariposan religion, the second with Mariposan romance. This symmetrical centre of the *Sketches* opposes three sketches on the virtues of Mariposa in matters of romance, love, marriage and family to three sketches on the failure of Mariposa's institutionalized religion to meet simply the needs of its Anglican parishioners. This structurally contrived, balanced opposition at the centre of *Sunshine Sketches* begins to suggest that Leacock's masterpiece is a more highly organized and complex work than has hitherto been shown.[3] And it is partly the purpose of the present chapter to show that the *Sketches* is the amplest illustration of Leacock's claim in its preface that true humorous literature is an "arduous contrivance" (*SS*, xi). More specifically, the organization – the plan – of the *Sketches* reflects the values of Leacock's humanism and toryism: the tory humanism that values continuity in human affairs, responsibility, tolerance, and organicism; that emphasizes balance and equipoise in all matters and insists upon the priority of the community over the individual – a community such as Mariposa, an individual such as Josh Smith.

The sketches proper are grouped into five thematic sections: 1) sketches one and two, concerning Josh Smith and Jeff Thorpe respectively, deal primarily with business, with the first including an important reference to and anticipation of the political concerns of the last two sketches; 2) sketch three portrays in microcosm the social life of Mariposa aboard the *Mariposa Belle*; 3) sketches four through six deal with the religious dimension to life in the town; 4) sketches seven through nine centre their concern on romance, love, marriage and family; and 5) sketches ten and eleven depict the political life of Mariposans and the practices of their candidates for the national legislature. Viewed thus, the two-sketch business and political portions of the *Sketches* can be seen structurally to contain the social, religious, and romantic concerns of the book. This is what might be expected in the fiction of a political economist, and the exigencies of such a writer's priorities offer a reason why the social-microcosm sketch, "The Marine Excursion," is not the first sketch, as might be expected. The structure of the *Sketches* mirrors the priorities of life within Mariposa and, in a pragmatic sense, Leacock's priorities: the realities of business and politics appear first and last, and at the heart of the book is found what may be called the spiritual realities of religion and love.

Excepting for the moment "The Marine Excursion" and the three-sketch Pupkin-Pepperleigh romance, we see that *Sunshine Sketches* deals humorously with those three taboos of genteel conversation: business, religion, and politics. Josh Smith is central to all three in Mariposa; he is peripheral only to the love interest. Smith, the principal character of the first and last sketches, can be conceived as straddling, so to speak, the Mariposans in a manner similar to his bestriding of the stubborn beam of the church's burning driving shed. With regard to the practical aspects of Mariposan life, *Sunshine Sketches* is Smith's book; with respect to the heart of Mariposa, it is Pupkin's and Zena's. Ralph Curry has written that Leacock had intended the Pupkin-Pepperleigh romance to be "the central theme to unify" *Sunshine Sketches*.[4] The love story is certainly central, but it does not serve as a unifying device. Quite possibly the attraction of Smith, the hard-nosed realist, seduced the worldly Leacock away from his intended plans for the romance. Only the voices of the prefacer and the narrator precede the looming figure of JOS. SMITH, PROP. Only the Envoi narrator figures after Smith's silent appearance on the victory platform in sketch eleven, "The Candidacy of Mr. Smith."

Josh Smith can in fact be viewed as *Sunshine Sketches'* closest approximation of a "hero" and its most convincing argument for a unity of plot. He moves through this time-suspended work, seemingly knitting together by his actions the frequently fraying fabric of Mariposan life. He runs the hotel that temporarily becomes Mariposa's commercial showpiece. He contracts for eggs with Jeff Thorpe's "woman" and thereby financially assists the bankrupt barber. He saves the *Mariposa Belle*. He burns down Dean Drone's debt-ridden church for the redemptive insurance money, then single-handedly prevents the fire from spreading to the tinderbox town. And he champions the Conservative fight for protectionism against Liberal leanings towards trade reciprocity with the United Stades, thereby saving, by ironic extension, the British Empire. What more could a reader ask of a hero? Regardless, it is the primary purpose of this chapter to show that Smith acts in every instance for patently self-serving reasons. Smith is a masterfully deceptive interloper: he moves into Mariposa, exploits its deluded residents, and by the end of the eleventh sketch is on his way out.

Sunshine Sketches is not, however, a novel, an observation which has often been uncritically lamented by Leacock's critics. Only by torturing beyond recognition such aspects of the traditional novel as character development and plot can it be claimed that Leacock's series of sketches is a novel, or a "proto-novel," or something else that reveals the critics' lack of appreciation for the linked series of stories.[5] But like the best short story cycles (Joyce's *Dubliners*, Sherwood Anderson's *Winesburg, Ohio*, and Alice Munro's *Who Do You Think You Are?* for example), *Sunshine Sketches* possesses thematic unity and, as has been shown, an underlying structure that is itself emblematic of Leacock's tory humanism. The prefacer's use of the phrase "an arduous contrivance" should alert the reader that *Sunshine Sketches* may be something more than a collection of simply sunny and unconnected sketches.

Authorial contrivance first manifests itself in the first sentence of the preface, wherein Leacock thinks it advantageous to introduce "his work" by introducing himself (*SS*, vii). Like the narrator of the sketches, who insists that the reader learn to *see* Mariposa properly before proceeding to meet Josh Smith, Leacock contrives that the reader become acquainted with the author's version of himself before proceeding to what he insists is imaginative fiction. The prefacer portrays himself in terms that are by turns equally boastful and self-effacing. In fact, his thumbnail autobiography is as charming as is his narrator's portrayal of Mariposa, as charming and as incongruous. He ironically inflates his own importance, thinking it "extremely likely" that there might have been a "particular conjunction of the planets" at the time of his birth (*SS*, vii). The narrator of the sketches tends also to employ mock-heroic, inflated comparisons, as is evidenced in his opening description of Mariposa (*SS*, 1–3). And like the narrator's Mariposa, which occupies a medial position between city and hinterland, the Leacock of the preface feels himself to be "singularly fortunate" in his position as university professor because it provides a middle way of a kind: "The emolument is so high as to place me distinctly above the policemen, postmen, street-car conductors, and other salaried officials of the neighbourhood, while I am able to mix with the poorer of the business men of the city on terms of something like equality" (*SS*, ix). This process of ironic inflation and deflation (or explosion) is a technique shared – if not overworked – by the narrator of the sketches.

Before the prefacer will relinquish the reader to the adeptly ironic and overly concerned narrator of the sketches, he must disclaim that either Mariposa or its inhabitants are real or based on living individuals. (Leacock's remarks in this instance anticipate his defence of Dickens' method of characterization; namely, his claim that caricature and selective realism are the surest means of achieving universality, a quality which Leacock understood to be one of the chief purposes of literary art.) The prefacer insists that not only Mariposa but also "the Reverend Mr. Drone, ... Mullins and Bagshaw and Judge Pepperleigh and the rest" are compilations or types. But it is the prefacer's unapologetic anticipation of Josh Smith that is of especial interest. The remarks occur emphatically last in the comments about the book's characters: "As for Mr. Smith, with his two hundred and eighty pounds, his hoarse voice, his loud check suit, his diadmonds, the roughness of his address and the goodness of his heart – all of this is known by everybody to be a necessary and universal adjunct of the hotel business" (*SS*, xii). Certainly Smith learns in the first sketch that a good heart is an asset to the hotel business. As the narrator notes following an instance of Smith's self-enriching philanthropy, "Mr. Smith learned, if he had not already suspected it, the blessedness of giving" (*SS*, 21).

In its subtle anticipation of the political concerns of the last two sketches, the first sketch develops most purposefully towards Smith's further realization "that the hotel business formed the natural and proper threshold of the national legislature" (*SS*, 34). Smith progresses from a political apprenticeship of sorts in the first sketch to his election victory in the last. In a loose sense, this is plot and character development. The prefacer's comment on Smith's good heart as it relates to the hotel business should alert the reader to be wary of him. (Indeed, in the subtlety of its irony, the prefacer's seemingly innocuous statement should alert the reader to be wary of appearances in general.) Unguarded readings of the prefacer's comment on Smith have misled many critics to view him as a commendable character, or to view him, in William H. Magee's opinion, as "the amiable representative of the small town at its best."[6]

Although the prefacer, the narrator of the sketches proper, and the Envoi narrator should be distinguished one from the other, such distinctions become blurred at the realization that all three share a similar style, especially in their use of inflated (mock-heroic) comparisons and an ironic voice of a purity that makes discriminations difficult. As already noted, the prefacer, like the narrator, boasts then undercuts. He was head boy at Upper Canada College and is a graduate of the University of Toronto, which education left him "intellectually bankrupt" (*SS*, viii). He received a Ph.D. from the University of Chicago and attained a sort of intellectual closure wherein "no new ideas can be imparted to him" (*SS*, ix). He is a member of a number of learned societies which, "surely, are a proof of respectability" (*SS*, ix). He has lectured internationally on Imperial organization, the impressiveness of which is undercut by the subsequent conflation/concatenation of the "Union of South Africa, the Banana Riots in Trinidad, and the Turco-Italian War" (*SS*, x). If such "proof of respectability" has not prepared the reader for fiction written from an ironic and conservative point of view, Leacock states plainly, "In Canada I belong to the Conservative party" (*SS*, x). He then undercuts the value of his political affiliation and the integrity of politics generally, by ironically complaining that he has received no political patronage, and, in so doing, implicitly boasting of his honesty. Such ironic undercutting is here called "pure" because Leacock can, finally, only be understood as holding to both views – the involved and the disenchanted – though certainly he keeps them at arms' length. It can be concluded that the preface reveals a Leacock who is, perhaps because ironically aware of the ultimate vapidness of his boasted accomplishments, "deeply conservative in a human sense." This is a characteristic of Canada's humorists which Northrop Frye has designated "the prevailing tone of Canadian humour every since" Thomas McCulloch.[7]

Like the prefacer, the narrator of the sketches maintains his Mariposa and Mariposans at an ironic distance. Perhaps this is because he is guiding "you" through Mariposa and is therefore forced to be more immediately aware of the incongruity between appearances and reality. At other times, such as when the *Mariposa Belle* is sinking, the narrator becomes fully Mariposan. This last point suggests another characteristic of the narrator. He has trouble at times with the chronological development of his narrative, such as when he prematurely and disingenuously reveals the climax to "The Marine Excursion" sketch: "But when you write about Mariposa, or hear of it, if you know the place, it's all so vivid and real, that a thing like the contrast between the excursion crowd in the morning and the scene at night leaps into your mind and you must think of it" (*SS*, 73). What the narrator has in mind is everybody's "crowding so eagerly to be in the accident" (*SS*, 70). He reflects on the incongruity: "Perhaps life is like that all through" (*SS*, 70). Such attempts to complicate and universalize his story reflect the complexity of the narrator, who can be omniscient, cleverly ingenuous, and frankly disingenuous. Donald Cameron has concluded that "Leacock evidently conceived of the narrator as an intelligent man feigning simplicity."[8] Although generally valid, Cameron's characterization is surely an oversimplification, for the narrator of the sketches is chameleon-like, and his changeableness serves a number of authorial purposes, foremost among which is that it prevents the continual ironic undercutting from degenerating, in Leacock's opinion, into one-dimensional caustic satire.

If satire that castigates with reference to a rigid moral norm had been Leacock's intention in the *Sketches*, then surely an adolescent, naïvely innocent, or persistently ingenuous narrator would have served better – Mariposa as seen by a Huck Finn, a Lemuel Gulliver, or even an Incomparable Atuk. But such a narrator would not have suited Leacock's purpose, for the satiric norm that operates within the book is provided, as Northrop Frye has observed, "by Mariposa itself." Frye writes that the reader often finds "in Leacock, a spirit of criticism, even of satire, that is the complementary half of a strong attachment to the mores that provoke the satire. That is, a good deal of what goes on in Mariposa may look ridiculous, but the norms or standards against which it looks ridiculous are provided by Mariposa itself."[9] In *Sunshine Sketches*, Mariposa is at once the object of much satire and the satiric norm, morally lacking and the moral norm. The foils to these norms are Josh Smith and, to a lesser degree, the auditor in "L'Envoi" – the auditor because he has forgotten the worthwhile of Mariposa while developing in himself its faults, Smith because of his blatant avaricious materialism and individualism.

Before the narrator will introduce Josh Smith, "you" must have your perspective adjusted. You must learn to see Mariposa properly, with "the eye of discernment" rather than "the careless eye." Seen with the careless eye, Mariposa is a slumbering little town: "But this quiet is mere appearance. In reality, and to those who know it, the place is a perfect hive of activity." What the narrator offers to illustrate Mariposa's activity – that is, to contradict its slumbering appearance – seems, however, to prove that the town is not a hive of activity. The "perfect jostle of public institutions" is obviously not "comparable to Threadneedle Street or Broadway"; nor do the four men working on the sausage machines in the basement of Netley's butcher shop argue for "a busy, hustling, thriving town." It would be a mistake, though, to assume that the narrator is satirizing only the affectations of Mariposans. As the sketches to follow prove, Mariposa seen from within *is* a hive of activity. The reader's perception of the town depends on perspective, or point of view, as the narrator well knows. Of course Mariposa appears to slumber "if you come to the place fresh from New York." So, too, might London, Ontario, appear relatively languorous in the sunshine if perceived by a visitor fresh from the bustle of the bigger London. As a consequence of such a juxtaposition, "your standard of vision is all astray" (*SS*, 3-4). By way of contradicting appearances, the narrator, in a pre-introductory reference to Josh Smith, presents Smith as standing with his eyes closed, presumably slumbering in the sunshine like the town itself. As the first sketch will amply demonstrate, however, Smith's brain never idles and is, if ever anything is, a "hive of activity" buzzing about the main chance.

The narrator proceeds in circumlocutory fashion toward the slouching figure of Smith, almost as though he were reluctant to confront and disturb him. All that the narrator digresses upon concerning Mariposa relates to the incongruity between appearances and reality. The Mariposa Local, as opposed to the express train, "is a real train" (*SS*, 7). The shanty-men who come down from the "lumber woods" are "calculated to terrorize the soul of a newcomer who does not understand that this also is only an appearance" (*SS*, 8). In reality, the shanty-men are farmers; after a spell in Mariposa, they undergo a transformation "and turn back again into farmers" (*SS*, 8). Even electricity (a benefit of technological modernity) is "turned into coal oil again" (that is, an energy closer to the organic) by the time it enters Mariposa (*SS*, 8). It would seem, then, that in Mariposa things are not what they first appear, though in another sense they are what they appear to be. With respect to Mariposa, this must remain in large part the equivocal kind of "truth" that *Sunshine Sketches* depicts.

The narrator begins the paragraph that introduces Smith in a tentative vein: "If, then, you feel that you know the town well enough to be admitted into the *inner life* and movement of it, walk down this June afternoon half-way down the Main Street – or, if you like, halfway up from the wharf – to where Mr. Smith is standing at the door of his hostelry" (*SS*, 9, emphasis added). It appears from this that Smith has somehow situated himself at the "inner life and movement" of Mariposa. He and his hostelry are located halfway along Main Street, Missinaba Street. The narrator adopts the Mariposan name for the street and invites the reader to enter Mariposa physically. Having done his best to adjust the reader's perspective to an ambivalent Mariposan point of view, the narrator ironically reveals his acceptance of that perspective and guides the reader/tourist towards the imposing and ominous figure of Smith, that "strange dominating personality ... that somehow holds you captive" (*SS*, 10).

Smith, like all that is connected to the Mariposa of the narrator's introductory remarks in the first few pages of "The Hostelry," undergoes within the space of one paragraph a transformation from the appearance of "an over-dressed pirate" to "one of the greatest minds in the hotel business" (*SS*, 10). Smith's facility at manipulating his and his hotel's appearance allows him to undergo a similar transformation in the eyes of the Mariposans (*SS*, 18–22). Simplicity of style and an imposing appearance assist Smith to do so. Having situated himself at the "inner life" of Mariposa, he is adept at exploiting the residents' respect for appearances. Unlike the former proprietors of the hotel, who affected such names for the transient establishment as the Royal, the Queen's, and the Alexandria, Smith simply hangs a sign bearing the legend, "JOS. SMITH, PROP." Simplicity in the abbreviations coupled with the assertive block lettering help provide "living proof that a man who weighs nearly three hundred pounds is the natural king of the hotel business" (*SS*, 11). That is, Smith's appearance as a hostelry king serves in Mariposa for the reality.

Before proceeding to his account of Smith's professional dilemma in the matter of the threatened liquor license, the narrator refocuses attention on Smith's appearance and contrasts this to "reality": "His appearance, to the untrained eye, was merely that of an extremely stout hotel keeper walking from the rotunda to the back bar. In reality, Mr. Smith was on the eve of one of the most brilliant and daring strokes ever affected in the history of licensed liquor" (*SS*, 13). (Note that the relation between Smith and his hostelry – their shared fate – is reinforced rhetorically by the progression of the "extremely stout hotel keeper" from the "rotunda to the back bar," a description that suggests further a rearview of Smith.) The narrator desires to keep before the reader the incongruity between Smith's appearance and his aspirations. Smith appears to be an "extremely stout hotel keeper." He looks like a buffoonish, over-dressed pirate, which, with emphasis on the piratical, he proves himself to be. Yet the narrator's description of the stroke that Smith is contemplating as "one of the most brilliant and daring" is equally a statement of truth, for this stroke is immediately associated with the "Ladies' and Gents' Cafe" (*SS*, 13), which is, as the subsequent sketches prove, *the* greatest illusion that Smith conjures into reality. The "caff" saves Smith's liquor license and temporarily maintains him in Mariposa. It also awakens his political ambitions, thus indirectly opening his avenue out of Mariposa. And as the narrator suggests in the above passage, the caff is but *one* of Smith's most brilliant and daring strokes; another is the "stroke!" (*SS*, 141) of his axe on the main supporting beam of dean Drone's driving shed; and as the arsonist who fires into reality Dean Drone's metaphoric "beacon," Smith is responsible also for Drone's "stroke" (*SS*, 146). Smith's "brilliant and daring stroke" with the caff reflects and resonates throughout *Sunshine Sketches*.

In the conversation of Smith, Gingham, and Henry Mullins – the first section of dialogue in *Sunshine Sketches* – Smith introduces what he knows to be the decisive factor in determining Mariposan opinion: the city. "If I have to quit," threatens Smith, "the next move is to the city" (*SS*, 16). It should be noted, though, that Smith already has in mind the idea of the Caff, the Rats' Cooler, and the Girl Room: "But I don't reckon that I will have to quit. I've got an idee that I think's good every time" (*SS*, 16). Smith's "idee" is to construct an impressive piece of the city in Mariposa, or at least to conjure up temporarily the illusion of a city hotel. Mullins' question to Smith, "Could you run a hotel in the city?" (*SS*, 16), demonstrates the open-mouthed awe that the magical word "city" evokes from Mariposans. It also betrays a "gosh-Josh" admiration of Smith that underscores the Mariposans' childish impressionableness and justifies Smith's addressing the assembled as "Boys" (*SS*, 16). As the narrator observes parenthetically in the second sketch, "In Mariposa all really important speeches are addressed to an imaginary audience of boys" (*SS*, 58). Like children, Mariposans are fascinated by appearances, particularly bigness, such as Smith's physical size, and the impressive trappings of such urban schemes as a "whirlwind campaign." This misinformed emulation of things that are big and related to the city continually gets the Mariposans into trouble and allows Smith to dupe them.[10]

"Bigness" is in fact the key concept in Smith's reply to Mullins' question: "There's big things doin' in the hotel business right now, big chances" (*SS*, 16). Smith dangles before the assembled (Mullins, George Duff, Diston, and Gingham) the picture of what they as Mariposans will miss if he moves: the Caff, the Rats' Cooler, and the Girl Room. He concludes: "If I go to the city that's the kind of place I mean to run" (*SS*, 17). But as he has previously hinted, Smith has no "idee" of going to the city, at least not yet. He employs the enticing vision of a hotel in the city as a lure (though he may also be sounding his audience's response to his "idee"). In either case, the open-mouthed fish are hooked when, further enticing his prey, Smith offers a free drink to Gingham: "What's yours, Gol? It's on the house" (*SS*, 17). It would be galling indeed to let such a "king" slip away to the city.

The revocation of his license compels Smith not to leave Mariposa but to carry out his plan for the Caff and the Rats' Cooler. When ordered to "close down" (*SS*, 24), Smith, in one of the book's most significant inversions, expands his business. That Smith is in full control even at this point in the first sketch, that he calculates which negative Mariposan illusions will best serve his needs, is substantiated by the flashback that elucidates his dilemma. This flashback, which concerns Smith's life prior to his arrival in Mariposa, explains how he has come to figure in the "inner life" of the little town. "But stop –" the concerned narrator interjects as Billy arrives with the telegram (*SS*, 17). "You" could not enter *Sunshine Sketches* until Leacock, as prefacer, had offered his terms for allowing you to do so. You could not proceed into Mariposa and toward Smith until the narrator had adjusted your perspective; that is, until the narrator had taught you to see with the "eye of discernment." And now, "it is impossible for you to understand" Smith's predicament without a fuller knowledge of his background (*SS*, 17).

The reader learns that Smith is *in* though not *of* the little town in the sunshine, *in* and casting a looming shadow. He has come from the north, having risen from the position of cook in a lumber camp to running a river driver's boarding-house, and, thence, to holding a "food contract for a gang of railroad navvies on the transcontinental," after which "the whole world was open to him" (*SS*, 18). The implications of this latter remark should recall the prefacer's ironical lament about his "failure" in Canadian politics – he never received a contract "to construct even the smallest section of the Transcontinental Railway" (*SS*, x). Thus the echo effectively distances the character of Smith from Leacock and suggests, perhaps, that Smith is corrupt and already knows something of political patronage. Moreover, Smith's association with the timber trade suggests the lawlessness characteristic of the timber trade along the Ottawa River (and elsewhere) in the mid-nineteenth century. (Here, the "river driver's boarding-house" is understood to suggest rivers as actively a part of the timber trade as the Ottawa.)[11] At this point in his mythical rise, Smith arrives in Mariposa and picks from the whole world "the 'inside' of what had been the Royal Hotel" (*SS*, 18). Notably, Smith does not want the "loafers and shanty men" for customers (*SS*, 19). These men are, as already noted, "only an appearance"; in reality, they are local farmers who have worked in the "lumber woods" and are simply on a binge before returning to their farms. Or, to state bluntly what the kindly narrator's account of Smith's past strongly suggests, Smith uses and discards people.

It is Smith's attention to the details of his and his hotel's appearance that drives away the low-lifers and secures the relatively high-class trade. By assuming the appearance of an "over-dressed pirate," Mr Smith had become a local character. Mariposa, like the whole world *after* his contract with the transcontinental, "was at his feet"

(*SS*, 20). Mr Smith overcomes lingering "*opposition … by a wide and sagacious* philanthropy" (*SS*, 21, emphasis added). By buying ten dollars' worth of free rides for the Mariposan children from a visiting merry-go-round operator, Smith effectively ingratiates himself with their parents – to the extent that they stand "four deep along [his] bar" (*SS*, 21). The narrator anticipates the reader's mistaken presumption that Smith's original gesture was truly motivated by kindly intentions: "Mr. Smith learned, if he had not already suspected it, the blessedness of giving" (*SS*, 21). If any doubts linger, the narrator removes them by beginning the following paragraph, "The *uses* of philanthropy went further" (*SS*, 21, emphasis added). Not a man to store up riches in heaven, Smith proceeds to donate to every organization in town, knowing full well that what he gives in his "sagacious philanthropy" will be returned at least a hundred-fold.

Instead of conveying to the reader a sense of Smith's anxiety, then, the flashback leaves little doubt that he will be more than adequate to any situation. When Billy returns with the unfavourable verdict, the telegram announcing that Smith must "close down," it comes as no surprise that Smith acts quickly, forcefully, and deviously. There is something of the furious in the manner in which the additions to Smith's Hotel take shape, something of demoniacal energy, of the construction of Pandemonium, in the way his "idees" assume form: "Then the excavation deepened and the dirt flew, and the beam went up and the joists across. … Spacious and graceful it looked as it reared its uprights into the air" (*SS*, 25). Smith informs the curious, baffled and forgetful Mariposans that the additions are "a caff – like what they have in the city," a Rats' Cooler and "a 'girl room,' like what they have in the city hotels" (*SS*, 26). The description of the completed additions further presents Smith's Hotel as having undergone a sort of magical transformation: "Not only was the caff built but the very hotel was transformed. Awnings had broken out in a red and white cloud upon its face, its every window carried a box of hanging plants, and above in glory floated the Union Jack. The very stationery was changed" (*SS*, 26). The impressionable and sensation-seeking Mariposans fall down, figuratively, before this gilded "caff" which Smith has shaped from their golden dreams of city life.

Smith brazenly reverts to names for his transformed hotel that are as affected as those used by former proprietors. His establishment is now called "Smith's Summer Pavilion" and is advertised in the city as "Smith's Tourists' Emporium and Smith's Northern Hotel Resort" (*SS*, 26). By enticing weekend sportsmen from the city, Smith demonstrates his ability to exploit the illusions of city dwellers with

regard to the benefits of a northern holiday as readily as he manipulates the illusions of the semi-rural Mariposans with respect to city
life. Smith's ruse in exploiting the city dwellers anticipates his ploy
in having notice of his election victory prematurely wired from the
city – a tactic that assures his victory as surely as the flocking of the
city dwellers to his Tourists' Emporium assures his esteem in the
wide eyes of the Mariposans. Smith's successful manipulation of
the city dwellers hints further that Mariposa may ultimately prove
to be too small a pond for this swelling toad.

The transformed hotel is of course false, illusory. Only Smith,
"who knew it by instinct, ever guessed that waiters and palms and
marble tables can be rented over the long distance telephone" (*SS*,
27). The French chef is as transient as are the artifically-deflated
prices of his meals. The Rats' Cooler, into which you "step from the
glare of a Canadian August to the deep shadow of an enchanted
glade" (*SS*, 39), is not only an ephemeral enchantment but a questionable one: "He who entered the Rats' Cooler at three of a summer
afternoon was buried there for the day" (*SS*, 30). Golgotha Gingham,
ever with an eye on trade, "spent anything from four to seven hours
there of every day. In his mind the place had all the quiet charm of
an interment, with none of its sorrows" (*SS*, 30). The Rats' Cooler,
with its "German waiter noiseless as moving foam" (*SS*, 30), momentarily holds the reality of "a Canadian August" and of Mariposan
life at bay. But it is a figurative crypt, a place much frequented by
the undertaker Golgotha Gingham. The Rats' Cooler is the home of
suggestively black magic. Only Smith, who bears the burden of
expense for this delusory charm and enchantment, understands the
real situation. When he sits down with Billy at the end of the day
to assess the situation, his language with reference to his clientele
is revealingly crude: "Billy, just wait till I get the license renood,
and I'll close up this damn caff so tight they'll never know what hit
her. What did that lamb cost? Fifty cents a pound, was it? I figure
it, Billy, that every one of them hogs eats about a dollars worth of
grub for every twenty-five cents they pay for it. As for Alf – by gosh,
I'm through with him" (*SS*, 30). It has cost Smith dearly to serve
underpriced lamb. In terms of the relation between Mariposa and
Mr Smith, the Mariposans are the lambs, Smith the wolf in "shepherd's plaid trousers" (*SS*, 9). And as the last sentence of the above
speech again shows, Smith thinks nothing of using and discarding
people, in this case, Alphonse, the "French Chief" (*SS*, 27).

The reader might therefore expect that the illusion of the caff and
the Rats' Cooler also will vanish when they have served their purpose, leaving behind but a rack of their former selves. Although the

primary purpose of the additions had been the renewal of Smith's license, the successful illusion inadvertently endows Smith with an aura of prestige that transforms his vision of himself. At the height of his hotel's popularity, some of the awed and excited Mariposans "wanted to make him the Conservative candidate for the next Dominion election" (SS, 33). Their reason for so wishing is associated, not with Smith's political acuity, but with his having "done more to boom Mariposa than any ten men in town" (SS, 33). The potential for self-advancement latent in this blind boosterism is not lost upon the perceptive Smith. In fact, Smith's transformation of his hotel effects nothing less than a transformation of Smith: "There was a quiet and a dignity about his manner that had never been there before. I think it must have been the new halo of the Conservative candidacy that already radiated from his brow. It was, I imagine, at this very moment that Mr. Smith first realized that the hotel business formed the natural and proper threshold of the national legislature" (SS, 34). "Halo" and "radiated" suggest that Smith here attains an ironic apotheosis, or, at least, a political canonization of sorts.

But Smith does become Mariposa's elected representative, and not simply because the electors are blind to their own interests. Mariposa does not obviously provide an absolute moral norm. The moral norms of the book can be induced only after a careful consideration of the events portrayed, after an appraisal of what motivates its characters, and after a thoughtful assessment of the narrator's relentlessly ironic commentary. Mariposa is anatomized humorously _and_ satirically. Its ambitions are Smith's writ small, and its reflective faults are heightened by Mariposan ineffectuality. Put simply, if Mariposans did not possess serious shortcomings reflective of Smith's glaring faults, he would not be able to manipulate and exploit them as he does. What Mariposans do possess in opposition to Smith is a concern for their community, a concern which is second nature to them. It might also be said that Smith brings out the worst in the Mariposans, the shadows.

Whereas the first sketch deals with real business, the second deals with illusory business. The parallel and opposition is suggested at the beginning of "The Speculations" by the location of Jeff Thorpe's little barber shop "just across the street from Smith's Hotel" (SS, 37). The eighth paragraph of the sketch, comprising one sentence, repeats and emphasizes the relation between Thorpe and Smith: "The barber shop, you will remember, stands across the street from Smith's Hotel, and stares at it face to face" (SS, 39). Jeff's barber shop, like Smith's Hotel, is located at the centre or "inner life" of

Mariposa, "halfway down the Main Street – or, if you like, halfway up from the wharf" (*SS*, 9). In contrast to the taciturn Smith, however, Jeff is distinguished for his loquacity, conversation being in fact "the real charm" of his barber shop (*SS*, 41). This "real charm" – leisurely, communal intercourse – bespeaks opposition to the delusive, dark enchantments of Smith's Rats' Cooler. And unlike Jeff, who loses all the money he makes from mining speculations, Mr Smith profits by the boom. Smith, the realist, is not seduced by the romance of northern riches: "You see, Mr. Smith had come down from there, and he knew all about rocks and mining and canoes and the north country" (*SS*, 46). Rather than speculating wildly, Smith realizes a tidy profit by shipping potatoes to the northern speculators. Jeff, on the other hand, "had looked at so many prospectuses and so many pictures of mines and pine trees and smelters, that ... he'd forgotten that he'd never been in the country" (*SS*, 46). The opposition between Smith, the real businessman, and Jeff, the speculative dreamer, is made plain: "Mr. Smith, I say, hung back. But Jeff Thorpe was in the mining boom right from the start" (*SS*, 46).

It would be naïve, however, to assume that this opposition between real and illusory business is simply for the purpose of exposing the baseless fabric of the latter and chastising the ruthlessness of the former. In business matters, the relation of the real to the illusory is more complex than a state of simple structuralist opposition. The illusion, Jeff's dream of riches, moves towards and becomes reality, only to revert to the illusive reality operative in Mariposa. The movement of Jeff's dream from illusion to reality, to Mariposan reality, is parallelled both thematically and temporally by Smith's caff, which briefly materializes only to dissipate.

Jeff's barber shop has a false front. It is the type of building that Sinclair Ross will later employ in his *As For Me and My House* to symbolize small-town affectation (though perhaps "hypocrisy" would be the better word for Ross's "Horizon"). The narrator describes Jeff's false-fronted shop as "a form of architecture much used in Mariposa and understood to be in keeping with the pretentious and artificial character of modern business" (*SS*, 39). It is to be doubted, however, that the Mariposans "understand" their architecture in this evaluative sense. No doubt they simply take the appearance for the reality. The assessment of "modern business" as "pretentious and artificial" is a statement that stands out stylistically from the page. Here, the narrator suggests that it is big business, not the mistaken Mariposans or their pathetically affected architecture, that is truly "pretentious and artificial." In effect, this incongruous remark is an implicit statement of theme. The plot of this sketch – the rise and fall of Jeff's financial fortunes – is relatively unimportant. Leacock cared little for plot.[12] His narrator has already revealed the central twist of the sketch: "As I say, it was when Jeff made money that they saw how gifted he was, and when he lost it – " (SS, 38). The narrator has ironically subverted the development of his story in order to allow his readers to concentrate on the contrasted aspects of "The Speculations," on its characters and its theme.

With the exception of "L'Envoi," no other sketch so insistently contrasts the city and Mariposa. In each instance of contrast the narrator favours Mariposa: "In Mariposa, shaving isn't the hurried perfunctory thing that it is in the city. A shave is looked upon as a form of physical pleasure" (SS, 40). City dwellers do not even have time to read their newspapers, "but in Mariposa it's different" (SS, 41). Where Mariposan life is distinguished for its physical pleasures and leisurely pace, Mariposans are individuated to an extent unknown in the city. The city financiers whom Jeff imagines to be working his undoing are lumped together as "that unseen nefarious crowd in the city" (SS, 49). And the narrator remarks with only a hint of condescending, mitigating irony, "After all, the capitalists of the world are just one and the same crowd" (SS, 53). Although the Mariposans may judge a man by his material possessions (SS, 38, 58), the pleasurable, leisurely atmosphere of the small town more than compensates for this human failing of its residents.

The narrator of "The Speculations" reveals a patronizing interest in keeping Jeff in his barber shop and content with his leisurely life in Mariposa. The narrator "liked it about Jeff that he didn't stop shaving" after he made his killing in the market (SS, 55). What the narrator does not like is the seeming shift in Jeff's interests, a threatened transformation in self-regard reminiscent of that which elevated Josh Smith to aspiring MP in the first sketch. The narrator notices "a sort of new element in the way Jeff fell out his monotone into lapses of thought that I, for one, misunderstood. I thought that perhaps getting so much money, – well, you know the way it acts on people in the larger cities. It seemed to spoil one's idea of Jeff that copper and asbestos and banana lands should form the goal of his thought when, if he knew it, the little shop and the sunlight of Mariposa was so much better" (SS, 56). Jeff does not "know it," the value of his life in Mariposa, but the relatively sophisticated narrator does know it. Of the many ironies in this sketch, one of the most telling is that Jeff's failure and loss is – from the narrator's point of view – his salvation. Although the conclusion is somewhat pathetic, the narrator is justified in admonishing, "Pathetic? tut! tut! You don't know Mariposa" (*SS*, 60). By this point, though, the careful reader does know Mariposa and can view Jeff's situation with the kind of ironic vision that the narrator and narrative demand.

Jeff is much better off in his leisurely paced environment, where people are individuated. The small-town barber, with his commendable if unsophisticated notions of advertising for "incurables" and giving "an acre of banana land in Cuba to every idiot in Missinaba county" (*SS*, 59), would not have lasted long or happily in the outside world, where philanthropy (as seen from Smith's use of it) is a euphemism for self-interest. Jeff ends where he began, poor though not significantly worse off. The conclusion to "The Speculations" emphasizes the brave face with which Jeff and his family accept their lot. Jeff must work a longer day but he is accustomed to such work; his daughter Myra bravely and admirably relinquishes her affected ambition of becoming an actress (*SS*, 61). It is Jeff's work habits, his communal function, that save him from despair. The Carlylean-Victorian work ethic aside, it must be faced that Jeff is also aided by Mr Smith.

The final irony of "The Speculations" resides in its closing allusion to Josh Smith's caff. The reader learns that Jeff's rise and fall has been concurrent with Smith's threatened fall and rise. Jeff is helped financially when Smith contracts with "Jeff's Woman" for seven dozen eggs a day. "You see it was just at this time that Mr. Smith's caff opened" (*SS*, 61). The coincidence of events suggests, in the least, that Mariposa at this time must indeed have been a "hive of activity." Real business, as practiced by Smith, transpires concomitantly with the illusion of business (market speculation) as practiced by Jeff. The caff, which was itself finally an illusion, served to further Smith's real business and political ambitions. Jeff's paper fortune, an appearance that moved towards reality only to vanish, served to effect his financial undoing and to return him to where he began. Thus the final reference to Smith and his caff can be seen to contrast Smith's progress to Jeff's stationary position in Mariposa. Smith is moving forward and outward; Jeff, like the accident-prone *Mariposa Belle*, returns to where he began. It may be that Smith's progress is contingent upon Jeff's stability. It may also be that Leacock is suggesting that some good – the helpful egg contract – results from Smith's rampant individualism and crass materialism. But as for Smith's motives, it is probable that his seeming benevolence is further evidence of his exploitive selfishness, his desire to keep Mariposa relatively stable for his own purposes. And Smith knows, even as he contracts for the eggs, that the caff will remain in full operation and in need of extra eggs only so long as it is useful to him. Jeff and "the Woman," like the shanty men, the German waiter, and the "French Chief," will soon have to fend for themselves.

This is not to say that Mariposa is guiltless. Jeff is obsessed with riches because that is one standard of value in Mariposa: "It was a favourite method in Mariposa if you wanted to get at the real worth of a man, to imagine him clean sold up, put up for auction, as it were" (SS, 58). Nevertheless, for all of Mariposa's faults, Leacock's narrator bears it an obvious affection that is seldom withheld. Smith is the only major character in Sunshine Sketches who is never treated with overt affection. Smith does not belong to Mariposa and only temporarily resides in Mariposa. Although Mariposa may not provide an unequivocal moral standard against which Smith can be measured, Smith embodies a selfishness in the shadow of which the virtues of the community shine and can be generously assessed. The reader would be mistaken to slight Jeff's intention to use part of his illusory fortune for charitable purposes. In terms of philanthropy versus selfishness, Jeff's humanitarian motives count for everything, his mistaken method and misplaced ambitions count for little (if the source of such rich humour can be called "little"). As was shown in the discussion of the first sketch, every instance of Smith's "philanthropy" illustrates his materialism and individualism. Smith's election to the national legislature illustrates an inevitable consequence of the relation between business and politics, and implies that political office is but the tacky laurel for those who are ambitious, energetic, and cunning enough to exploit that relationship.

Smith's election victory, "the crowning triumph of Mr. Smith's career" (SS, 244), is of a piece with his earlier triumph in the matter of the caff, which was itself "one of the most brilliant and daring strokes ever affected in the history of licensed liquor" (SS, 13). Like the earlier triumph, his election victory is the product of his industrious manipulation of Mariposan delusions of grandeur. But the narrator, who insisted in the opening sketch that the reader could not meet Smith until he had learned to see Mariposa properly (that is, until "you" had discarded the mere appearance in favour of the inner reality), cautions in "The Great Election" that "you can't understand the election at all ... unless you first appreciate the peculiar complexion of politics in Mariposa" (SS, 214).

The narrator adopts the Mariposan perspective from the opening of this sketch, a perspective which may be termed a determinedly Mariposcentric point of view: "I saw it all [the election] from Missinaba County which, with the town of Mariposa, was, of course, the storm centre and focus point of the whole turmoil" (*SS*, 213). Having thus identified himself with the Mariposans, the narrator reasons that in "the great election Canada saved the British Empire, ..." and so onward (or inward) until he begins to conclude "that those of us who carried the third concession, – " (*SS*, 214). The narrator arrests the tendencies of his Maripocentric thinking, realizing that he is about to conclude, ludicrously, that little Mariposa "saved the British Empire."

The narrator then reveals the basis of Mariposan political opinion: "As soon as they grab the city papers out of the morning mail, they know the whole solution of any problem" (*SS*, 215). The informed reader can now begin to "appreciate the peculiar complexion of politics in Mariposa." It is of course this fact of city orientation that Smith exploits for victory. And yet, the narrator can remark, fully cognizant as he is of the derivation of Mariposan political opinion, that politics in Missinaba County "is not the miserable, crooked, money-ridden politics of the cities, but the straight, real old-fashioned thing that is an honour to the countryside" (*SS*, 219). As is soon revealed, this is the truly ironic or backhanded compliment. Leacock harboured no illusions about practical politics, whether urban or rural (as chapter one of the present study has shown). In "The Great Election" his narrator proceeds to illustrate that politics in Missinaba County is nothing but bribery and patronage (*SS*, 219), where voting is a simple matter of herd mentality: "Nobody cares to vote first for fear of being fooled after all and voting on the wrong side" (*SS*, 244). Although the herd mentality is but the other face of the coin whose stamp is the commendable sense of community, it must be conceded that in political matters Mariposa gets the MP it deserves.

Employing a narrative strategy that parallels the movement of the opening sketch, the narrator of "The Great Election" concludes his general analysis of Mariposan politics with the statement, "So now, I think, you understand something of the general political surroundings of the great election in Missinaba County" (*SS*, 221). Reminiscent of the way in which the circumlocutions of the first sketch centred finally on Smith, here the ironic anatomy of political life leads to an introduction to "John Henry Bagshaw, ... the sitting member, the Liberal member, for Missinaba County" (*SS*, 221). Bagshaw can be viewed as Smith's mirror image. Whereas Smith has situated himself at the "inner life" of Mariposa and is moving towards the politically representative, Bagshaw is the political representative returning involuntarily to the inner life.

Perhaps Bagshaw loses the election because he has been away from Mariposa for too long (twenty years interrupted by intermittent compaigning returns) and so has lost touch to some extent with the pulse that fancies itself the throbbing of a metropolis. In any event, the Liberal Bagshaw, running on the issue of trade reciprocity with the United States, attempts to win through traditional patronage only. Smith, the Conservative champion of protectionism and "the Empire," stands upon a somewhat wavering platform. An opportunist, he knows nonetheless that the small Canadian town of Mariposa will unseat a Liberal who threatens the British connection. (Leacock considered that protective tariffs within the British Empire were necessary for its economic and political unity.[13]) Smith wins, though, not because of his changeable policies or his Imperialism, but because he has his victory prematurely telegraphed from the city. (Leacock, a Conservative and public defender of protectionism in the 1911 general election, must have held little hope for the possibility of integrity in politics, as he humorously implies in his preface, and as the portrayal of the virtuous, though ineffectual, Edward Drone would suggest.) By exploiting Mariposan awe of the city, Smith assures the overly cohesive electorate that a vote for him will not be a vote "on the wrong side," the losing side. Bagshaw, "the old war horse" and "old jackass" (SS, 221), fails to exploit this apparently recent ambivalent city reverence, and so he loses the election.

Accordingly, Smith's campaign draws much of its incidental credibility from things civic and from references to bigger things. He answers the question on Imperial defence by claiming that he is "fer" whatever "the Conservative boys at Ottaway think" (SS, 236). He inflates impressive "statissicks": "'Shove it up to four,' said Mr. Smith. 'And I tell you,' he added, 'if any of them farmers says the figures ain't correct, tell them to go to Washington and see for themselves'" (SS, 241). By contrasting the success of Smith's political strategy to Bagshaw's failure to realize the importance of "the city," Leacock may be suggesting an even greater shift in Mariposan orientation towards the city. Since one of the repercussions of this presumed shift is Smith's election – through prematurely telegraphing news of his victory from the city – it follows that the tendency away from provincial self-sufficiency is not a commendable development. The implication is certainly there in the tactics of the two campaigns and in Smith's telling coup. Yet such an interpretation is beside the point. Partisan politics is an unseemly business, complete with the mathematical trappings of business – "statissicks" and "figures" (SS, 240). In the final analysis, there is little to choose between Smith and Bagshaw.

Bagshaw is presented as a formidable opponent. In a Maripocentric sense, he is "one of the greatest political forces in the World" (*SS*, 221). The illustrations of his political prowess which follow this childish superlative concern Bagshaw's adept (and Smithian) manipulation of appearances. He maintains the appearance of residency in his riding while being in reality an absentee farmer. He sends hogs to the "Missinaba County Agricultural Exposition and World's Fair" (Maripocentrism), accompanying them in his corduroy breeches with a straw in his mouth. "After that," observes the narrator, "if any farmer thought that he was not properly represented in Parliament, it showed that he was an ass" (*SS*, 222). Bagshaw's personal tokenism extends equally to business, religion, and education, to be capped by the revelation that he keeps "a little account in one bank and a big account in the other, so that he was a rich man or a poor man at the same time" (*SS*, 223). Bagshaw's physical presence in Mariposa is literally significant: "You could see, if you knew the signs of it, that there was politics in the air" (*SS*, 224). The narrator's observation is revealingly to the point: in many ways *Sunshine Sketches* is an encyclopedia of humorous signs, the significance of which "you" are taught to read.

Bagshaw's political strategy is one of the more surprising instances of inversion in the *Sketches*, though even it is surpassed by that flexible secondary plank in Smith's platform – "temperance and total prohibition" (*SS*, 230). Bagshaw would rather run on the issue of graft than on the tariff question, not because he can prove that the Conservatives are corrupt but in order to *publicize* his free dispensing of political patronage (*SS*, 226). His reasons for so desiring reveal the limits of his manipulative skills relative to Mr Smith's and provide a damning indictment of Mariposan political life: "Let Drone have plenty of material of this sort and he'll draw off every honest unbiased vote in the Conservative party" (*SS*, 226). That is, Drone will lose by a landslide.

If *Sunshine Sketches* has a climax with regard to the opposition between Mariposa and Mr Smith, it occurs at Golgotha Gingham's timorous announcement to Bagshaw that the Conservatives "are going to put up Josh Smith" (*SS*, 228). Bagshaw, nobody's fool, realizes immediately the Herculean task before him and comes "as near to turning pale as a man in federal politics can" (*SS*, 229). Appropriately it is Gingham, the undertaker, who informs Bagshaw of Smith's candidacy, thus figuratively sounding Bagshaw's death knell. The news is a blow to Bagshaw and of such import that the narrator, in a manner reminiscent of Fielding, Sterne, and Dickens, announces that he must close his chapter. What follows in the eleventh sketch, "The Candidacy of Mr. Smith," is the opening of a new chapter in Mr Smith's life. In this final sketch, Smith is insistently called "Mr. Smith." To some extent, the "joshing" is past, and the change to the formal "Mr." further distances the familiar narrator from this apparently transformed, "over-dressed pirate."

It is crucial to an appreciation of Mr Smith's progress to realize that he risks his standing in Mariposa by running for federal office. Before the reader learns that Smith is "put up" by the Conservatives, the narrator notes that "hotel keepers," along with "office holders, and the clergy and the school teachers" are "allowed to claim to have no politics" (SS, 216). The implication is that they must appear – "claim" – to be disinterested in order to maintain their sinecures. Smith's profession is remarked upon twice when Bagshaw learns that he is to be the Conservative candidate: "Smith! the hotel keeper," exclaims Bagshaw (SS, 228); and the narrator, following a few mock-heroic metaphors, remarks redundantly "that the Conservatives had selected Josh Smith, proprietor of Smith's Hotel" (SS, 229). Bagshaw and the long-empowered Liberals either have not learned or have forgotten what Smith realized in the first sketch: that "the hotel business formed the natural and proper threshold of the national legislature" (SS, 34). The election is, then, a must-win. And because Smith is so successful a hotel keeper, it is a will-win competition for him.

Displaying a subtle symmetry, the sketches proper begin and conclude with telegrams: Smith is victimized by the first, the victor with the second. Furthermore, the telegram from the city which proclaims Smith's victory is but a more sophisticated version of the "caff" of the first sketch. The effectiveness of both caff and telegram depend upon the awe with which Mariposans view things metropolitan. Neither caff nor telegram has a basis in reality; both are illusions conjured up by Smith and based upon a cluster of Maripocentric characteristics, the most easily distinguished of which are affectation, envy, physical appetite, and the provincial herd mentality. This may sound like an indictment of Mariposa equal to Robertson Davies' ungenerous assessment.[14] It is not intended as such.

The crucial distinction to be made between Smith and Mariposa is that the negative characteristics just rehearsed are evoked, cajoled, and exploited by Smith for the gratification of those same, and apparently sole, attributes of himself. Smith possesses no redeeming features. Mariposa does. In opposition to Smith, Mariposa's most obvious virtue is its nature as an interdependent community. This opposition was made clear in the contrasting first two sketches, a contrast between real business as practiced by Smith for his own enrichment and the illusory business of Jeff Thorpe, whose evanes-

cent fortune was to be used partially for local philanthropic purposes, and whose real business, barbering, provides a meeting place
for leisurely communal intercourse. To suggest an indecent, rather
un-Leacockian *double entendre*, Smith's rapacious relation to Mariposa
can best be surmised from his instructions to his supporters to hold
back their votes: "Wait till she begins to warm up and then let 'em
have it good and hard" (*SS*, 245).

The seven middle sketches of *Sunshine Sketches* treat the social,
religious, and romantic dimensions of life in this riding which Mr
Smith carries before him then leaves behind him. But the removal
of JOS. SMITH, PROP., does not threaten Mariposa with collapse. If
anything, Mariposa props up Smith; or Smith is a "prop" in the
theatrical sense, a colourful villain in the melodrama of Mariposan
life. The following analysis of the third sketch, "The Marine Excursion of the Knights of Pythias," will demonstrate once again – this
time with a nationalist twist to the theme – the opposition between
Mariposa and Mr Smith, showing further that Smith is unnecessary
to the life of the community.

There are repeated hints throughout "The Marine Excursion" that
the sketch should be considered as presenting a microcosm of social
life in Mariposa. The narrator remarks that "the Mariposa Belle always seems to me to have some of those strange properties that
distinguish Mariposa itself" (*SS*, 68). One of these properties is, like
the town's population figures, the steamer's variable size as a function of perspective: "After you've been in Mariposa for a month or
two, ... she gets larger and taller" (*SS*, 68). The image of the steamer
as a kind of floating Mariposa is humorously underscored in the
behaviour of the passengers aboard her; they occupy themselves
exactly as they would at home, particularly the older women who
"all gravitated into the cabin on the lower deck and by getting round
the table with needlework, and with all the windows shut, ... soon
had it, as they said themselves, just like being at home" (*SS*, 74–5).
It will be recalled, however, that in both the preface and the first
paragraph of the opening sketch, Mariposa was established as *the*
small Canadian town. That the steamer, symbolic of Mariposa, also
represents something essentially Canadian is indicated by the Py-
thian band's departure song, the "Maple Leaf for Ever" (*SS*, 74), and
by the recurrent singing of "Oh Canada." Most notable is the politically telling, "I think that it was just as they were singing like this:
'O-Can-a-da,' that word went round that the boat was sinking" (*SS*,
83). And there is of course the final block-lettered transcription of
the singing as the boat "steams safe and sound to the town wharf"

– "O-CAN-A-DA" – the last syllables of the sketch (*SS*, 93). "The Marine Excursion" suggests that *Sunshine Sketches* was indeed the only fiction that Leacock wrote on commission for a specifically Canadian audience. [15] Pertinently, it is during the sinking of the *Mariposa Belle* – which craft, by extension, becomes a symbolic "ship of state" – that Leacock's narrator becomes most fully Mariposan.

When the steamer begins to sink, the narrator grows alarmed, despite his knowledge of the lake's depth and the periodic recurrence of these sinkings. "Safe!" he exclaims. "I'm not sure now that I come to think of it that it isn't worse than sinking in the Atlantic" (*SS*, 86). He proceeds to work himself into an identifiably Mariposan frenzy: "– safe? Safe yourself, if you like; as for me, let me once get back into Mariposa again, under the night shadow of the maple trees, and this shall be the last, last time I'll go on Lake Wissanotti. … Safe! oh yes! Isn't it strange how safe other people's adventures seem after they happen?" (*SS*, 87). Such frenzy must be seen as a lapse from the narrator's usual ironic coolness and earlier omniscience with regard to the lake's depth. His change serves three important functions: firstly, he has dramatically and personally illustrated his continuing insistence on the crucial matter of perspective or point of view; secondly, by so exposing himself to the reader's laughter, the narrator has identified himself wholly with the Mariposans in this microcosmic sketch of community and country; and thirdly, the remarks that immediately follow contrast him and the alarmed Mariposans to a composed Mr Smith: "I don't see how some of the people took it so calmly; how Mr. Smith, for instance, could have gone on smoking and telling how he'd had a steamer sink on him on Lake Nipissing and a still bigger one, a side-wheeler, sink on him in Lake Abbitibbi" (*SS*, 87). When the steamer settles down on the reed bank, the narrator, along with his fellow Mariposans, dismisses the previous alarm: "Danger? pshaw! fiddlesticks! everybody scouted the idea" (*SS*, 88). He soon reverts to his characteristic ironic self. But the momentary identification with the imperilled Mariposans, coupled with the contrast to Smith's calculated calm, subtly underscores the central tension of *Sunshine Sketches:* the opposition between a cohesive, interdependent community and a self-serving individual. This desire on the part of Leacock's narrator to identify himself with the Mariposans in opposition to Mr Smith – here achieved by manipulation of the narrator's character – has been evident from the beginning of "The Marine Excursion."

The narrator begins this sketch with praise for "Excursion day!" (*SS*, 63) and proceeds to a series of inflated comparisons between things Mariposan and other wonders of the world.[16] He cares for none of these other spectacles: "Take them away," "I don't want them," "I'd shut my eyes." He concludes his introduction with a somewhat petulant demand: "I want to see the Mariposan band in uniform" (*SS*, 64). His reason for desiring to be part of the excursion is one that he has noted before in the *Sketches*, the sense of community: "That's the great thing about the town and that's what makes it so different from the city. Everybody is in everything" (*SS*, 66). Everybody may well participate in everything in Mariposa, but everybody's motivation for so doing in "The Marine Excursion" is different from Mr Smith's.

The narrator remarks particularly on the apparent oddity of Smith's participation in the excursion: "Do I say that Mr. Smith is here? Why, everybody's here" (*SS*, 65). Apparently Smith does not belong in the communal outing. Yet he is there, along with generous helpings of liquor and food. There should be little doubt, however, concerning the motivation behind Smith's generosity. His largesse is either for the benefit of his hotel business or for the feathering of his fledging political ambitions. Although the other passengers are roundly and humorously satirized for the self-obsessiveness of their pastimes aboard the steamer, they are, nonetheless, presented as a viable community enjoying an annual social outing. Smith, in contrast, plays "freezeout poker with the two juniors in Duff's bank" (*SS*, 79). As the reader must suspect, Smith's winning is assured.

When enough passengers have been "rescued" from the grounded steamer, Smith raises her and wins a twenty-five dollar bet from Mullins, the head of Mariposa's other bank. This is Smith's only motive for "saving" the *Mariposa Belle*. Smith, "who has had steamers sink on him in half the lakes from Temiscaming to the Bay" (*SS*, 93), stays atop the *Mariposa Belle*. He manages to steer her safely into dock because he is, as the narrator has pointedly remarked, "shrewd" (*SS*, 92). Smith's monetary motivation for raising the steamer places him in marked contrast to those Mariposans who put out heroically in lifeboats to attempt a rescue. For all the inversions and ironies of the rescue attempt, Leacock's narrator is sincere in his appraisal of the rescuers: "After all, the bravery of the lifeboat man is the true bravery – expended to save life, not to destroy it" (*SS*, 90). Although Donald Cameron fails to take account of the central tension in *Sunshine Sketches* – the opposition between Mariposa and Mr Smith – his study of the book correctly perceives the essential values evinced by Mariposans: "The recognition of each other's humanity is an impulse which Mariposa consciously values.[17] There is, perhaps, no reason to attribute a consciousness of their humanitarian values to Mariposans. It is enough that they possess an ingrained instinct for comunual life.

The Mariposans are, as usual, ineffectual in their rescue attempt, though not completely so. They do manage to get enough passengers off the steamer to allow Smith to raise it. As is their habit, though, the Mariposans work their own undoing, which in this instance entails their diminution and Mullins' loss of twenty-five dollars. All this results in the greater glory of, the propping up of Josh Smith, *whom the Mariposans do not need*. The *Mariposa Belle* "sank every now and then" in Wissanotti's six feet of water and was somehow raised, presumably before Smith's arrival in Mariposa (*SS*, 85). The Mariposans' shouts for a new pilot to steer them safely into dock – "Smith! Get Smith!" (*SS*, 93) – have been shrewdly orchestrated by Smith. Moreover, the cry echoes forward to their election of Smith in the last sketch, after which Mr Smith goes to "Ottaway" to held guide the ship of state. The view of the *Mariposa Belle* – the incongruous "Beautiful Butterfly" – as a microcosm of both community and nation makes it likely that Leacock is deliberately employing the traditional ship-of-state trope. Men such as Josh Smith who understand the mechanical workings of the ship of state, the bowels of the Beautiful Butterfly, opportunely exploit the ignorance of the passengers/citizens who are not so ready and able to plug and pump and pilot.[18]

As was the case with the illusory caff and telegram, the sinking of the *Mariposa Belle* is an instance of an illusion upon which Mr Smith capitalizes: the steamer sinks but does not fully, or *really* sink, and Smith exploits to his enrichment and aggrandizement the appearance of its sinking. No doubt Smith's answering the call, "Get Smith!" does as much for his stature in Mariposa as did his "booming" of Mariposa with his caff. His steering the steamer safely into dock contributes to the Mariposans' impulse "to make him the Conservative candidate for the next Dominion election" (*SS*, 33).

The six sketches that follow "The Marine Excursion" continue to contrast the material values embodied in the individualistic Smith with those of the community, with the added and ominous suggestion in the sketches on religion that these latter values are being forgotten. The sketches on religion further point up the problems that arise when metropolitan schemes are assimilated to Mariposa by its impractical and incompetent citizens. Here again Smith figures centrally in the resolution of a Mariposan dilemma which, though not in this instance of his making, is the result of those material values he has come to personify. Opposed to the negative appraisal of misdirected Mariposan religion are the three sketches on romance and love, wherein Mariposan adherence to appearances serves a communally redeeming purpose. Opposed also to Smith's outward movement, the three sketches on love offer the inward movement of Peter Pupkin. And, finally, "L'Envoi" presents two stationary figures in an urban Mausoleum Club who attempt an imaginative return to Mariposa which, with respect to the auditor in "L'Envoi," ends in failure.

Religion and Romance in Mariposa – En Voiture!

The Rev. Mr Drone, minister of the Church of England Church in Mariposa, is introduced sitting in his garden and "reading" drowsily in Greek. The narrator asks a leading question: "For what better could a man be reading ... than the Pastorals of Theocritus?" (*SS*, 96). Since Greek would seem to be all that this pastor "reads" (and as his muddled biblical references would further suggest), the reader might well answer, "His bible." It is unnecessary to recall Leacock's frequent invidious remarks on classical literature to observe that Dean Drone is wasting his time and neglecting the pastoral duties of an Anglican minister. The prefacer provided the pertinent gloss with his remarks on "languages, living, dead, and half-dead," the acquisition of which left him knowing "nothing of the outside world" and "intellectually bankrupt" (*SS*, viii). As developments reveal, Drone's ill-spent time threatens to bring about the literal bankruptcy of his Church of England Church.

But Dean Drone has time on his hands, a common workday being characterized by a meeting with "the Early Workers' Guild at eleven-thirty" (*SS*, 98). His most revealing traits are a "curious liking for machinery" – a liking that may give mechanical associations to the name Drone – and an affinity with children that would be mistakenly termed child-like (*SS*, 98–9). The Rev. Mr Drone is childish, not simply in his fondness for mechanical toys but also in his petulant reluctance to let other, real children play with them (SS, 99). As the traditional expression has it, Drone is something of a "dog in a manger."

Leacock's narrator attempts to soften his characterization of this foolish minister by appealing to the reader's – to "your" – sympathies. Dean Drone is a widower: "And when your Sunday walk is to your wife's grave, as the Dean's was, perhaps [death] seems different to anybody" (SS, 99). The implication seems to be that Drone is but human and mortal; the further suggestion is that the "you" who is suddenly and colloquially projected into Drone's situation should sympathize with the minister rather than satirically belittle his faults. The logic of such a proposition may be elusive, but the appeal to the reader's sympathies is not proffered by Leacock as a rational equation. Nonetheless, Drone's pride in his toys and his Greek – the gold medal in Greek which "is there in its open box on the rectory table, in case of immediate need" (SS, 101) – hints at his spiritual pride. This pride finds fullest expression in the new, ostentatious church, the central image of sketches four through six. Since the new church eventually serves to chastise symbolically Drone and the Mariposans, Leacock no doubt employs the pathetic appeal of Drone's dead wife in order to soften the harshness of the treatment that follows. It would be a mistake, though, to view the frequent touches of pathos here and throughout *Sunshine Sketches* as intrusive, or as instances of Leacock's nodding. Leacock believed that humour should utilize pathos to mitigate pointed satire. In the sketches on religion, he frequently and unapologetically solicits the reader's sentimental emotions in order to counter an overly-rational satiric view of Drone. Such a de-emphasis of the aggressively rational intellect, along with an abiding respect for traditional institutions, is characteristic of Leacock's tory humanism.

But the new church is much more than a testimony to Drone's and Mariposa's pride and incipient materialism: it also constitutes a denial of the past. It has replaced "the little stone church that all the grown-up people in Mariposa still remember, a quaint little building in red and grey stone" (SS, 100). Furthermore, the new church has effectively destroyed the old cemetery. The reader should therefore question the extent to which "the grown-up people in Mariposa still remember" their old church, for only "the Mariposa children still walk round and read the headstones lying flat in the grass and look for the old ones, – because some of them are ever so old – forty or fifty years back" (SS, 100). Forty or fifty years constitutes a lengthy history only in the eyes of children. Yet this span of time would appear to be all the past that is possessed by a Canadian town such as Mariposa, and the Mariposans are destroying even this relatively present past. By defacing the old cemetery, the Mariposan Anglicans for whom Drone is the spiritual leader are violating emblematically Edmund Burke's conception of the social contract. "Society is indeed a contract," writes the father of toryism: "As the ends of such a partnership cannot be obtained in many generations, it becomes a partnership not only between those who are living, but between those who are living, those who are dead, and those who are to be born."[1] The new church, particularly with regard to its defacement of the old cemetery, portentously associates the Mariposans with the people of Burke's aphoristic admonishment – "People will not look forward to posterity, who never look backward to their ancestors."

The stone from Mariposa's quaint old church was "devoutly sold to a building contractor, and, like so much else in life, was forgotten" (*SS*, 105). In view of Leacock's reverence for institutions that have proven their worth, this disposal of the stone from the old church is, as Drone suspects, a "sacrilege" (*SS*, 105). The plan had been to incorporate the old stone into the new church. This discarded plan symbolizes the central concern of *Sunshine Sketches*: the worthwhile from the past (from "Mariposa") must be recollected and carried forward if there is to be any hope for a full and continuous life in the present and the future. In the matter of Mariposan religion, this is not proving to be the practice.

Leacock's narrator leaves little doubt about the needlessness of the new church and the error of the motives behind its existence. The new edifice is "a large church with a great sweep of polished cedar beams inside, for the special glorification of the All powerful, and with imported tiles on the roof for the greater glory of Heaven and with stained-glass windows for the exultation of the All Seeing" (*SS*, 102). A moment's reflection should reveal the incongruity between mistaken aspiration and vain achievement in Mariposa's new Anglican church. In Leacock's view, strong cedar beams do not glorify the All Powerful, nor do imported tiles reflect glory to Heaven. And whether or not the All Seeing is exulted by stained-glass windows, it is certain that all those who are inside the church, admiring the cedar beams and thinking of the tiles and gazing at the windows, will not be able to see into the Book of Nature beyond the opaque windows. Malcolm Ross has summarized popular reaction to the similar importation of High-Church Anglican architectural practices into the Maritimes in the late-nineteenth century: "To stain a window was perhaps to stain a soul."[2] In Leacock's view, affected architecture takes the Anglican Church away from its roots – astray of the *via media*. More than simple materialism, this is the deeper error of Drone and his congregation. And this original error leads to the commission of others.

Notice though that Drone's church is a "high" church even in spatial terms. The first sentence of "The Ministrations" informs the reader that "the Church of England Church in Mariposa is ... a little *up* the hill from the *heart* of the town" (*SS*, 95, emphasis added). (Interestingly, the church is situated where Jeff Thorpe envisioned a home for incurables: "on the hill behind the town – the very place for these incurables" [SS, 60].) "The New Church – towered ... It stood so high" (*SS*, 106). The pastor of this "high" church, the Rural Dean Drone, rather than tending to his Christian pastoral duties, sits reading his pagan pastorals at a "rustic table" (*SS*, 95, 97, 100). But the "table," which is suggestive of the traditional Anglican altar, no more reminds Drone of his religious roots and the error of his ways than do the old stone church and the forgotten cemetery.

In accordance with this suggestive satire against High Anglicanism, there is subtle and straight-forward anti-Catholic satire. When the congregation begins to turn against Drone, "Yodel, the auctioneer, ... narrated how he had been to he city and had gone into a service of the Roman Catholic church: I believe, to state it more fairly, he had 'dropped in,' – the only recognized means of access to such a service. He claimed that the music that he had heard there was music, and that (outside of his profession) the chanting and intoning could not be touched" (*SS*, 109). The ritualism of Roman Catholic worship is associated, in so far as Yodel's opinion of Latin hymns is concerned, with an inferior kind of auctioneer's yodelling. Such ritualism removes worship from the community, from the "heart of the town," because it "could not be touched." Pertinently, Drone's one contribution to the efforts to raise money is a "magic lantern lecture" on "Italy and her Invaders" (*SS*, 116). Even if the "magic lantern" (an early version of the slide projector) is not meant to suggest in a derisive fashion the tabernacle light of the Catholic altar (which testifies to the "Real Presence" of Christ at the altar), the import of "Italy and her Invaders" should be clear: not only is Drone actively interested in the things of Italy (Roman Catholicism) but he is permitting her "Invaders" (High Anglican practices) to establish a position in Mariposa. Thus does Leacock, by means of spatial imagery (the location of the church), symbolism (the rustic table), and humorous implication (Yodel, the magic lantern lecture), gently indict Drone for leading his flock away from the roots of Anglicanism and towards a High Anglicanism that is suggestively associated with Roman Catholicism.

Drone's belief that a knowledge of logarithms could resolve the fiscal dilemma of his parish is but self-deception. To a great extent Drone's misplaced faith illustrates Leacock's observation on the failure of economics "The fault of economics was the assumption that what *can only be done by the Spirit* could be done by material interest" (*LL*, 106). Drone is much lacking in the Spirit. He is unconcerned with *Logos*, the Word of the Bible which, with the Book of Nature, is the true evidence of the Creator's works. "At the Anglican college" where Drone had been trained, "they had simply explained that Logos was a word and Arithmos a number, which, at the time, seemed amply sufficient" (*SS*, 102–3). But Drone, in his fascination with mechanisms and logarithms, no longer found this explanation *ample* enough. Forgetting his training (and his Bible), he mistakes quantity for quality and changes from a small church to a big church.

Two learned allusions further illustrate this failing of Drone's. The minister had preached for twenty-five years that "his one aim" was to rear a larger Ark in Gideon" (*SS*, 104).[3] As Russell Brown and Donna Bennett have noted, Drone here confuses *Gideon*, the Old Testament hero (Judg.7:16–21), with *Gibeon*, an Old Testament location that is described, significantly, as "the great high place" (I Kings 3:4).[4] Brown and Bennett proceed to point out that the Ark of the Covenant "was returned to the Israelites at Gibeon after its capture by the Philistines (described in I and II Samuel). Since the Ark is built to exact and divinely revealed specifications (Exod.25:10–22)," they point out, "the idea of aspiring to 'a larger Ark' would be highly inappropriate." The second learned allusion that points up Drone's confusion of quality and quantity occurs in one of his sermons when he is parading his knowledge of Greek: "'The original Greek is "Hoson," but perhaps you will allow me to translate it as equivalent to "Hoyon"'" (*SS*, 111). To quote once again from Brown's and Bennett's scholarly notes, "Both words mean 'what', but to think them interchangeable would be a schoolboy error, since '*hoson*' refers to quantity ('what amount') and '*hoyon*' to quality ('what kind')."[5] Thus does Drone's schoolboy error prove especially revealing, since the source of all his troubles, the big church, is the direct result of his confusion of quantity and quality.

In its largest sense, this confusion epitomizes the Mariposan awe of big things and the confusion of appearances and reality. In the matter of the new church, material appearance is confused with spiritual reality. Accordingly, in a short emphatic paragraph the narrator makes clear the true cause of the fiscal predicament: "But to think that all this trouble had come through the building of the new church" (*SS*, 104). Despite the windy intentions of glorifying God, the narrator makes equally clear the true inspiration of the imposing edifice: "You could see and appreciate *things* from the height of the new church, – such as the size and the growing wealth of Mariposa, – that you never could have seen from the little stone church at all" (*SS*, 106, emphasis added). This is an appreciation of things from a Realtor's point of view. The new church is held up as a testimony to Smith's and the city's god – Mammon.

It is not only Drone's mistaken ambition, pride, and ineptitude that land his parish in woeful financial straits: he also embezzles church funds (*SS*, 103–4). This latter revelation is indeed a searing indictment. Yet Leacock's narrator mitigates the fault by attributing to Drone the beginnings at least of a guilty (perhaps religious) conscience: "Sometimes as he went down the street from the lighted precincts of the Greater Testimony and passed the Salvation Army, praying around a naphtha lamp under the open sky, [the debt] smote him to the heart with a stab" (*SS*, 110). The simplicity of the Army's evangelical service – the "naphtha lamp" in contrast to Drone's "beacon" (and perhaps to his magic lantern) – begins Drone's penance, punishment, and problematic salvation. The Salvation Army, devoted to the kind of pastoral work that should concern the "Rural Dean" (*SS*, 3), prays "under the open sky," a natural cathedral. But Drone has been, as the first reference to him reveals, more concerned with "going home to get his fishing rod after a mothers' auxiliary meeting" (*SS*, 3) than with pastoral work. More concerned with fishing for fish than for men, more interested in the pagan shepherds of pastorals than with the Good Shepherd, more absorbed by mathematical angles than by angels, Drone is ill-suited to fulfil his pastoral duties.

When the Whirlwind Campaign fails, Drone does full penance over his letter of resignation. He acknowledges further that his remaining and equally mistaken pride in his facility with language is unfounded: "Then the Dean saw that he was beaten, and he knew that he not only couldn't manage the parish but couldn't say so in proper English, and of the two the last was the bitterer discovery" (*SS*, 138). Appropriately, Drone's obsession with words and literalness – with Greek, with the meaning of "mugwump," and with his letter – rather than with the spirit of the Word, is associated with his mismanagement of the church. Drone's taste in church architecture finds here a literary parallel in his "fine taste for words and effects" (*SS*, 136). But when Drone attempts to write in "proper

English," in the language of the Church of England, his words become merely "one set of words and then ... something else" (*SS*, 135). At every turn, Drone is defeated by that which caused his problems: high affectation in word and deed.

Drone's final punishment is the stroke that he suffers when he perceives that his church is burning (*SS*, 139). As a result of this stroke, his mind becomes so "clear" that he is relegated to instruct only the "Infant Class." In the last paragraph of "The Beacon on the Hill," the narrator again attempts to mitigate Drone's self-inflicted situation by referring again to the deceased Mrs Drone and to the Dean's growing closeness to her (that is, to death): "And sometimes, – when his head is very clear, – as he sits there reading beneath the plum blossoms he can hear them singing beyond, and his wife's voice" (*SS*, 148). This concluding paragraph did not appear in the version of the sketch originally published in *The Montreal Star*.[6] There is some evidence to suggest that Leacock may have appended this pathetic touch as a result of his mother's unfavourable reaction to the thinly disguised depiction of her truly gentle and tolerant Orillian minister.[7] More importantly, though, Leacock believed that true humour exists in an area between satire and sentimentality. In the instance of the three sketches under discussion, the humorous satire against Drone could be considered harsh indeed. The pathetic reference to his approaching death at the conclusion of "The Beacon" admirably serves the kindly purpose of the humorist and humanist Leacock.

But long before Drone's final punishment is visited upon him, his effectiveness in resolving the dilemma of his church's finances had been removed, and the interest of the sketches had similarly shifted, from a person (Drone) to the Mariposans generally.

When the Rev. Mr Drone begins to look to his parishioners for help, the narrator imagines that his "appeals went out from the Ark of Gideon like rockets from a sinking ship" (*SS*, 110). The image should recall the plight of the sinking *Mariposa Belle*, "signalling for help and ... sending up rockets" (*SS*, 91). The financially foundering Ark of Gideon will also ultimately require the services of Mr Josh Smith. But before Smith is called upon to effect yet another "rescue," the congregation must attempt its own version of fiscal salvation. With the possible exception of the "'endless chain' of letters" (*SS*, 114), all of these salvaging operations, these machinations, culminating in the farcically disastrous Whirlwind Campaign, are drawn directly from the city. The bazaar held by the Girls' Auxiliary requires "special costumes that were brought up from the city" (*SS*, 115). The equipment for the "magic lantern lecture" comes "up from the city" (*SS*, 116). The idea for the Whirlwind Campaign itself comes to Mullins when "he happened to be present in one of the big cities and saw how they went at it there to raise money" (*SS*, 118). True to Mariposan form, Mullins only "*saw* how they went at it" in "one of the big cities." He does not understand the inner workings of a metropolitan fund-raiser but, Mariposan to the core, he is fascinated by the external features or trappings of a Whirlwind Campaign – by the appearance. Accordingly, the initial description of the Mariposans' execution of the scheme that Mullins witnessed in the city employs diction suggestive of the way in which the Mariposans habitually mistake deceptive appearances for reality, words such as "unostentatious," "pretence," and "pretext" (*SS*, 121). Whereas in the city the appearance of casualness serves to civilize the covert monetary convassing, in Mariposa the appearance serves for the reality. The Mariposans *are* merely eating, drinking, and fishing when they should be canvassing contributions.

"The Whirlwind Campaign" proceeds relentlessly, like "The Speculations," to contrast Mariposa and the city. Although the narrator offers no alternative to the Campaign, early in this sketch he disingenuously suggests a reason for the Campaign's pending failure: "It may be that there are differences between Mariposa and the larger cities that one doesn't appreciate at first sight. Perhaps it would have been better to try some other plan" (*SS*, 121). Although they believe that they are operating "as the *big* city men do when there's an important *thing* like this under way" (*SS*, 122, emphasis added), the Mariposans obviously are not proceeding correctly. They are children playing at civic fund-raising, with little notion of the business end of soliciting donations. The following comments on the relation between efficaciousness and businessmen imply ironically that in this instance of Mariposan confusion ignorance is bliss: "It's all right to talk about education and that sort of thing, but if you want driving power and efficiency, get business men. They're seeing it every day in the city, and it's just the same in Mariposa. Why, in the big concerns in the city, if they found out a man was educated, they wouldn't have him, – wouldn't keep him there a minute. That's why the business men have to conceal it so much" (*SS*, 123). That this insinuating plutocratic mentality is "just the same in Mariposa" echoes the overriding concern of the previous sketch, "The Ministrations": the importation into semi-rural and little Mariposa of the big city's materialistic values (High Anglicanism) encouraged Drone and his congregation to forsake the old stone church and cemetery in favour of the ostentatious "Brighter Beacon" (*SS*, 104). Yet, the comment that the situation is "just the same in Mariposa" refers to a similar *willingness* to adopt a crass, materialistic orientation, not in this case to an ability to do so. The Mariposans are incapable of fully realizing a metropolitan scheme of things, as their handling of the Whirlwind Campaign testifies. They are capable only of aping the appearance, which "failing" is superbly illustrated by Mullins' telegram of support to himself, the telegram "informing him that he had heard of his project and assuring him of his liveliest interest in what he proposed" (*SS*, 125–6).[8] The only man in Mariposa who is as adept as city businessmen at concealing, if not his education, then at least his guile, is Josh Smith. Only Smith profits materially from the Whirlwind Campaign.

The Mariposans overreach each other in writing donation cheques that are conditional on the Campaign fund reaching ever greater amounts. The conditions are of course virtually impossible to meet. But in Mariposa a benefaction that is conditional upon a highly improbable reality is, like appearance itself, equivalent to reality. When "Mullins stood up and announced that the conditional fund had reached a quarter of a million" (*SS*, 127), the Whirlwind Campaign achieves a kind of success – all the success, in fact, that it is destined to attain. That success is in no sense financial. The Whirlwind Campaign promoted sociability and gregariousness, for as the narrator notes: "I don't say it didn't do good. No doubt a lot of the men got to know one another better than they ever had before" (*SS*, 129). And although the narrator undercuts this concession by remarking that he heard "Judge Pepperleigh say that after the campaign he knew all of Pete Glover that he wanted to" (*SS*, 129), the ironic undercutting negates neither the initial concession nor a similar, earlier observation (*SS*, 127–8), nor the narrator's first assessment of the Campaign which, "in many ways ... couldn't have been a greater success" (*SS*, 121).

The gregarious cohesion of the community may not completely offset the selfish motives evidenced by the Mariposans (their self-aggrandizement and their appetite), yet their behaviour does present them in terms of a human community. Although the conditions that they place upon their contributions assure their financial security and boosterish vanity, these conditions are nevertheless in pointed contrast to Mr Smith's conditional donation: "Mr. Smith had given them two hundred dollars in cash conditional on the lunches being held in the caff of his hotel. ... So Mr. Smith got back his own money, and the crowd began eating into the benefactions" (*SS*, 129). Smith's donation of real money – "in cash" – enriches him, assists the failure of the Campaign, and increases his standing in Mariposa.

The final irony of "The Whirlwind Campaign" is that the committee's failure – "the financial, the bookkeeping side of the thing" (*SS*, 128) – reflects Drone's similar failure with the finances of his beacon. It appears that Drone is, in the matter of his inept bookkeeping, but representative of his financially inept parishioners. The assessment of the Campaign's failure just quoted is the narrator's generous appraisal. He restates his truer assessment of the Campaign's failure: "The real trouble about the Whirlwind Campaign was that they never clearly understood which of them were the whirlwind and who were to be campaign" (*SS*, 129). The "real trouble," which has been apparent from the beginning, is that the Mariposans cannot distinguish the appearance of a Whirlwind Campaign from the reality. The campaign remains, in fact, an illusion incapably conjured up by Mullins and the Mariposans to redeem Drone's false beacon. Their motive is commendable; their actions are at once laughable and pathetic. Unlike Smith's caff – an illusion of sorts that serves Smith – the Campaign whirls great amounts of hot air to no real purpose, then dissipates, having done no real harm. From its realization in the city, the Whirlwind Campaign undergoes, like so much else imported to Mariposa, transformation to an appearance that then attempts to function as reality. Yet this appearance serves a purpose: it calls forth feelings of gregariousness that contrast to Smith's individualistic avariciousness. What the Mariposans really needed to redeem their church was a return to the Anglican *via media*, a retreat from High-Church ostentation, a recovery of the inspiration of *pneuma* and the Word, as opposed to the whirlwind. As events progressed, though, such a recovery was never even considered.

The movement from illusion to reality in "The Beacon" is an instance of the metaphoric made literal. (This is a traditional device of satire which is perhaps most fully executed in Jonathan Swift's *A Modest Proposal*.) With Leacock, the technique has its rhetorical counterpart in what he terms the "Face Value Technique," a technique which "consists in the contrast between the face value of the words or phrases as usually used and the logical significance of it." The "Face Value Technique" and its "converse" are two of the stylistic mainstays of Leacock's humour (*HTT*, 36).[9] One humorous example of the "Face Value Technique" from "The Marine Excursion" must serve to exemplify his practice. In the following passage, Miss Cleghorn's wistful expression of admiration for a scene is taken at "face value" by the narrator: "The scene is all so quiet and still and unbroken, that Miss Cleghorn, – the sallow girl in the telephone exchange, that

I spoke of – said she'd like to be buried there. But all the people were so busy getting their baskets and gathering up their things that no one had time to attend to it" (SS, 80–1). Making the metaphoric literal is characteristic not only of Leacock's technique of humour but also of his general mode of thinking. Such thinking, the essence of which is irony, is best approached in terms of illusions becoming realities and vice-versa. In "The Beacon," the illusion or metaphoric "beacon" becomes a real, literal fire. And this outbreak of threatening reality in Mariposa offers the final, searing judgment on what began in "The Ministrations" as humorous satire on Drone's and Mariposa's affectations in matters of religion. Drone's ostentatious new church figures symbolically as a denial of the past, as a violation of the Burkean social contract, and as a testimony to High affectation, pride, and materialism. The new church is a threat to Mariposa. It must come down.

Leacock's implicit resistance to the new church, which parallels his narrator's belief that Jeff Thorpe is better off remaining in his barber shop, illustrates the trenchant resistance to change that Northrop Frye has noted to be characteristic of humour in Canada: "The attitude of encouraging a farming population to stay at home (we notice that 'home' is already becoming a magic word in Mc-Culloch) ... is the traditional attitude of clerical paternalism in both Protestant and Catholic parts of Canada."[10] Leacock's Mariposa may not comprise a "farming population" (though Missinaba County does), and Leacock is not a cleric, but Frye's perception remains valid with reference to Leacock's affectionate (SS, xii), paternalistic, and somewhat condescending attitude towards the Mariposans. (And to ancitipate, in no work of Canadian fiction is "home" more richly metaphoric than in the Envoi to Sunshine Sketches.) In this sense, the movement of the beacon image from metaphor to literalness throws a condemnatory light on the Mariposans' urge to change home, which is to leave home in a spiritual sense. When the metaphoric beacon on the hill breaks "into a very beacon kindled upon a hill" (SS, 139), it serves specifically to illuminate the error of High Anglican affectation and serves generally to highlight the folly of Mariposa's materialistic ambitions. This symbolic illumination of error is presented, once again, in comparison to the shady dealings of Mr Smith, whose motives for acting as he does in "The Beacon" are not made explicit. Smith seems to function in "The Beacon" as he did in "The Marine Excursion," as a sort of deus ex machina. In fact, Leacock's narrator stands in ironically appreciative awe when Smith appears to fight the fire that he and "Mr. Gingham's assistant" started (SS, 146).

The firefighting is described as follows: they "fought it, with the Mariposa engine thumping and panting in the street, itself aglow with fire like a servant demon fighting its own kind" (*SS*, 140). The Mariposans fight furiously because "the fire could leap into the heart of Mariposa." The brigade is led by Mr Smith, by whom the narrator is suddenly fascinated and to whose actions he wishes especially to direct the reader's attention: "Most of all I wish you could have seen Mr. Smith" (*SS*, 141). Much is transpiring in this scene. As leader of the firefighters, Smith is imagined to be fighting the fire with fire, and both fires are imaged as "demons." Figuratively, Smith is battling a spiritual pride equal to his own materialistic ambitions. Moreover, this fire which Smith started threatens "the heart of Mariposa," the place where, it will be recalled, Smith's Hotel is located. Smith is fighting the fire, then, to save his own hotel and the material possessions of those destined to become his constituency – his base. The fire brigade *never* fights to save the church: "They fought the fire, not to save the church ... but to stop the spread of it and save the town ... Most of all they fought to save the wooden driving shed behind the church from which the fire could leap into the heart of the town" (*SS*, 140). It is strongly suggested, moreover, that Smith acts in answer to a call from Mullins and the church's sidesmen (Gingham and Nivens). These men have had access to the church's financial records, and they had taken particular notice of the "fire insurance" (*SS*, 103). After the fire, "the wardens and sidesmen and Mullins, the chairman of the vestry, smiled and chuckled at the thought of" the insurance money (*SS*, 145). At this point the opposition between Mariposa and Mr Smith becomes one of facing mirrors.

As the analysis of the two previous sketches, "The Ministrations" and "The Whirlwind Campaign," has shown, Leacock's narrator strongly disapproves of the new church and of the Mariposans' discarding and forgetting of the old stone church, which, "like so much else in life, was forgotten" (*SS*, 105). The new church must come down, by hook (axe) and by crook (Smith). By employing Smith to burn it down, Leacock effectively points up the relation between the agent of destruction – and the motivations behind the beacon's existence – pride, affectation, and materialism. Consider the narrator's ecstasy over the destruction of the church and Smith's transfigured appearance: "See him there as he plants himself firm at the angle of the beams, and with the full impact of his two hundred and eighty pounds drives his axe into the wood! I tell you it takes a man from the pine country of the north to handle an axe! Right, left, left, right, down it comes, with never a pause or stay, never missing by a fraction of an inch the line of the stroke! At it, Smith! Down with it!" (SS, 141). Although Leacock's narrator ironically celebrates Smith's actions – "At it, Smith! Down with it!" – it would be as mistaken to conclude that he approves of Smith, even in this instance, as it would be to think that he admires the new church. (In fact, the "with" of "Down with it!" may reveal the narrator's wish that Smith fall with the driving shed and so rid Mariposa of its two most threatening blights.) In the matter of the church Smith is useful for his destructive efficaciousness, a quality that once again places him in contrast to the habitually ineffectual Mariposans. The narrator emphasizes this contrast in an indirect reference to the failed Whirlwind Campaign, paying Smith what seems like a compliment, until the ironic point of its reference to Bismarck, Gladstone, and Taft is understood: "Your little narrow-chested men may plan and organize, but when there is something to be done, something real, then it's the man of size and weight that steps to the front every time. Look at Bismarck and Mr. Gladstone and President Taft and Mr. Smith, – the same thing in each case" (SS, 142).[11] Arson, the "something real," is opposed to the illusory and ineffectual Whirlwind Campaign. But the illusory Campaign did, as has been seen, evoke feelings of communal purposefulness, whereas Smith's real actions accomplish a moral inversion. In fact, the scene of his transfiguration on the angled beams of the driving shed can be read as a grotesque paraody of the Crucifixion.

Smith starts the fire "in April" (SS, 140), which is the time of the Crucifixion. He does so with the help of "Gingham's assistant" (SS, 146) – the assistant of the Gingham whose Christian name is Golgotha, "the place of the skull" (Mark.15:22) where Christ was crucified. The narrator describes the scene of the church's fall as follows: "Then when the roof crashed in and the tall steeple tottered and fell, so swift a darkness seemed to come that the grey trees and the frozen lake vanished in a moment as if blotted out of existence" (SS, 143). The blotting darkness suggests St Mark's (and the other Evangelists') descriptions of Christ's death: "There was darkness over the whole land" (Mark.15:33). Not only is the scene of the fire a parody of the Crucifixion but Smith can also be seen to function as a hideous parody of Christ. By his death, Christ ransomed mankind and provided *assurance* of heaven; by burning down the beacon, Smith ransoms the indebted parish and indirectly provides the redemptive *insurance* money. Smith, in league with Golgotha Gingham, is associated with death and destruction rather than with life. As a parodic saviour, he is also, in his "huge red helmet," something of a Satanic figure; his "voice ... dominates the fire itself"

(SS, 142), a fire which earlier is termed "a great Terror of the Night" (SS, 140). In fulfilment of Smith's parodic function, the destruction of the church is followed by further inversions: what should be experienced as a catastrophe is felt to be a "luxury of excitement ... just as good as a holiday" (SS, 144); the beacon is worth more when extinguished than when beaming; and "a little faith and effort" (SS, 145) resolves into faith in illegality and the efforts of Smith as arsonist and axeman.

The recourse to pathos at the conclusion of "The Beacon" may succeed in sentimentalizing the character of Drone (depending upon the reader's accession or resistance to the pathetic appeal). But this pathetic touching up of the sketch (an act of post-publication revision) does little to soften the stark picture of, and the bare prospects for, religious life in Mariposa. Leacock described "the humour of the highest culture, the humour of the future," as the humour "of disillusionment, of loss of faith, and of the wide charity of mind that comes with the shattering of narrower ideals, not yet replaced" (HH, 205–6). Although he effectively deploys Smith to remove the ostentatious beacon, he does not replace the beacon with a more viable alternative. The Mariposans use their ill-gotten insurance money to build yet another, perhaps higher, new church. They employ one "Mr. Uttermost" (SS, 146), who is no doubt more worldy and far less humane than that gentle and mistaken soul, the Rev. Mr Drone. Leacock does not employ his humour to avoid the disillusioning reality of the mistaken beacon, the arson, and the new church. On the contrary, his humour makes the disillusionment bearable. It is a measure of the integrity of Leacock's humorous vision that he did not avoid the conclusion to which the three sketches on religion pointed: the loss of a truly communal place of worship in Mariposa. However (and it is a crucial "however"), by contrasting the beacon to the old church, Leacock does imply that the religious life of a community can remain viable only by maintaining a sense of continuity with the past and by incorporating the traditional values into the new, an incorporation which the Mariposans fail to achieve. Not unlike the Carlyle of *Sartor Resartus*, Leacock seems to see "the one thing needful" as a *straightforward* and *simple* Christian faith.[12] In the passage that relates the fate of the stone from the quaint old church, Leacock's narrator touches one of the most elegiac chords in *Sunshine Sketches*: "The stone of the little church was laid reverently into a stone pile; afterwards it was devoutly sold to a building contractor, and, like so much else in life, was forgotten" (SS, 105). "Stone" that is "devoutly sold" is a richly allusive and ironic image. In Mariposa's parodic Anglican community, the Rev. Mr Drone leans upon Mullins, the banker, "as upon a staff," and Mullins leans "against" Drone, "in matters of doctrine, as against a rock" (*SS*, 116). The stone of the true church (and Leacock is alluding no doubt to the pun whereby Christ made Peter the foundation rock of His church) gives way to what is ultimately a capitalist edifice; the original spiritual contract is symbolically sold with the stone to "a building contractor." The three sketches on Mariposan religion are replete with inversions, reversals, undoings, hideous parodies, and very fine humour.

It was perhaps the bleak outlook resulting from the sketches on religion that led Leacock to follow them with the three sketches that portray most positively the virtues of life in Mariposa: "The Extraordinary Entanglement of Mr. Pupkin," "The Fore-ordained Attachment of Peter Pupkin and Zena Pepperleigh," and "The Mariposa Bank Mystery." Although Leacock did not possess faith in the conventionally religious sense, or faith in conventional religious institutions, the three-sketch Pupkin-Pepperleigh romance demonstrates that he believed in the redemptive "enchantments" of love.

In the three sketches dealing with love, movements between the real and the illusory accentuate the positive charms of life in Mariposa. Here, though, the movements generally are between the romantic and the realistic, and vice-versa. Whereas in the sketches on religion the Mariposans mistakenly discard the old in favour of the new, Peter Pupkin and Zena Pepperleigh succeed in fusing the romantic and the realistic. Smith, who acts only for himself and often functions to point up the foolish ineffectuality and emergent materialism of Mariposans, figures only peripherally in the love story. His customary manipulative role is undertaken by an indigenous Mariposan, Judge Pepperleigh, and by an appreciative outsider, Pupkin Senior.

Unlike Smith, the outsider who moves into Mariposa and is destined to move out, Peter Pupkin is an outsider moving inwards to a permanent place in the "enchanted" heart of the community. Smith comes from Canada's northern timber frontier and settles in Mariposa as the embodiment and enlarged reflection of much that threatens the community. In contrast, Peter Pupkin, the latest issue of Loyalist stock from the Maritime provinces, settles permanently in Mariposa to become an example of the best that the community has to offer. Although useful in the matter of bringing down the beacon, Smith, the frontiersman, threatens the values of the community. Pupkin, from the longer-civilized Maritime provinces, marries a native Mariposan and with her fortifies the community with an "enchanted baby" (SS, 211). Consistent with the values of Leacock's toryism, those who help to "fore-ordain" the attachment of Pupkin and Zena – Judge Pepperleigh and Pupkin Senior – are the representatives of law and order and old money.

The three sketches devoted to Mariposan love present a systematic blurring of the line between illusion (or romance) and reality. Each instance of confusion demonstrates that real love is partially founded on romantic illusions, and that romance has an ironic basis in reality. In effect, these sketches suggest that love depends upon the interdependency of the romantic and the realistic. The broad outlines of the movements from illusion to reality, and vice-versa, can be sketched as follows: the romantic perception that makes of commonplace occurrences "extraordinary entanglements" leads to extraordinary love; the romantic notion of a "fore-ordained attachment" results in actuality, for the romance is to some extent fore-ordained by Judge Pepperleigh and Pupkin Senior; and the illusory bank mystery serves a real purpose by bringing about a resolution to Pupkin's romantic dilemma. By confusing and fusing the romantic and the realistic, sketches seven through nine best illustrate Leacock's credo: "You cannot tell a love story just as it is – because it isn't ... When a young man sees in his girl an angel, and a young girl sees in her lover a hero, perhaps they are seeing what is really there" (HTW, 106). Leacock's attitude, revealed in this comment and in his narrator's attitude towards the lovers, is one of unapologetic affection and indulgence. Granted, Pupkin's love for Zena is at first a romantic, "puppy love"; yet the "kin" in the hero's name (Pup/kin) should suggest more than his relation to a pup. Pupkin's surname suggests that the romantic love he struggles to realize is "kin" to, and matures into, what Leacock apparently viewed as real love. Because the romance sketches deal also with love in its various phases, the first of the three sketches, "The Extraordinary Entanglement of Mr. Pupkin," begins, not with a discussion of the principles involved, but with a portrayal of mature, married love, of the temperamental Judge Pepperleigh and his wife. Love is also, as will shortly be seen, "kin" to Leacock's conception of the function of kindly humour: love, especially romantic love, like humorous literature, offers enchantment against hard reality.

Before this three-sketch section of Sunshine Sketches addresses itself to the romantic love interest between Pupkin and Zena, it first considers other kinds of love: the love between a husband and wife, and a father's love for his daughter and his dead son. This is a narrative strategy to which the reader of the Sketches has grown accustomed: the prefacer knew "no way in which a writer may more fittingly introduce his work to the public than by giving a brief account of who and what he is" (SS, vii); to know Mariposa "you" had first to know Josh Smith; to know love in Mariposa, "you" must first become acquainted with one of the arrangers of the romance, Judge Pepperleigh.

The Judge is portrayed as a domestic terror of a kind, as explosively temperamental and irascible in his relations with his wife and daughter. Even "his spectacles flash like dynamite" (SS, 149). By arranging the romance, the Judge, the tory (and Conservative) bastion, serves an authorial purpose reminiscent of Josh Smith's razing of the unwanted beacon. In his association with law and order, Judge Pepperleigh stands in distinct contrast to the gamblers of the *Sketches*, to such men as Smith and Jeff Thorpe, who put their faith in chance and luck, things as inimical to Leacock's tory mentality as selfishness and machinery. After his characterization of the Judge, Leacock's narrator briefly relates the anxieties that Peter Pupkin suffers when approaching the house of such a man. And it is here, with his concluding remark, that the narrator effectively announces the theme of the three sketches to follow: "Still, that's what you call love" (SS, 152). But Pupkin's and Zena's is only one kind of love. The narrator turns immediately to other kinds.

The love between Judge Pepperleigh and his daughter Zena is, as shall be seen, the least interesting of these kinds of love. The Judge may throw her romantic novels over the grapevine (an act that is emblematic of his function as a realist), but such behaviour is more than compensated for by the displays of affection between father and daughter (SS, 153). Of greater interest is the Judge's undying love for his son Neil, a violent drunkard who was "so clever that he used to come out at the foot of the class in mathematics at the Mariposa high school through sheer surplus of brain power" (SS, 154). Judge Pepperleigh's love for his son is offered as a sincere emotion, as a worthy and viable paternal love – regardless of the seeming unworthiness of its object. (It is probable, however, that Neil is to be considered, in view of Leacock's toryism and Imperialism, as a partly positive figure: he died in service to his country in the Boer War [SS, 156], which means he died fighting for "the Empire" that Leacock loved.) But the truth about Neil does not matter. Neil is not the subject of the narrator's attention; the Judge's love for his son is. The Judge does not need to know that Neil was drunk when "he struck the Liberal organizer" and drunk when he rode off to war, "and now he never will. For if you could find it in the meanness of your soul to tell him, it would serve no purpose now except to break his heart, and there would rise up to rebuke you the pictured vision of an untended grave somewhere in the great silences of South Africa" (*SS*, 156). The Judge's love belies the reality because love lives, in Leacock's view, by necessary illusion. In matters of love the facts are best left unmentioned; the cold, Gradgrindian facts about Neil should be left to lie with him beneath the dirt of his untended grave.

Following the relation of the Judge's love for Neil, the narrator returns to relations between Pepperleigh and his wife. The narrator admonishes that if "you" have taken for reality the appearance of disharmony between these two, "It just shows that you know nothing about such things, and that marriage, at least as it exists in Mariposa, is a sealed book to you" (*SS*, 156). The full range of his theme is here announced: not only the various kinds of love are to be revealed, but love which leads to a Mariposan marriage. If "you" mistake the appearance of the Pepperleighs' marriage for the reality, you are thinking like one Miss Spiffkins, who seems overly concerned about Mrs Pepperleigh's lot in life. You would have presumptuously excluded from your appraisal the fact that the Judge and Mrs Pepperleigh sat and held hands on the night they received the news of Neil's death (*SS*, 157). This sentimental scene excuses much in the opinion of Leacock's narrator; in truth, the shared commiseration appears intended to redeem the Judge's irascible treatment of his wife: "Go and tell Miss Spiffkins that! Hydrangeas, – canaries, – temper, – blazes! What does Miss Spiffkins know about it all?" (*SS*, 157). Nothing, it would seem. For Leacock, the well-matched Pepperleighs exemplify married love. In a revealing passage from the posthumously published *Last Leaves*, he describes the "real adoring husband": "The real adoring husband overtalks his wife, overdominates her, pays with unexpected presents for easy forgiveness of his ill temper, and never knows that he adored her till it is too late, because now she cannot hear it" (*LL*, 4). The appearance of the Pepperleighs' marriage is not to be mistaken for the real love that unites them. Similarly, Judge Pepperleigh's love for his son is unfounded upon reality and is ultimately unassailable by it: "If you tried to tell Judge Pepperleigh about Neil now he wouldn't believe it. He'd laugh it to scorn" (*SS*, 157). This is the only use of scornful laughter that Leacock ever condoned. For Leacock, scornful laughter is simply, like Milton's "grim laughter," "the speediest way to see the truth vindicated."[13]

After the narrator has dealt with other kinds of love – connubial and paternal – he plays humorously upon the word "love" in the paragraph beginning (as has been his practice in introducing Mariposan subjects), "So I think that if you know Mariposa" (*SS*, 159). In this one paragraph, the narrator remarks twice on Pupkin's mistaken belief that he was "in love" with Miss Lawson and concludes,

"That wasn't LOVE!" (*SS*, 160). He then introduces his central theme, "real love," which is romantic love become real. (This paragraph only begins to reflect the relation between the romantic and the realistic which the love interest of the *Sketches* takes for its true subject.) The "sealed book" of Mariposan love and marriage, the book which the narrator is determined to unseal for "you," is finally a tale every bit as "enchanted" as those romance novels that seduce Zena away from her father's recommended reading, *The Life of Sir John A. Macdonald* (appropriately a biography that exemplifies a Canadian toryism).

The scene that concludes "The Extraordinary Entanglement," Pupkin's meeting and falling in love with Zena, makes clear the enchanting, transforming quality of love. Not only is "the whole world changed" for Pupkin as a result of meeting Zena (*SS*, 165), but the narrator, too, undergoes a change, a change that echoes his becoming thoroughly Mariposan when the *Mariposa Belle* sank (*SS*, 86–7). He begins the discussion of love's effect on Pupkin by revealing the commonplaceness of the ironic, "most peculiar coincidences" that bring Pupkin and Zena together. But as he moves from Pupkin's perception of the "whole world changed" to Pupkin's view of Mariposa, it becomes obvious that he sympathizes with the sentiments expressed and that he bemusedly, patronizingly, though not condescendingly, condones the workings of this romantic love: "And, for Pupkin, straight away the whole town was irradiated with sunshine, and there was such a singing of the birds, and such a dancing of the rippled waters of the lake, and such a kindliness in the faces of all the people, that only those who have lived in Mariposa, and been young there, can know at all what he felt" (*SS*, 165). The irradiation of sunshine offers here a contrast to the "darkness" that blotted out the trees and the lake in "The Beacon" (*SS*, 143). However, Mariposa is "irradiated with sunshine" only when the vision is a lover's; Mariposans all have "kindly" faces only when seen with a lover's eyes – Pupkin's, the prefacer's, the narrator's, the Envoi narrator's, and Leacock's. Significantly, the sunshine of these *Sunshine Sketches* is contingent upon "an affection," as the prefacer finally admitted (*SS*, xii). And "kindliness," it will be recalled, is the key word in Leacock's definition of humour: "The essence of humour is human kindliness." It follows that love, like humour at its best, transforms reality, bathes its subjects in sunshine, and views humanity in as kindly a light as human folly will allow. In opposition to the failure of Mariposan religion, *Sunshine Sketches* offers redemptive romantic love. "Which fact is so important that it would be folly not to close down the chapter and think about it" (*SS*, 166).

"The Fore-ordained Attachment" introduces Zena Pepperleigh and begins in earnest the depiction of the relation between romance and reality. Zena, who is typical of "all the girls in Mariposa" (*SS*, 168), is overly fond of chivalric tales and romantic daydreaming. Her father, the Judge, acts as a check upon these tendencies. When Zena hears her father approaching, she lunges for the *Pioneers of Tecumseh Township* and starts "reading it like mad" (*SS*, 168). The narrator, too, tempers the romantic with the realistic: the "unstilled yearning in [Zena's] violet eyes" is made somewhat less intense, and she is revealed to be but a fallible and mortal woman, by the healthy bite that she takes from an apple (*SS*, 167). What the Judge and the narrator do in these instances is typical of the entire love story: romantic inclinations need the ballast of realistic concerns to achieve the desired balance. The resulting ideal, "enchanted" love realizes thereby a synthesis of the magical and the mundane. In the love story this synthesis of the romantic and the realistic allows the Pupkins to move steadily and purposely forward, in contrast to Mariposa's waywardness in religious matters.

It is, nonetheless, the romantic perspective bequeathed by Zena's reading of quest romances that elevates, "the ordinary marriages of ordinary people" to the "enchanted" (*SS*, 169). And if the word "enchanted" has seemed to be overused here, consider the following remarks of the narrator on the relation between the ordinary and the enchanted: "So it is that each one of them [the girls of Mariposa] in due time marries an enchanted prince and goes to live in one of the enchanted houses in the lower part of the town. ... I don't know whether you know it, but you can rent an enchanted house in Mariposa for eight dollars a month, and some of the most completely enchanted are the cheapest. As for the enchanted princes, they find them in the strangest places" (*SS*, 169–70). Such enchantment is a charm against disillusioning reality. (And notice that the narrator includes mundane detail – the houses that "rent" ... for eight dollars a month.") But "to be able to find" the enchanted princes in commonplace occupations, "you have first to read ever so many novels about Sir Galahad and the Errant Quest and that sort of thing" (*SS*, 170). The adjectively diminutive "ever so many" – and the consequent attitude of indulgent condescension that it reveals – should not be allowed to obscure the point: romantic literature is essential if the imagination is to transform the humdrum.

It would seem that for Leacock women bring the romance and "poetry" to love and marriage. It was enough for Pupkin to see Zena "wearing a white shirt waist and a crimson tie" (*SS*, 165) to fall "clean, plumb, straight, flat, absolutely in love with her" (*SS*, 166). Pupkin falls in love supposedly because of a biological imperative. Zena, on the other hand, must imbue Pupkin with the trappings of her romantic heroes. Her triumph is that she succeeds in doing so. Although she knows the mundane facts of Pupkin's life in Mariposa, she seizes upon the one element of mystery attached to him – his origins – and lets her imagination work its magic until she sees "a dim parallel between the passing of the bicycle and the last ride of Tancred the Inconsolable along the banks of the Danube" (*SS*, 172). This interplay of the romantic and the realistic, a commendable feat of imagination, augurs well for love and marriage. But complications arise, of course. A romance would not be a Leacockian romance without its conventions being parodied as they are simultaneously exploited and elevated. In this second sketch of the three-sketch love story, the complications arise ironically from Pupkin's adoption of Zena's romantic standards. Pupkin, adhering literally to romantic convention, feels himself unworthy of Zena and contemplates suicide as the most appropriate termination to his anguish.

Because he wholeheartedly adopts Zena's romantic standards, Pupkin develops what may be termed a fear of reality. In one of *Sunshine Sketches'* characteristic inversions of the conventional, Pupkin is shown fearing that Zena will refuse to marry him not because his family is poor but because it is wealthy. This threat from unromantic affluence is termed "cold reality" (*SS*, 179). As is often the practice in the *Sketches*, the reality that threatens Mariposa and its representatives is projected onto "the city": Pupkin feels threatened by a poet "up from the city, probably" (*SS*, 188); he is driven to his final attempt at suicide because "Zena had danced four times with a visitor from the city" (*SS*, 195); and, after the bank mystery, Pupkin's new role as hero is threatened by the investigating detectives who "come up from the city" (*SS*, 203). It is at this critical juncture that Mr Smith makes his brief appearance in the lengthy love story.

Smith and the city detectives "take to" one another immediately because "hotel men and detectives have a general affinity and share in the same impenetrable silence and in their confidential knowledge of the weaknesses of the public" (*SS*, 204). Although it is improbable that the freeloading, drinking detectives ever would have solved the bank mystery, Smith nonetheless puts an end to their "investigations" by cautioning them not to "ask too close as to what folks was out late at night: in this town it don't do" (*SS*, 204). Following Smith's advice, "those two great brains," the detectives, "left for the city on the five-thirty" (*SS*, 204). It might appear that Smith has purposely removed the final obstacle to Pupkin's apotheosis to romantic hero. It is at least as probable, however, that Smith's remarks refer ironically to the time when *he* was "out late at night" to burn down the beacon and to the dedicated Mariposan drinkers who frequent his after-hours speak-easy.

In any event, Leacock's narrator has made his position clear with reference to the threat of the city in a passage that contrasts the Mariposan girls to their city rivals: "The Mariposa girls are all right. You've only to look at them to realize that. You see, you can get in Mariposa a print dress of pale blue or pale pink for a dollar twenty that looks infinitely better than anything you ever see in the city, – especially if you can wear with it a broad straw hat and a background of maple trees and the green grass of a tennis court" (*SS*, 169). The Mariposan girls are more attractive because they "wear" with their simple dress a more becoming environment than do their urban counterparts. Zena and Pupkin have little to fear. "The grinding capitalistic tyranny of the banks in Mariposa" actually assists the success of marriage by making it difficult for "ever so many mature and experienced men of nineteen and twenty-one" to wed prematurely (*SS*, 178). And Zena's dance partner from the city, by driving Pupkin to his last pseudo-suicide attempt, inadvertently brings about the opportunity for Pupkin to attain the status of hero. Leacock portrays Pupkin's and Zena's love not only as invulnerable to the threats of reality and the city but also as indirectly assisted by external reality. This favourable interdependency is underscored by the realization of Pupkin's greatest fear, that his wealthy father will visit Mariposa.

Pupkin lives in terror of this visit because he anticipates the loss of Zena's good opinion and because he is anxious lest his father take the appearance of Mariposan life for the reality. His father will treat Jim Eliot "like a druggist merely because he ran a drug store" and speak "to Jefferson Thorpe as if he were a barber simply because he shaved for money (*SS*, 182). Pertinently, Pupkin's concerns are a combination of the individualistic and the communal. He is afraid that his father will not be sensitive to the reality of illusive aspiration in the Mariposans, to those buried lives upon which the narrator commented with such irony in "The Beacon on the Hill" (*SS*, 136). The narrator is speaking the simple truth when he notes that such a lack of appreciation for the niceties of appearances and reality "could ruin young Pupkin in Mariposa ... and Pupkin knew it" (*SS*, 182). It is to Pupkin's credit that he knows it. But he does not know that there are those who have been working behind the scenes for the happy resolution of the complication. These people, Judge Pepperleigh and Pupkin Senior, possess the healthy grasp on reality that the lovesick Pupkin lacks at this point.

Upon his arrival in Mariposa, Pupkin Senior admirably demonstrates that his son's apprehension was unfounded. The father smokes a corn-cob pipe with Judge Pepperleigh, visits Jeff Thorpe, hunts ducks, and plays poker for small stakes (SS, 210–11, unlike Smith who fleeces the junior bank tellers and takes twenty-five dollars from Mullins). Pupkin Senior, unlike the auditor of "L'Envoi," is fully capable of returning to and courteously adapting to life in the little town. And he genuinely enjoys Mariposa, for "they had to send him telegrams enough to fill a satchel to make him come away" (SS, 211). Pupkin Senior is the representative of long-established big business, old money, and the world outside Mariposa at its best. Relative, say, to steel manufacturing, his business ventures – fishing and forestry – are not dehumanizing (SS, 181). He is also, to a greater extent, even, than Judge Pepperleigh, a representative of law and order, having served selflessly as Attorney General. As the narrator comments, "Attorney General! Why there's no money in that!" (SS, 181). Pupkin Senior shares much, in fact, with E.P. Leacock, Leacock's "Remarkable Uncle," whose way with the humble classes Leacock described as follows (and the emphasis is Leacock's): "E.P. was on the conservative, the *aristocratic* side, but along with that was hail-fellow-well-met with the humblest. This was instinct. A democrat can't condescend. He's down already. But when a conservative stoops, he conquers" (RU, 4). Most important, Pupkin Senior has passed on to his son the real heroic virtues that make possible the resolution to the romantic complication. It is this inheritance of real virtue that so fittingly complements Zena's romantic vision and makes their union possible.

Appropriately, practical financial concerns banish the maudlin thoughts of suicide from Peter Pupkin's mind and establish him as a suitable Mariposan hero. *Sunshine Sketches* is, after all, the work of a conservative political economist – a realist who is also a romantic idealist. When in the bank Pupkin suspects that Missinaba County's harvest money is threatened, he forgets "all about the maudlin purpose of his first coming" and "for the moment all about heroes and love affairs … He only knew that there was sixty thousand dollars in the vault below, and that he was paid eight hundred dollars a year to look after it" (SS, 197). Following this tribute to the virtues of work and duty (those Carlylean-Victorian virtues), the narrator eulogizes the Loyalist courage that Pupkin Senior has bequeathed his son: "His heart beat like a hammer against his ribs. But behind its beatings was the blood of four generations of Loyalists and the robber who would take that sixty thousand dollars from the Mariposa bank must take it over the dead body of Peter Pupkin, teller"

(*SS*, 198). The emphasis here on the physical – "heart," "ribs," "blood," "body" – suggests, however ironically, that the real cannot be denied, that Pupkin's very physical, Loyalist pedigree will triumph over his assumed "maudlin" imagination. Such sound Loyalist stock comprises for Leacock the *real* stuff of heroes, of which even a "teller" may partake. Thus Pupkin's courage allows him to "be turned into such a hero as even the Mariposa girls might dream about" (*SS*, 198).

Reminiscent of the way in which Jeff Thorpe's failed finances did not tarnish his charitable intentions, it is finally of no consequence to Pupkin's heroic stature that there was really no bank robbery. It is enough that Pupkin thinks the harvest money is in jeopardy. (And for a tory such as Leacock, as for Oliver Goldsmith and Thomas Chandler Haliburton, agriculture should form the basis of society.) Pupkin's heroism fires his resolve "to propose straight out" to Zena in a manner "supposed to belong only to people in books" (*SS*, 208). That is, the romance has become the real in what the Envoi narrator calls "such a book as the present one" (*SS*, 255), while yet remaining a story romance. Pupkin's courage, an inheritance from his Loyalist father, brings about his ironic apotheosis and the consummation of the love story. Of equal importance, however, is the role played by the other father, Zena's, for Judge Pepperleigh also works behind the scenes to further his daughter's and Pupkin's love.

It may be that the portrayal of Judge Pepperleigh owes something to the characterization of Prospero in Shakespeare's *The Tempest*. The Judge, a kind of front-porch Prospero, acquiesces to the fact that the lovers cannot permanently be kept apart, yet he apparently believes that their union should not be achieved too easily, perhaps "less too light winning / Make the prize light" (*Tmp*.I.ii.452–3). Reminiscent of the deceptively surly manner of Prospero towards Ferdinand, the Judge "used to sit and sneer at Pupkin after he had gone till Zena would throw down the *Pioneers of Tecumseh Township* in a temper and flounce off the piazza to her room. After which the judge's manner would change instantly and he would relight his corn cob pipe and sit and positively beam with contentment" (*SS*, 178). The Judge's contentment at the course events are taking is every bit as snugly smug as is Prospero's. Both are responsible for bringing the respective suitors to their daughters; and though neither is ultimately responsible for the love that buds, both choose to cast a passing shadow across its blossoming. It would not be straining the comparison to suggest further that Judge Pepperleigh may well be an authorial persona in the sense of those readings of *The Tempest* that view Prospero as a dramatic projection of Shakespeare. (More

correctly, it may be that Pepperleigh and Pupkin Senior taken together comprise a fictional projection of Leacock, with the Judge
representing the Orillian Leacock and Pupkin Senior being Montreal's Leacock.) It can be observed further that Leacock quotes directly from Prospero's speech beginning, "We are such stuff" to
illustrate what he conceived to be the point at which the highest
humour *begins* (HH, 232). These resemblances are noted to emphasize the associations for Leacock between humour and love: both
are dependent upon the romantic perspective and both must selectively fuse with the realistic; moreover, humour and love are closely
associated with a disposition towards "kindliness," and they bestow
an enchantment that alleviates the ordinariness, the disillusionments, of hard reality. The romantic love between Pupkin and Zena,
which leads to an "enchanted" marriage, should be understood to
be every bit as magical as the marvels of *The Tempest* – the true magic
of which is forgiveness and love.

Unlike Shakespeare's lovers, who must venture their deceptively
hard-won gains in Miranda's brave new world, Leacock's lovers are
allowed to remain in the insular and, in these three sketches at any
rate, permanently "enchanted" town of Mariposa:

> So Pupkin and Zena in due course of time were married, and went to
> live in one of the enchanted houses on the hillside in the new part of town,
> where you may find them to this day.
>
> You may see Pupkin there at any time cutting enchanted grass on a little
> lawn in as gaudy a blazer as ever.
>
> But if you step up to speak to him or walk him into the enchanted house,
> pray modulate your voice a little – musical though it is – for there is said
> to be an enchanted baby on the premises whose sleep must not lightly be
> disturbed. (SS, 211)

The conclusion to the love story possesses a fairy-tale quality. The
"in due course of time" itself suggests the "once upon a time" of the
fairy tale whose married lovers live happily ever after. But the repetition of "enchanted" suggests more than charm and delight. It
argues that this enchanted family has been bespelled by its author,
temporally suspended in his fiction to serve as a permanent exemplar
of the best in Mariposa. Mariposa is not an idyllic town, but it allows
for the existence of idyllic love.

Leacock has written elsewhere that in the real world (as opposed
to a fictional world) the enchantments of romantic love are impermanent: "All lovers – silly lovers in their silly stage – attain for a
moment this super-self, each as towards the other. Each sees in the

other what would be there for all the world to see in each of us, if we could but reach it" (*RU*, 206–7). The imagination that conceives of romantic lovers as living permanently in an enchanted world temporarily abandons itself to the subjective orientation of the lovers. This is the case with Leacock's narrator at the conclusion of the love story. Surely it would be critically perverse to distort the conclusion by forcing it onto some Procrustean bed of distorting irony. *Of course* Leacock parodies the conventions of romance throughout the sketches on Mariposan love: the adventurous hero, the beautiful heroine, the providential coincidence, the happy ending, and so on. But as Jerome H. Buckley has observed of Oscar Wilde's ironic portrayal of women who evoke pathos, "We may suspect the playwright of deliberately burlesquing the distress of his heroines; but we can hardly assume that he would have us regard his most calculated pathos as completely ironic."[14]

As is often the case in Leacock's humour, the sketches on love present an instance of extremes being modulated: the realistic tempers the romantic and vice-versa. The three sketches have tempered the disheartening conclusions that were drawn from the previous three sketches, which portrayed Mariposa as extremely affected, materialistic, and dishonest in matters of religion. By effectively excluding Mr Smith from the love interest, the sketches on romance, love and marriage have revealed the town in its most positive light, functioning as a cohesive community towards a commendable goal – a new Mariposan citizen (who will help, incidentally, to justify the town's tendency to inflate its census figures). All of which is to say that Leacock's enchanted love story is also a chant in the religious sense. It is, as it were, a number of humorously-intoned variations on a single theme, romantic love, variations which are chanted to counter the dispiriting failure of Mariposan religion.

"L'Envoi: The Train to Mariposa" takes the completed picture of Mariposa and throws a new light on *Sunshine Sketches* by applying its perceptions of the little town to life in the city. In a manner that parallels the movements between reality and illusion within each previous sketch, there is in "L'Envoi" a quite literal traffic between reality and illusion – "the train to Mariposa."

As this train crosses the bridge over the Ossawippi and moves ever closer to Mariposa, the Envoi narrator exclaims, "We must be close now!" In a manner that resembles a technique of the dramatic monologue, the auditor interrupts his anticipation with an unrecorded, though apparently apprehensive, remark. The narrator considers the cause of his companion's anxiety: "What? It feels nervous and strange to be coming here again after all these years? It must indeed. No, don't bother to look at the reflection of your face in the window-pane shadowed by the night outside. Nobody could tell you now after all these years. Your face has changed in these long years of money-getting in the city. Perhaps if you had come back now and again, just at odd times, it wouldn't have been so" (SS, 263). The mirror image here focuses the concerns of "L'Envoi": self-identity in relation to Mariposa. The Envoi narrator admonishes his auditor for the relentlessness of his "money-getting in the city," a relentlessness that has told on his features, making him unrecognizable to those who have remained in touch with their Mariposan roots. However, the Envoi narrator is not suggesting that his auditor go home again, only that he should "perhaps" have "come back now and again, just at odd times."[15] Note, also, that the nostalgically maudlin and simplistic perception of Mariposa as "home" (SS, 256–7) is not the Envoi narrator's; it is, rather, the homesick auditor's.

The reader of the Sketches may experience at "L'Envoi" a sense of dislocation similar to its auditor's sense of displacement. Here, for the first time since the preface, the reader is outside of Mariposa. He is situated now in the "dull" Mausoleum Club, and like the auditor, he may yearn to return to colourful Mariposa. But before such an imaginative return can be attempted, the Envoi narrator, in a manner reminiscent of the practice of the prefacer and the narrator of the sketches, must first correct his auditor's misperceptions.

The Envoi narrator initially suggests his auditor's displacement and ignorance of Mariposa by remarking continually on what he "knows" and does not "know" (SS, 255–6). The auditor does not know – or remember – that there is a train to Mariposa, though he came "from the little town" and once spent many an evening yearning after the returning train. The auditor does not have a definite reference for the repeatedly emphasized word, "home." Home once referred to Mariposa, but now home "means that 'big red sandstone house … in the costlier part of the city," or "'Home' means, in a way, this Mausoleum Club" (SS, 255). And, finally, home can once again mean Mariposa when the auditor sits "reading in a quiet corner somewhere such a book as the present one" (SS, 255). Essentially, Sunshine Sketches is a reminder of what "home" is, and "L'Envoi" is a concluding lesson in how memories of Mariposa should be employed. But the reader would be as ignorant as the auditor to presume that Mariposa-as-home is an ideal to be set apart in some musty, nostalgically maudlin corner of a Mausoleum Club – an ideal that is occasionally dusted off and shined up. The reader, who is familiar with Mr Smith and with Drone's "beacon," should know better. The Envoi narrator is determined to correct just such a mis-perception of Mariposa. He does not want his auditor to misread *Sunshine Sketches* and misapply the lessons that it contains.

The Envoi narrator proceeds to recount his auditor's career. Upon first arriving in the city, the auditor, a homesick boy, had planned to "make money," to become "really rich," and then to return to Mariposa and build an ostentatious house – the best that money could buy" (*SS*, 256). The Envoi narrator remarks that such a house would be "much finer in true reality, than the vast palace of sand-stone with the porte-cochère and the sweeping conservatories that you afterwards built in the costlier part of the city" (*SS*, 256). No doubt the narrator's perception is to some extent "true reality": such a house in Mariposa would be "much finer" than a "palace of sandstone" in the city. The ostentatious house that the auditor had dreamed of building in Mariposa dwindles, however, in comparison with the enchanted home of Peter and Zena Pupkin, which home is located in the "newer part of town" (*SS*, 211). "Cost" has little to do with the relative enchantments of a Mariposan home; in fact, it can effect enchantment inversely, for, as the reader knows, "some of the most completely enchanted [homes of Mariposa] are the cheapest" (*SS*, 169). Or to state the point directly, the auditor's early ambition betrays his dream as the gaudy dream of the *nouveau riche*: the small-town boy makes a pile and returns to impress the locals.

The salient characteristics of the auditor are his desire for wealth and his mistaken, nostalgic perception of Mariposa as "home." The auditor changed when he left Mariposa and lost a part of himself. A large part of the cause for his change and loss is that to which the narrator later refers in the central passage on self-identity – "these long years of money-getting in the city." The auditor's obsessive desire for material riches suggests further that he possesses some-thing of a Smithian bent. His ambition also recalls Jeff Thorpe's mistaken desire for impressive wealth and Dean Drone's mistaken faith in his ostentatious beacon. And yet, though the auditor is uninformed in his nostalgic perception of Mariposa and mistaken in his desire for riches with which to build an impressive home in Mariposa, he is nonetheless still thinking of Mariposa. Mariposa remains his reference point. The more threatening trouble arises when he begins to forget Mariposa.

The Envoi narrator regrets that his auditor has "half forgotten Mariposa, and long since lost the way to it" (*SS*, 256–7). He notes that his auditor is in this respect "only like the greater part of the men in this Mausoleum Club in the city" (*SS*, 257). And it is here especially that "Mariposa" acquires a degree of abstraction, for it is difficult to conceive that "practically every one of [the Mausoleum Club members] came from Mariposa once upon a time" (SS, 257). Rather, "Mariposa" is intended to suggest collective origins and the past, an interpretation supported by the fairy-tale "once upon a time" which assists temporal suspension. (As the prefacer concluded, "the inspiration of the book ... is large enough" [SS, xii].) Like the auditor who "half forgets" his origins, the members of the Mausoleum Club are "half ashamed to own" their beginnings in "Mariposa" (SS, 257). Just as the earlier comparison of houses recalled the enchanted houses of the three-sketch love interest, the most favourable treatment of Mariposa, so here the restrained criticism of forgetting and disowning remembers the three sketches on Mariposan religion, the most unfavourable treatment of Mariposa. The auditor and his fellow clubbers are forgetting "Mariposa" in a manner that parallels the way Mariposa discarded the quaint old church which, "like so much else in life, was forgotten" (SS, 105). In an attempt to induce his auditor to remember correctly his origins and the value of Mariposa, the Envoi narrator begins to recall for him some of Mariposa's allurements and to lead him to board, in his imagination, the train to Mariposa. Only such an imaginative re-affiliation with his origins can offset "the long dull evening" (SS, 257) of the Mausoleum Club – a place that, judging from his anxious reaction to his reflection in the window of the train to Mariposa, negates the auditor's fully integrated personality.

The Envoi narrator first entices his auditor with a sensuous appeal. The auditor is asked if his club meals can compare to the fish and fowl that he once caught near Mariposa (SS, 257). (Perhaps memory must begin so, with the body, in order to counter the maudlin musings of the mistaken mind. Certainly Proust thought so.) By a sudden leap of imagination, the narrator and his auditor are aboard the train to Mariposa. "The joke is" (SS, 258) that the city dwellers do not realize that the suburban train transforms into the Mariposa train. This may well be "the joke" – the humorous purpose – of Sunshine Sketches, for, like the train, the book itself provides access to Mariposa. Sunshine Sketches provides the opportunity for an imaginative return to "Mariposa" – to the past, to home, to origins. The community is transformed in Leacock's humorous vision so that it is perceived simultaneously as more real and more illusory, as ironically revealed and colorfully heightened. It may be, moreover, that the shift to the train is not so sudden a leap of imagination. The Envoi narrator began by recalling Mariposa and then unapologetically required his auditor (and the reader) to board the train.

Without informed memories of Mariposa, an imaginative return is not possible.

By feigning ignorance of the appropriate, fashionable terminology, the narrator not only insinuates an opposition between himself and his travelling companion but also identifies himself with the temporarily displaced Mariposans aboard the train: "Those people with the clothes that are perfectly all right and yet look odd in some way, the women with the peculiar hats and the – what do you say? – last year's fashions? Ah yes, of course, that must be it" (SS, 258). While in the city, the Mariposans are not individualized. When the narrator points out "one of the greatest judges that ever adorned the bench of Missinaba County" and "that clerical gentleman … who is explaining to the man with him the marvellous mechanism of the new air brake (one of the most conspicuous illustrations of the divine structure of the physical universe)" (SS, 258–9), the references are, of course, to Judge Pepperleigh and Dean Drone, although neither is named. In a sense, Pepperleigh and Drone are here accorded a degree of abstraction similar to "Mariposa," in accordance, perhaps, with the prefacer's claim that his characters are types (SS, xi–xii). More important, the references to Pepperleigh and Drone pointedly recall the most favourable treatment of Mariposan life (the romance) and the most disillusioning aspect of life in the little town (the beacon). Only as a result of temporal and spatial distance – such as the auditor has interposed – is Mariposa remembered incorrectly as the ideal "home" or as an untroubled idyllic community. As the train moves towards Mariposa, the two characters of Pepperleigh and Drone emerge hazily to suggest the good and the bad of Mariposan life. "But of course you hardly recognize them while the train is passing through the suburbs and the golf district and the outlying parts of the city area" (SS, 259).

As the train departs from city environs, it undergoes a transformation reminiscent of the electricity which "turned into coal oil again" by the time it entered Mariposa (SS, 8). The electric locomotive "changes its character" and turns into an "old wood engine … with sparks enough to light up a suit for damages once in every mile" (SS, 259). Metaphorically, the city and the present, set afire by the retreating train, are left in the distance as the train to Mariposa enters the country and the past and continues "thundering and pounding towards the north" (SS, 258), "up to the higher ground of the country of the pines and the lakes" (SS, 260). It is at this juncture that the Envoi narrator instructs his auditor to "look from the window as you go" (SS, 260). And there are hints that the auditor's fleeting journey towards Mariposa/home reflects his country's, Canada's, ongoing struggle for the preservation of a distinctive identity vis-à-vis the United States of America.

In a passage that anticipates the ultimate indictment of the auditor for having half-forgotten Mariposa, the Envoi narrator regrets that it is not a lack of opportunity that has kept the auditor away from Mariposa:

As you sit back half dreaming in the car, you keep wondering why it is that you never came up before in all these years. Ever so many times you planned that just as soon as the rush and strain of business eased up a little, you would take the train and go back to the little town to see what it was like now, and if things had changed much since your day. But each time when your holidays came, somehow you changed your mind and went down to Naragansett or Nagahuckett or Nagasomething, and left over the visit to Mariposa for another time. (SS, 260)

Rather than coming up to the country of his origins and affirming his bond with its changing reality, the materialistic auditor has spent what free time he could steal going down to vacation in the United States. (Narragansett is a resort town and its adjoining bay in Rhode Island; "Nagahuckett" appears to be a conflation of the names of two other US resort areas, Naugatuck in Connecticut and Nantucket Island off Massachussetts.) Compared to the mellifluous "Mariposa" – the Spanish word for butterfly – the US names onomatopoeically suggest the grinding gears of a machine. These areas are the vacation spots that the auditor has chosen – "you changed your mind and went down."

The Envoi narrator then contrasts this "Nagasomething" to the Mariposan countryside that the auditor has been avoiding: "At every crossway we can hear the long muffled roar of the whistle, dying to a melancholy wail that echoes into the woods; the woods, I say, for the farms are thinning out and the track plunges here and there into great stretches of bush, – tall tamarack and red scrub willow and with a tangled undergrowth of brush that has defied for two generations all attempts to clear it into the form of fields (SS, 260–1). This is suggestively a view of the country (to borrow from the title of an Al Purdy poem) north of Toronto.[16] This view is offered in opposition to "the city," but it is contrasted also to those vacation spots in the US that were referred to in the immediately preceding paragraph. A recalcitrant land that defies "all attempts to clear it into the form of fields" is a strikingly poetic image that echoes for-ward to several later Canadian works. Here is an approach to the

Canadian landscapes of Lawren Harris, F.R. Scott, and A.J.M. Smith, and Leacock has captured the spirit of the land in one seemingly endless sentence. (Of course, the implications arising from the image of a land resistant to "the form of fields" are ones to which later modernists such as Margaret Atwood have devoted much literary exploration.) For Leacock the Canadian hinterland – "the higher ground of the country of pines and the lakes" (*SS*, 260) – is the place "where the town of Mariposa has lain waiting for you ... for thirty years" (*SS*, 261). Mariposa has lain waiting to reaffirm the auditor's sense of self and identity. Mariposa waits as the place to which city dwellers (Mausoleum Clubbers) may yet return, and should return, to revitalize their lives – both individual and collective. But the auditor has "half forgotten" Mariposa, having dismissed the train to Mariposa to ride instead the "Empire State Express" and the aptly named "New Limited" (*SS*, 261). The auditor is aboard the train to Mariposa only because the Envoi narrator has brought him there. By extension, the representative auditor is aboard only because "such a book" as *Sunshine Sketches* has provided memories and induced imaginings of Mariposa. Still, Leacock does not portray the auditor as a hopeless case. The auditor is on the train in a "half dreaming" state, which suggests an equal mixture of romance and reality and, consequently, the possibility of transcendent, yet accepting, insight into his condition. Furthermore, the positive side to "half forgotten" is that the auditor has "half remembered" Mariposa and so has read such a book as *Sunshine Sketches*.

Significantly, when nearing Mariposa, the Envoi narrator feels none of his auditor's anxiety. Having alternated his narrative mode from "you," to "they," to "you" (*SS*, 255, 257, 258), the narrator finally clarifies his own position in a passage that employs the first person, thereby stressing his identification with the Mariposans as the train approaches its destination. He refers to some other of the world's fast trains and proceeds in what has previously been termed a Maripocentric manner:

But what are they to this, this mad career, this breakneck speed, this thundering roar of the Mariposa local driving hard to its home! Don't tell me that the speed is only twenty-five miles an hour. I don't care what it is. I tell you, and you can prove it for yourself if you will, that that train of mingled flat cars and coaches that goes tearing into the night, its engine whistle shrieking out its warning into the silent woods and echoing over the dull still lake, is the fastest train in the whole world.

Yes, and the best too, – the most comfortable, the most reliable, the most luxurious and the speediest train that ever turned a wheel. (*SS*, 262)

In a sense the "wheel" is coming full circle. The Envoi narrator's childish petulance and pride in *his* "Mariposa local" as the best, most comfortable and speediest "train in the whole world" is of course quintessentially Maripocentric. Most important, he desires to be so wholly Mariposan because the Mariposans aboard the train are "the most genial, the most sociable" of people; having shed "that dull reserve" of the city, they call to one another by name "as if they were all one family" (*SS*, 262). There is no need at this point to rehearse the numerous times within the *Sketches* when the virtues of such a communal familiarity – in contrast to Mr Smith and "the city" – proved overwhelmingly attractive to the narrator of the sketches.

In the passage that describes the auditor's anxiety over his own reflection, the narrator at once sympathizes with his apprehensiveness and forthrightly reveals its causes. The indictment is twofold: the auditor is guilty of an over-emphasis on "money-getting" and of going down to the US intead of occasionally returning to the typically Canadian and somewhat northern town of Mariposa. The two offences – materialism and a US bias – are suggestively related. Leacock may well be implying that the obsessive desire for material gain nurtures an affinity for the "home" of liberal individualism. Such a relationship is suggested in "L'Envoi," though it would be mistaken to over-simplify. The auditor lives, after all, in a Canadian city. Rather, *Sunshine Sketches* disparages unrestrained individualism and crass materialism in favour of the humane virtues of the Mariposan community. And yet, individualism and materialism are gaining ground in Mariposa; these are two of the changes the auditor would have noticed had he "come back now and again, just at odd times." Had he met Smith or attended services in Drone's (or Mr Uttermost's) new church, he would have seen that "things had changed" (*SS*, 260). Perhaps the incongruity between his mistaken nostalgic memories of "home" and the reality of change for the worse would have prompted him to perceive and arrest such developments within himself.

In fulfilment of his credo that humour be "kindly," Leacock portrays the Envoi narrator's final position as one of sympathetic identification with his auditor's plight. "L'Envoi" could have ended with the train's arrival in Mariposa, with "the cry of the brakemen and the porters:

MARIPOSA! MARIPOSA!" [17]

The cry recalls the conclusion to "The Marine Excursion," that other, most Canadian of the sketches: "O-CAN-A-DA!" (*SS*, 93). The cry

"Mariposa" would seem similarly to offer a fitting conclusion to *Sunshine Sketches*, but only if the reader is unrealistically predisposed to the escapist, idyllic literature that enjoyed such popularity at the turn of the century. A physical and permanent return to Mariposa was never the Envoi narrator's intention, either for himself or for his auditor. The auditor should have returned "now and again" (*SS*, 263). For the book to have terminated with the train *in* Mariposa would have been to leave the reader with a falsely comfortable impression, an impression that satisfies an emotional indulgence similar to the auditor's mistaken nostalgia. And, of course, a successful return to and entry into Mariposa would have devalued the criticism of materialism and uninformed memories that the Envoi narrator levels at his auditor.

The final paragraph (the postcript, as it were) of "L'Envoi" serves two critical purposes: first, it shows that the Envoi narrator sympathizes with the plight of his auditor. The narrator adopts the narrative mode "we," thus effectively unifying himself and his auditor back in the Mausoleum Club at precisely the point where an escape into an idealized "Mariposa" appeared imminently realizable: "And as we listen, the cry grows fainter and fainter in our ears and we are sitting here again in the leather chairs of the Mausoleum Club, talking of the little Town in the Sunshine that once we knew" (*SS*, 264). With Maripocentrism as its communally binding force, the little Town in the Sunshine gathers to its enchanted heart those residents who have visited the city. Leacock closes his "circle of affection," but he sympathetically leaves his philosopher-guide, the Envoi narrator, with the auditor.[18] The pair, now a community of two within the world of the Mausoleum Club, are returned to the real world. The conclusion of "L'Envoi" displays Leacock's humanism: an imaginative and visionary journey out of the self and the present to a northern, ideal community – "The country of the Ought to be" – is followed by a return to "a land of baser men."[19] A conclusion that left the narrator and his auditor in "Mariposa" would have suggested a *contemptus mundi* that was foreign to Leacock's humanistic vision.

The second purpose of the "postcript" is to emphasize what has become increasingly clear throughout "L'Envoi": there is no literal "train to Mariposa." In the context of "L'Envoi," there is no real Mariposa. Mariposa is geographically real to the narrator of the sketches, but it is not to the Envoi narrator. For the Envoi narrator, "Mariposa" is an abstraction, the extrapolation finally from "seventy or eighty" Canadian towns, as the prefacer protested (*SS*, xi). "We are sitting here in the leather chairs of the Mausoleum Club," which, of course, "we" never left physically. The real and only "train to Mariposa" is *Sunshine Sketches*. Imaginative literature, "such a book as the present one," provides access to a correct perception of the past, of origins both individual and collective; and it helps make available in the present the *informed* memories from which imagination can fashion a vision of the future.

The Envoi narrator stresses the importance of periodic imaginative "returns" to Mariposa and demonstrates that, in imagination, by means of realistically and romantically informed memories, he is quite capable of reaffirming his bond to Mariposa. If Mariposa remains only "the little Town in the Sunshine that once we knew," if "we" forget and deny our origins, then "we" are condemned to remain entombed in a Mausoleum Club, waxing nostalgically and with mistaken eloquence on misconceptions of Mariposa as "home." It is just such an ignorance of Mariposa that allows the auditor to fancy that he possesses the proper feelings, thereby freeing himself to pursue competitively his materialistic, individualistic ends. However, the threatened fracturing of the representative auditor's identity, which he experiences when his face is reflected on the window of the imaginative train, is but one of the consequences of forgetting Mariposa. Without realistically informed memories of Mariposa, the auditor also lacks the material of imagination from which to fashion a future based on a correct understanding of the worthwhile from his and his country's past. The Envoi narrator has shown, as has *Sunshine Sketches*, how such an imaginative recreation operates – how, in Margaret Avison's expression, the "optic heart must venture."[20]

"*Quo vadimus?*" asked Leacock with regard to mankind's moral development (*ELS*, 52). In *Arcadian Adventures With the Idle Rich*, he offers a humorous vision of present tendencies in "the City," an American city.

CHAPTER FIVE

Arcadian Adventures: *The City of the End of Things*

Lurid and lofty and vast it seems;
It hath no rounded name that rings,
But I have heard it called in dreams
The City of the End of Things.

Archibald Lampman, "The City of the End
of Things"

Arcadian Adventures With the Idle Rich has often been compared rewardingly with *Sunshine Sketches*.[1] Taken together, the two books reveal the range of Leacock's fictional concerns: his perception of the need to recover the values that he associates with small communities and his apprehensions at the sort of metropolitan society that may develop in the absence of these values. Where the *Sketches* steadily and affectionately looks to the past – or homeward – *Arcadian Adventures* peers at the present (c. 1914) and humorously satirizes its tendencies. The *Adventures* can also be seen to present a vision of the sort of society that emerges when the implicit warning of the *Sketches'* "L'Envoi" is unheeded. The essence of that warning is the need to return northwards periodically to a symbolically Canadian "Mariposa" and not to drift southwards to the plutocratic decadence of an equally symbolic United States of America. Mariposa remains, in effect, the implicit norm against which the plutorian Arcadia is to be judged.

In *Arcadian Adventures* Leacock apparently felt no need to introduce himself as the self-effacing bastion of toryism; certainly the volume contains no preface to establish an attitude toward the fiction or to predetermine the reader's attitude (such manipulation is usually Leacock's intention in a preface[2]). The narrator's attitude towards the plutorians is relatively easily discerned compared with the narrative stance in the *Sketches*. From the beginning of chapter one, "A Little Dinner with Mr. Lucullus Fyshe," the reader knows which way the irony of *Arcadian Adventures* is intended to cut. The following remarks on the location of the Mausoleum Club relative to "the tangled streets and little houses of the slums" are a case in point: "In fact, if you were to mount to the roof of the Mausoleum Club itself on Plutoria Avenue you could almost see the slums from there. But why should you? And on the other hand, if you never went up on the roof, but only dined inside among the palm-trees, you would never know that the slums existed – which is much better" (*AA*, 11). Here, the narrator informs the reader that there will be no discomfitting climbing up on roofs to gain a disconcerting view of the world beyond Plutoria Avenue. The perspective is to be limited to Plutoria Avenue and its extensions (such as The Grand Palaver Hotel and Mr Newberry's Castel Casteggio in "The Love Story of Mr. Peter Spillikins"). As the narrator invitingly remarks, "The whole world as seen from the boulevard of Plutoria Avenue is the very pleasantest place imaginable" (*AA*, 10). The intention of such ironic observations is obvious. Indeed, in terms of Northrop Frye's useful distinction between irony and satire, Leacock's irony in the *Adventures* approaches "militancy." "Satire is militant irony," writes Frye: "Its moral norms are relatively clear, and it assumes standards against which the grotesque and absurd are measured." The reader immediately suspects that Leacock dislikes and is perhaps repulsed by the plutorian indifference to poverty and the working world. The reader of the *Sketches* can seldom be certain of its narrator's attitude toward the Mariposans, which uncertainty, Frye argues further, suggests "irony with relatively little satire."[3] The narrator's ambivalence in the *Sketches* makes that book a masterpiece, and not a minor one, of ironic humour. Leacock's more militant irony in the *Adventures* makes it the work of a satirist, albeit a relatively kindly and humanistic one.

In *Arcadian Adventures*, Leacock's narrator refers intermittently to the poorer sections of the City, focusing the reader's attention on those who work and those who are victimized by plutocratic greed. The selective perceptiveness that he initially and ironically commends in the plutorians and implicitly recommends to the reader suggests, by inversion, the moral norm within *Arcadian Adventures*: those who work, those who are not the *idle rich*. The closing phrases of the book return to "the others – in the lower parts of the city," who rise early in the morning "to their daily toil" (*AA*, 310). In terms of the book's structure, the self-serving activities of the "idle" plutorians are framed by opening and closing references to the poor and the workers. Similarly, the activities of the Mariposan community are framed by opening and closing sketches (excepting "L'Envoi") dealing with the business and political machinations of Mr Josh Smith. The workers and the slum-dwellers of *Arcadian Adventures*, like the Mariposans who provide the standard against which Mr Smith is to be measured, offer an understated moral norm by which the plutorians are to be judged.

In Leacock's social-political writings, the workers and the victimized poor provided a sharp contrast to the idle rich. In *The Unsolved Riddle of Social Justice*, for example, he regrets the disparity between rich and poor: "Few persons can attain to adult life without being profoundly impressed by the appalling inequalities of our human lot. Riches and poverty jostle one another upon our streets. The tattered outcast dozes on his bench while the chariot of the wealthy is drawn by. The palace is the neighbour of the slum. We are, in modern life, so used to this that we no longer see it" (*UR*, 14). When representatives of the working classes intrude upon the plutocratic Arcadia, as is the case with Tomlinson, they can place on view the true ethical and intellectual bankruptcy of the idle rich, or, as is the case with Norah, "the Little Girl in Green," they can serve as the pathetic victims of the indifference to human suffering that lies behind rampant material acquisitiveness.

No doubt it is such authorial sureness that makes the narrator's ironic voice less difficult to interpret in the *Adventures* than is the voice of the *Sketches*. The reader of the *Adventures* can safely believe that what the narrator ironically reveals is what Leacock thought of the plutorians. In *Arcadian Adventures* the issues are more cut and dried and offered for display, as it were. Or, to put the matter differently, when Leacock wrote fiction about what he believed were his country's origins in "Mariposa," he offered much in equivocal terms; when he set his humorous satire in the United States, he presented a scathing, unqualified anatomy of the body and end-product of liberal individualism.

Before embarking on an analysis of the subjects treated in the adventures of *Arcadian Adventures*, it should be observed that they are the same as those portrayed in the *Sketches* and that the organization of the *Adventures* parallels the *Sketches*.[4] *Arcadian Adventures* contains eight chapters, which can readily be grouped, like the eleven chapters of the *Sketches*, into five thematic sections: business, society, romance, religion, and politics. The *Adventures* begins with the theme of business, with chapters one through three dealing with Mr Lucullus Fyshe's dinner and Tomlinson's financial wizardry. The book ends with political dealings in "The Great Fight for Clean Government." The *Sketches* begins with Mr Smith's business ventures and concludes, excepting "L'Envoi," with his political intrigues. Chapter four of the *Adventures*, "The Yahi-Bahi Oriental Society of Mrs. Rasselyer-Brown," is a depiction of plutorian society in microcosm. As such, it corresponds to the third sketch of *Sunshine Sketches*, "The Marine Excursion." Jefferson Thorpe has his partial counterpart in Tomlinson, whose activities are the concern of chapters two and three in *Arcadian Adventures*: both Jeff and Tomlinson make and lose illusory fortunes. Moreover, Tomlinson immediately follows the introduction of Fyshe, who is to Plutoria what Smith, who is followed by Jeff, is to Mariposa – the prime mover and most manipulative schemer. Chapter five of the *Adventures* depicts the short-sighted love affair of Mr Peter Spillikins. Chapters six and seven concern religious matters. And chapter eight, as has been remarked, concludes the book with a dissection of plutorian politics. *Sunshine Sketches* ends where *Arcadian Adventures* begins, in a Mausoleum Club, suggesting perhaps that they mirror as well as continue one another.

The one important difference between the organization of the two books is in the sections dealing with love and religion. In the *Sketches*, the trimphant love of Pupkin and Zena – their enchanted home and baby – follows the failure of institutionalized religion to meet simply the needs of Mariposan Anglicans. In the *Adventures*, the successful religious venture follows the failure of Peter Spillikins to realize that for him true love resides only with Norah, "the Little Girl in Green." The financially rewarding church merger underscores the cause of Norah's suffering, which is plutorian greed and guile. Norah is the one character in the *Adventures* to whom Leacock's authorial heart is most pathetically devoted. Love of the kind enjoyed by Pupkin and Zena is impossible in a plutocratic world, where a "gold-digger" such as Mrs Everleigh can take the short-sighted Spillikins by the nose and lead him away from the promising "green girl." More correctly, romantic love between a plutorian and a member of the humbler classes is impossible. Finally, the relative importance of love in Mariposa and Plutoria is mirrored structurally not only in the organization of chapters but also in the space allotted to romantic concerns. In the *Sketches* three chapters are devoted to the love interest; in the *Adventures* only one is.

In *Sunshine Sketches* money is chiefly the obsession of Mr Smith, an ascendant plutorian. Every aspect of life in *Arcadian Adventures* is a going business concern. Although the book is most accessible when approached as humorous satire on plutorian business, society, romance, religion, and politics, all of these aspects of life in the City are directly determined by the first subject – money matters. Claude

Bissell has called the *Adventures* a "fictional companion piece" to Thorstein Veblen's *The Theory of the Leisure Class*.[5] But Leacock's insistence on the "money-getting" motive behind all plutorian action,[6] rather than emphasizing the spending of money, makes Alexis de Tocqueville's fascinated and denigrating *Democracy in America* as likely a companion piece: "At first appearance this people seems to be a company of merchants gathered together for trade; and as one dips further into the national character of Americans, one sees that they have sought the value of all things in this world only in the answer to this one question: how much money will it bring in?"[7] Again, it is the blatancy of the pecuniary motives behind all plutorian "idle" action that makes the ironic voice of the *Adventures* relatively easy to understand. Similarly, because avarice and idleness are so obviously satiric targets, the norm *within* the book is represented by those who work in non-plutorian pursuits, or the norm is represented by those who are simply not *the idle rich*.

Leacock's tory-humanist satiric norm is, however, more richly affirmative than the idle/workers description suggests. As the first chapter of this study argued, Leacock's fictional characters can be understood as existing on a continuum between "Mariposa" and "Plutoria." The characters of the *Sketches* and *Adventures* partake to varying degrees in Leacock's tory-humanist norm, the norm which is characterized by the following human attributes: community, family, interdependency, romantic love, tolerant politeness, respect for tradition, reverence for the dead, and organicism. In *Arcadian Adventures* the negative extreme of "Plutoria" is represented by characters such as Lucullus Fyshe and Asmodeus Boulder, whose surnames suggest the cold-blooded and the inanimate – definitely the subhuman. Between the likes of Fyshe and Mariposans such as Judge Pepperleigh, there are Arcadian characters who approach Leacock's norm. For example, the British Duke of Dulham, though by no means wholly admirable, compares favourably to the native plutorians because of his politeness, his maintenance of a kind of feudal family that is based on agricultural pursuits, and his intention to borrow money rather than to accrue it ruthlessly. Tomlinson and his farming family personify Leacock's rural agrarian virtues in opposition to urban mechanistic Plutoria. And there are other characters, such as Mr Rasselyer–Brown, Peter Spillikins, and Dr McTeague, who are neither completely "Mariposan" nor extremely "Plutorian" and whose fates in the *Adventures* reveal much about the irresistible triumph of the plutocracy.

Comparisons and parallels between the narrators and the structures of, and some characters in, the *Sketches* and the *Adventures* reveal much about the basis of the Mariposan community and the plutorian anti-community. As will be shown further, these parallels ultimately support the thesis that "Mariposa," as it is understood by the Envoi narrator, is the necessary norm against which "Plutoria" must continually be judged if it is to be opposed.

Although *Arcadian Adventures* does not possess a preface, it offers in chapter one, "A Little Dinner with Mr. Lucullus Fyshe," an introduction to the plutorian Arcadia that recalls the *Sketches'* introduction to Mariposa. Just as the introduction to Mariposa adjusts the reader's perspective and proceeds towards Mr Josh Smith, the introduction to the City establishes the ironic perspective and leads to a presentation of Mr Lucullus Fyshe. Fyshe shares with Smith the ability to turn to his own advantage something that looms as a business setback: he avenges himself on his chief business rival, Asmodeus Boulder, by passing the solicitous Duke of Dulham into Boulder's greedy hands. Whereas the introduction to Mariposa induces the reader to see Mariposa indulgently, the introduction to the City's Mausoleum Club, scathingly presents a society where the one referent is money.

Children, those enchanted, positive figures in Mariposa, are exploited in the plutorian Arcadia to diversify business holdings; they are tax shelters, or they protect against anti-trust suits. Using the "here/there" convention of picturesque and pastoral description, Leacock's narrator describes the infant inhabitants of the ironically picturesque Arcadia as follows: "Here you may see a little toddling princess in a rabbit suit who owns fifty distilleries in her own right. There, in a lackered perambulator, sails past a little hooded head that controls from its cradle an entire New Jersey corporation" (*AA*, 10). The birds of Plutoria Avenue are "the most expensive kind of birds"; a roaring train is "earning dividends"; "the shepherds and shepherdesses consume preferred stock and gold interest bonds in the shape of chilled champagne and iced asparagus" (*AA*, 9, 10, 12). The plutorians of the opening adventure are presented as truly *idle* over their long lunches; even their cars – their machines – "move drowsily" (*AA*, 9).

In the opening pages of *Sunshine Sketches* the narrator asked the reader to view sympathetically the vanity that is based on true community pride and initiated him into a complex, ever broadening and constantly deepening vision of the little town. In contrast, the introduction to Plutoria presents the plutorians in a straight-forwardly ironical light. There is more to Mariposa than meets the "careless eye." There is less to Plutoria. All is facade. In his anatomy of Mariposa, Leacock's narrator indulgently indicates the affectations and vanities of an interdependent community: Mariposa exists most fully in the ironic double-vision. In *Arcadian Adventures*, Leacock's narrator uses a scalpel to exhibit the cash-stuffed head and entrails of the thing.

"A Little Dinner" hinges on the comic device of cross-purposes. The plutorians, Fyshe, Dr Boomer from the university, and Asmodeus Boulder, having heard that the Duke of Dulham is in the city, want him to invest in their various concerns. But the Duke is there to borrow money. When Fyshe, who gets first crack at fleecing the Duke, learns the truth, he passes him off on Boulder, who eagerly departs with the Duke for Wisconsin on an ersatz hunting trip. The plot of the story is relatively unimportant, as it often is in satire. The only meaningful action occurs in the kitchen of the Mausoleum Club, where a union of the waiters is organized and its members decide to strike. This action ruins Mr Fyshe's idle little dinner, presenting the opportunity for him to work his counter-scam on Boulder. But the reader does not learn the outcome of Boulder's and the Duke's expedition to the hunting lodge in Wisconsin. Parties at cross-purposes, action that is inaction, and irresolution appear initially to be the characteristics of plutorian business. There are, however, undercurrents at work in this first adventure.

Business transactions are served up in "A Little Dinner" with images of predator and prey. When Fyshe first gets wind of the Duke's intention to borrow money, he is "quick as a lynx" (*AA*, 44) with his scheme to bait Mr Boulder with the Duke. (Boulder had stolen prey from Fyshe; in "A Little Dinner" Fyshe strikes when the moment for vengeance presents itself.) The first chapter also concludes with images of predator and prey. The *Plutorian Citizen* reports that the Duke is about to leave with Mr Boulder for the Wisconsin woods and that "Mr. Boulder intends to show his guest … something of the American wolf" (*AA*, 46). On the train to Wisconsin, Mr Boulder sits opposite the Duke as though ready to pounce upon an unsuspecting sheep: "Mr. Boulder looked at him with fixed, silent eyes, and murmured from time to time some renewed information of the ferocity of the timber wolf" (*AA*, 47). Leacock then makes plain what the image suggests: "But of wolves other than the timber wolf, and fiercer still, into whose hands the Duke might fall in America, he spoke never a word" (*AA*, 47). The redundancy – the forced humour – emphasizes the word "America," thereby reinforcing the earlier mention of the "American wolf." Accordingly, the introductory satire of *Arcadian Adventures*, although directed against the rapacity and savagery of plutocrats generally, has for its subject a decidedly American target, that is, the capitalistic assumptions of the United States of America.

The City of *Arcadian Adventures* is an American city (perhaps Cleveland[8]): Canadian and Mexican currencies are considered foreign and inferior by the charlatan Yahi-Bahi (*AA*, 138); Dr Slyder sends his patients to Canada because it is "perfectly quiet, not a soul there, and, [he] believes, nowadays quite fashionable" (*AA*, 167). The second sentence of *Arcadian Adventures* describes the Mausoleum Club as "a Grecian building of white stone" (*AA*, 9), a description that introduces the parodic plutorian Arcadia (with attendant implications of pagan versus Christian pastoral), reveals plutorian pretentiousness in architecture, and suggests the architecture of revolutionary America's government buildings. Although plutocratic materialism is not limited to the United States, Leacock chose to locate his "city of the end of things" – his most unified and extensive satire on pecuniary materialism – in the United States of America. Douglas Spettigue has argued that "Mariposa is Canada, so is Plutoria; the one is what we were and are, the other what we are and will be."[9] But surely Leacock is pointing to an essential distinction between the sort of society that arises from the tradition of liberal individualism, Plutoria, and the kind of community that his tory-humanism favours, Mariposa. (Mariposa, it will be recalled, was the community that Leacock imagined when he was commissioned to write something specifically Canadian.) Moreover, the device of cross-purposes that informs the plot of "A Little Dinner" brings into play the parallel theme of a contrast between the old world of Britain and the new world of the United States. Here Leacock suggests that the ideal of democracy with which the United States began has come to be but another principle exploited, debased, and vulgarized by the plutorians.

The Duke of Dulham is not an attractive character. A representative of the British aristocracy that originally gained its wealth in ways perhaps more brutal than anything the plutorians do, he feels that borrowing money is "essentially low. He could have understood knocking a man over the head with a fire shovel and taking his money, but not borrowing it." The aristocracy comes to America to borrow money, "pledging for it their seats or their pictures, or one of their daughters – anything (*AA*, 29–30). The treatment of people, particularly family, as *things* is to be condemned from the point of view of Leacock's tory humanism. Exploitation of people is also, of course, one of the sins the plutorians regularly commit in their unending search for wealth and power (as it is one of Josh Smith's sins). But at least one difference between the plutorians and the

Duke is that the former think only of unending pecuniary gain, whereas the Duke thinks first, in his need to *borrow* money, of politeness. When the "Chinese philosophers dressed up to look like waiters" (*AA*, 12) strike, thereby ruining Fyshe's predatory business dinner, "Mr. Fyshe sat silent with his fist clenched. Dr. Boomer, with his great face transfixed, stared at the empty oyster-shells, thinking perhaps of his college days. The Duke, with his hundred thousand dashed from his lips in the second cup of champagne that never was served, thought of his politeness first and murmured something about taking them to his hotel" (AA, 43). When frustrated in his scheme to gain more money, Fyshe, who actually has nothing to lose, seems ready to do violence with "his fist clenched." Boomer, who has eaten a free plate of oysters, which in his college days he considered an "ample meal" (*AA*, 41), and who has selfishly indulged his academic obsessions, has gained by the encounter. Yet he sits in dumb shock. Only the Duke, who has much to lose if he misses his chance to borrow money, behaves politely, with genuine manners. Significantly, the last sentence of the above quotation contains the only favourable comment on anyone in "A Little Dinner." The Duke of Dulham partakes to some extent of Leacock's tory-humanist norm, especially so in contrast to such as Fyshe, Boulder, and President Boomer. The Duke suggests in a number of ways the favourable character of Pupkin Senior in the *Sketches*. Like Pupkin Senior, the Duke is an outsider who politely adapts to the milieu in which he finds himself. Like Pupkin Senior, the Duke represents old money and an older order whose values transcend the crassly capitalistic. And like Pupkin Senior, the Duke's ventures – mainly agricultural (*AA*, 26–7) – are not dehumanizing. Although Leacock had a lifelong dislike of unearned, aristocratic privilege, he nonetheless presents the Duke of Dulham as representative of the old tory order in opposition to "the new government of the money power." In his 1917 essay, "Democracy and Social Progress," he describes the ascendant plutocracy as being "without a soul. It [knows] nothing of the ancient pride of place and race that dictated a certain duty towards those below. The creed that was embodied in the words *noblesse oblige* has vanished with the nobility. The plutocrat, unfettered by responsibility, seem[s] as rapacious and remorseless as the machinery that has made him."[10]

If the Duke is hypocritically solicitous in order to preserve his somewhat feudal way of life, the plutorians are even more hypocritical in their relation to the Duke. The hypocrisy of such plutorians as Fyshe derives from an insincere belief in the levelling principle of democracy. When Fyshe first utters the name of the Duke, he does so "with that quiet, democratic carelessness which meant that he didn't care whether half a dozen other members lunching at the club could hear or not" (*AA*, 15). Fyshe consumes "a pint of Moselle in the plain, downright fashion of a man so democratic that he is practically a revolutionary socialist" (*AA*, 17). When the Duke arrives in New York, the city, "being an ordinary, democratic, commercial sort of place, ... made no fuss over him whatever," other than announcing his arrival, tracing his pedigree, and suggesting that he is investing in American Industrials (*AA*, 33–4)). And when Fyshe fumes because he assumes that a comment of Boomer's is a lament over the Duke's missed lunch, the narrator notes that Fyshe "was feeling in the sourest of democratic moods" (*AA*, 44). The repeated ironic use of "democratic" in these contexts suggests that the American democratic ideal is being both exploited and debased by the plutorians for individual gain. The plutorians are proof that a moneyed class exists in America, a class that is as privileged as the European aristocracy, though hypocritically deferential still to foreign aristocrats and lacking the redeeming social graces of those whom it obsequiously admires.

From the first chapter's picture of real business, the reader could comfortably conclude that these big businessmen exploit no one but each other. Yet it should be kept in mind that the opening paragraphs of the sketch contain a reference to the working poor and that the plutorians are *big* businessmen. Ruthless accruers and custodians of millions of dollars, the plutorians are portrayed as predatory financial animals with whom Leacock insists the reader reckon. The plutorians, with their mock-Grecian architecture, their parodic Arcadia, and their affected classical names (Lucullus, Asmodeus, Philippa, Juliana), stand in pagan opposition to the Judeo-Christian pastoral ideal of the Good Shepherd, in opposition to the ideals of responsibility and charity. More than simple financial animals, the plutorians are, in Al Purdy's apt conception, *The New Romans*. [11]

In chapters two and three of *Arcadian Adventures*, Leacock offers the figure of Tomlinson, the purported "Wizard of Finance," as the representative of an agrarian way of life that is an alternative to mechanistic Plutoria. Tomlinson provides a contrast and foil to the plutorians; though he represents the agrarian aspect of Leacock's tory-humanist norm, he takes no action against the plutorians. It is Fred Tomlinson who actively opposes the plutorians. The story of the Tomlinsons' sojourn in the City contains one of the book's most damaging indictments of the plutorians.

In the first chapter of *Arcadian Adventures*, the Duke of Dulham offers the sole contrast to the plutorians. He embodies much that is unattractive, but he has his politeness, his agrarian association, and his sense of duty to recommend him. In the book's second and third chapters, Leacock utilizes the naïve Tomlinson to contrast the present of the City and its tendencies to the familial stability of an agrarian way of life. The juxtaposition of city and country takes many forms in these two chapters, though it can be expressed generally in a number of paired opposites, such as rural innocence and urban sophistication, honesty and deception, virtue and vice, organic and mechanical. Tomlinson offers further a partial parallel to the *Sketches'* Jeff Thorpe, though Tomlinson is even more of an innocent in the court of Plutoria than is Jeff in his brief flirtation with the world of high finance. Tomlinson is representative of a rural extreme. His virtues – hard work, loyalty, honesty, and modesty – are the essence of virtue extracted, as it were, from the soil of an America that may be past or vanishing, though Tomlinson and his son do reassert these virtues at the conclusion of "The Arrested Philanthropy." (There is in fact much of Leacock's understanding of Abraham Lincoln in the gangling, homespun figure of Tomlinson [*AA*, 52].[12]) As a prototype of a kind, Tomlinson embodies rural agrarian virtue that is employed to throw into high relief the greed and shallowness of the equally caricatured plutorians of the mechanistic present.

The controlling metaphor of "The Wizard of Finance" is magic: illusion, appearance, and reality. As the word "wizard" suggests, the story of Tomlinson deals primarily with the incongruity between the way things appear in Plutoria and the way things really are. The contrast between appearance and reality is also, it should be recalled, the controlling metaphor of the *Sketches*. In *Sunshine Sketches* the appearance – affected, dull, boastful – is an unattractive manifestation of the real communal virtues that lie behind the appearance. This is also the case with Tomlinson: behind the appearance of a simple rustic and behind the persona of the "The Wizard of Finance" which the plutorians project onto him is a genuine man, "THE MAN TOMLINSON" (*AA*, 102). Precisely the reverse is true of the plutorians. In *Arcadian Adventures* generally, though most obviously in chapters two and three, the attractive appearance of Arcadia is shown to be but a green smokescreen through which streak the flaming hypocrisies of the greedy plutorians.

Images of magic and alchemy recur throughout the story of Tomlinson's deceptive fortune, emphasizing the illusory nature of plutorian appearances. The Tomlinson story deals primarily with the consequences of a transmutation of sorts: the metallurgically worthless bed of Tomlinson's creek is transformed into a gold mine; then, at the conclusion of chapter three, the Tomlinsons and nature change it back into the green of the farm. This latter transmutation is understood to be the truer or white magic, for as the narrator remarks, "nature reached out its hand and drew its coverlet of green over the grave of the vanished Eldorado" (AA, 113–4). Most important, it is Tomlinson's realization that his green farm is the true gold mine that makes him a true wizard: "For there was one aspect and only one in which Tomlinson was really and truly a wizard. He saw clearly that for himself and his wife the vast fortune that had fallen to them was of no manner of use. What did it bring them? The noise and roar of the City in place of the silence of the farm and the racket of the great rotunda to drown the *remembered* murmur of the waters of the creek (AA, 70, emphasis added). Tomlinson is a wizard, then, in so far as his memory of what has been taken from him helps extract him from the pandemonium of the Grand Palaver Hotel. Something of a Merlin figure, he carries within him the vision of the farm that has been taken from him: "If the eyes of the man are dreamy and abstracted, it is because there lies over the vision of this vanished farm an infinite regret" (AA, 54). It is Tomlinson's "vision" of "this vanished farm" that he and his son reconstitute – literally re-member – at the conclusion of "The Arrested Philanthropy." In this way the Tomlinsons are practitioners of white magic in opposition to the plutorians, who practice a sort of mechanistic black magic.

Leacock's narrator introduces the metaphor of false and true magic in his opening description of the Grand Palaver: "Aladdin's enchanted palace was nothing to it. It has a vast ceiling with a hundred glittering lights, and within it night and day is a surging crowd that is never still and a babel of voices that is never hushed, and over all there hangs an enchanted cloud of thin blue smoke such as might enshroud the conjured vision of a magician of Baghdad or Damascus" (AA, 50). The ceaselessly "surging crowd" (that is, the pushiness) and the "babel of voices" offset whatever "enchantments" even the Grand Palaver may possess. The hotel, which ignores the natural diurnal cycle, is all plutorian illusion for the sole purpose of financial profit. The "enchanted palace" is a "Pluto's Palace," or worse. The above description of the Palaver may contain, as did the description of the excavation for Josh Smith's "caff," echoes of Milton's description in *Paradise Lost* of Pandemonium:

> from the arched roof
> Pendant by subtle Magic many a row
> Of Starry Lamps and blazing Cressets fed
> With *Naphtha* and *Asphaltus* yielded light
> As from a sky. (1.726–30)

Like Pandemonium, built by those original "strip-miners," Satan's cohorts of darkness, the Grand Palaver is the product of such unnatural rapaciousness as the strip-mining of Tomlinson's creek. In *Canada: The Foundations of its Future*, Leacock observes that Canada contains "a store of minerals and metals that Pluto himself might envy. All hell can be raised in the bowels of northern Canada."[13] The sentences show that Leacock was of course capable of associating for satiric purposes Pluto (the plutocrats and Pluto's Palace), mining, and hell.

Leacock shows further that the Grand Palaver brazenly exploits the concept of "home" for the purpose of soliciting clientele: "The aim of the company that owns the Grand Palaver – and they do not attempt to conceal it – is to make the place as much a home as possible. Therein lies its charm. It is a home" (*AA*, 49). The verb of the emphatic sentence, "Therein lies its charm," is perhaps to be read in its sense of falsifying. The Grand Palaver's charms lie. Leacock makes this interpretation of the Palaver's home-like charms unavoidable; in the last summary sentence of the introductory paragraphs to "The Wizard," his irony approaches disdain: "And the clerks call for the pages, the pages call for the guests, and the guests call for the porters, the bells clang, the elevators rattle, till home itself was never half so homelike" (*AA*, 51). "Home" held an especially affirmative meaning for Leacock, a contention that requires no further argument than a direction to his use of the word in "L'Envoi." There, "home" is "Mariposa," the past, origins both individual and collective; in the *Sketches*' romance an enchanted home is the centre of the Pupkin family. But the City's Grand Palaver is a travesty of the concept of home. Plutoria exploits and debases all that it touches. Tomlinson is a wizard in "one aspect and only one": he remembers the value of home and is extracted by Fred, his son (family), from the false illusion of the Grand Palaver. (Even while residing in the Grand Palaver, the false home, the Tomlinsons maintain a sense of true home and family, calling each other "Mother" and "Father.") The Mausoleum clubbers of the opening chapter are, like their counterparts in "L'Envoi," guilty of forgetting, and thus denying the familial associations of, their homes: "It is as impossible to go back to plain water as it is to live again in the *forgotten* house in a side street that you inhabited long before you became a member" (*AA*, 13, emphasis added).

The "magical metaphor" is reiterated frequently in the course of the adventure concerning Tomlinson's fortune. The duped geologist, Gildas (whose name, while suggesting gold and gilt, also connotes a scatalogical image unusual in Leacock' writing), tests the salted gold "in a darkened laboratory, with blue flames playing underneath crucibles, as in a magician's cavern" (*AA*, 65). Unwittingly a tool of the deceiving businessmen, Gildas effects the initial transmutation of the "worthless" riverbed rock into gold. Tomlinson sits in the Palaver "with the Aladdin's palace of his golden fortune reared so strangely about him" (*AA*, 74). When he and his wife anticipate divesting themselves of their wealth, they sleep "in an Aladdin's palace filled with golden fancies" (*AA*, 108). In this last quotation, as elsewhere when the metaphor of magic is employed, the illusory gold of Tomlinson's wealth is contrasted to the true gold of his farm. Leacock makes this contrast most forcibly in dealing with Tomlinson's son, Fred.

Over-indulged by his bewildered parents, Fred has easily accommodated himself to the Palaver's sycophantic service and grown slothful, *idle*. The narrator remarks that "at present Fortune was busy taking from him the golden gifts which the fairies of Cahoga County, Lake Erie, had laid in his cradle seventeen years ago" (*AA*, 58). As a necessary preparation for the figurative transmutation of Tomlinson's farm from the false gold of the mining operation to the green of the original farm, Fred himself undergoes a transformation and reclaims those "golden gifts." The scene of Fred's reinvigoration is reminiscent of Peter Pupkin's apotheosis to Mariposan hero. Pupkin, it will be recalled, embraced the virtues of courage and duty when called upon to save the *harvest* money in the Mariposa bank, and his courage was understood to be a legacy of his Loyalist heritage. Fred, like Pupkin, is awakened by adversity. When he sees his father accosted, "The boy's soul woke within him"; "adversity laid its hand upon him, and at its touch his adolescent heart turned to finer stuff than the real gold of Erie Auriferous" (*AA*, 109). Fred turns to finer stuff than the real gold which is "salted" on Gildas. Fred's truer mettle comprises, like his father's, the elements of loyalty, courage, and respect for honest work. Fred is allotted the last words of the Tomlinson story. When his father considers tipping the doorman, or the "*chasseur*," or "*commissionaire*, or some foreign name to mean that he did nothing," Fred stops him with a dismissal that is surely intended for the *idle rich* generally: "Let him work" (*AA*, 111). Leacock's narrator reveals his position on the idleness of plutorian life as it is lived in the Grand Palaver, calling Fred's Carlylean advice an "admirable doctrine" (*AA*, 111).[14] No doubt Leacock would also apply Fred's advice to the idle, and again Carlylean, "captain[s] of industry" (*AA*, 52).

Perhaps even more than his father, Fred emerges as an instance of Leacock's norm. Whereas the father's bewildered innocence makes him ineffectual in opposing the plutorians, Fred adds reason and action to his stock of rural virtues. Fred puts on (and again Carlyle's "philosophy of clothes" comes to mind) his "rough store suit" (*AA*, 110); that is, Fred reaffirms his rural-agrarian virtues: duty, loyalty to family, courage, and, simply, a no-nonsense attitude. (Fred is, in fact, the truer Tomlinson, a name that may be a conflation of Thomas Jefferson and Lincoln – both of whom Leacock greatly admired – and, if so, suggestive of Fred's fusion of the agrarian ideal and virtuous action.) The father carries the "vision"; the son's soul wakes to it. There is much that is mythical in Leacock's portrayal of the Tomlinsons' "adventures" in the City. And there is something of the epical in their heroic exit: "With which admirable doctrine [the work ethic] the Wizard and his son passed from the portals of the Grand Palaver" (*AA*, 111).

By subtly manipulating the images of magical transmutation, Leacock indicates where the "real" gold resides – back on the farm, for the Tomlinsons at any rate. Nonetheless, the plutorians are (like Mr Josh Smith) adept at manipulating appearances for their own self-aggrandizement. Plutorian life and the Grand Palaver do appear charmingly resplendent. Leacock utilizes Tomlinson's sojourn in the plutorian Arcadia to chip further at this appearance of splendour. In doing so he frequently contrasts the sordid present of the City to what he repeatedly presents as a much more attractive past. The Tomlinson story is the section of *Arcadian Adventures* in which the past is most insistently called up to offer judgment on the present. Besides the primary contrast between the urban present and a traditional agrarian way of life, a number of other pertinent contrasts should be noted in the Tomlinson story. The primary target of Leacock's subsidiary satire is "modern" education – Plutoria University – though he manages in passing to prick a number of plutorian bubbles.

For example, the second paragraph of "The Wizard" contrasts the statues of the first and the present governors of the state in which the City is located ("governors" and "state" again emphasizing the American setting of the *Adventures*). The indictment of modern political methods speaks, metaphorically, for itself: "In the case of the governor of a hundred years ago one had to start from plain, rough material and work patiently for years to get the effect, whereas now the material doesn't matter at all, and with any sort of scrap, treated in the gas furnace under tremendous pressure, one may make a figure of tremendous size like the one in Central Square" (*AA*, 49). A writer of Leacock's political sophistication would not argue that the earlier politician was a man of greater integrity. His analysis of

Lincoln's political opportunism in the cause of freeing the slaves makes that amply clear.[15] Rather, the targets of the satire are political image-making, which is abetted by modern technology, and the tendency to megalomania in modern sensibilities (thus the repetition of "tremendous"). It is through the agency of modern technology that the modern politician assumes, in the metallic form of the statue, an imposing role in the urban landscape.

Leacock also makes passing satiric reference to modern developments in medicine and art. The demeaning effect that plutorian materialism has upon art is indicated in the first chapter, "A Little Dinner." To the solicitous Duke of Dulham, the pictures in the Mausoleum Club are "really good thing[s]" because "something in their composition, or else in the soft, expensive light that shone on them enabled him to see in the distant background of each a hundred thousand sterling. And that is a very beautiful picture indeed" (AA, 36). Both art and moral language, "good," are here debased. In "The Wizard" the innocent Tomlinson believes that he must now buy "Mother" the "very best" novels, "the ones that cost a dollar fifty, because he knew that out home she had only been able to read books like Nathaniel Hawthorne and Walter Scott, that were only worth ten cents" (AA, 57). Art, whether visual or literary, is either a means to material gain or evidence of what Thorstein Veblen termed "conspicuous consumption."[16]

Similarly, plutorians solicit Dr Slyder's medical services but to show that they possess the means to pay for them. Slyder's plutorian patients "always got well – there being nothing wrong with them" (AA, 60). Slyder's practice of prescribing "rest" for his idle, ennui-stricken patients is contrasted to "therapeutics in Cahoga County, where the practice of medicine is carried on with forceps, pumps, squirts, splints, and other instruments of violence" (AA, 60). Medicine in Cahoga County is associated with birth and the treatment of injuries sustained, no doubt, in the operation of farms. Leacock is suggesting ironically, and perhaps too subtly, that the rural medical practice is the better, a belief that he states explicitly, adding past to rural, in the autobiographical essay, "Fetching the Doctor."[17] The handiest cure for the restless plutorians would be that which Fred (who temporarily contracts the plutorian malaise) admonishes: "Let [them] work." By so prescribing, Fred serves as an admirable doctor, and his prescription encapsulates Leacock's "admirable doctrine." Arcadian Adventures emerges as more than an anatomy of the plutorian Arcadia. It is a diagnosis and prescriptive analysis of how the materialism of the present has infected the body of American society. Along with honest work, Leacock's satire continually suggests that a respect for the past would begin to provide tonic for the plutorian sickness of the hour.

"The Arrested Philanthropy of Mr. Tomlinson" begins in earnest the contrast between past and present that underlies those more obviously contrasted elements of the Tomlinson story – city and country, agrarian and metropolitan, Tomlinson and the plutorians – and it does so by contrasting Plutoria University to Concordia College. The idea of what a university should and should not be was a life-long concern of Leacock's. In such essays as "Literature and Education in America," "Oxford As I See It," and most extensively in *Too Much College*, he sets forth his program for an Arnoldian liberal arts education which should be "wide and humane." Opposed to specialization and vocational training, Leacock argues for a "smattering" of all subjects (*ELS*, 63).[18] But the reader requires no smattering of Leacock's other writings on education and the idea of a university to appreciate his satire on plutorian higher education. Plutoria University compares "favourably with the best departmental stores or factories in the City" (*AA*, 80). Its president Boomer is pleased that his students are reported to look "like plumbers" (*AA*, 81). Boomer's one idea of a university is a place of continual change (or turnover) in buildings and personnel, a place of unrelenting destruction, a going business concern. His opinion of Plutoria University is one with his view of its library, "for it was twenty years old and out of date (*AA*, 89). Such are the perverted ambitions that result from a false notion of progress. The past is destroyed even before it becomes the past in any real sense. "Twenty years," less than a single generation, is an appropriately contracted span of time to illustrate the short-sightedness of Boomer's historical vision. The span of time recalls the similarly ironic exaggeration of the age of tombstones in the old graveyard of Mariposa, which were "ever so old" at "forty or fifty years" (*SS*, 100). In fact, the nostalgically elegiac treatment of the older Concordia College offers one of *Arcadian Adventures'* closest and most revealing parallels to the *Sketches*.

Concordia College bears a relation to Plutoria University that is strikingly similar to that which the quaint old church in Mariposa bears to Dean Drone's ostentatious beacon. Leacock's narrator states plainly that "the changes both of name and of character from Concordia College to Plutoria University was the work of President Boomer" (*AA*, 81). Concordia College, a name suggesting collective, harmonious effort, "had no teaching of religion except lectures on the Bible" (*AA*, 81–2). Plutoria University dispenses "lectures also on Confucianism, Mohammedanism, Buddhism, with an optional course on atheism for students in the final year" (*AA*, 82). In "The

Devil and the Deep Sea," Leacock considers the relativistic approach to morality and ethics to be the cause of what is ultimately a loss of faith (*ELS*, 49–50). With reference to its curriculum, Boomer's Plutoria University is at fault for its liberally pluralistic approach to education: it "taught everything and did everything ... It offered such a vast variety of themes, topics, and subjects to the students, that there was nothing that a student was compelled to learn" (*AA*, 82). Rather than fulfilling its proper role as a university through concentrating on the education of its students in shared ideas and values of the Judeo-Christian and tory-humanist ("wide and humane") traditions, Boomer's Plutoria is a factory of dissipative busyness. Like the mistaken Dean Drone, who fails in his role as spiritual leader, the mistaken Boomer fails in his role as intellectual leader. Like Drone with his brighter beacon, Boomer has ambitions for bigger buildings, buildings that bring new debts and destroy the very traditions that they should embody.

In a manner that recalls the treatment of the old stone church in the *Sketches*, Leacock offers the historical continuity that Concordia College represents: "It was indeed a dilapidated building; yet there was a certain majesty about it, too, *especially when one reflected* that it had been standing there looking much the same at the time when its students had trooped off in a flock to join the army of the Potomac, and much the same, indeed, three generations before that, when classes were closed and the students clapped three-cornered hats on their heads and were off to enlist as minute men with flintlock muskets under General Washington" (*AA*, 86, emphasis added). "Dr. Boomer's one idea was to knock the building down and to build on its site a real *facultas* ten storeys high, with elevators in it" (*AA*, 86). The value of Concordia College resides in its "wide and humane" curriculum and the aura of history that clings like vines to the college. The building may appear "dilapidated," yet it possesses "a certain majesty," "especially when one reflected." To ascribe majesty to an admittedly modest building is an act of associative memory. In the narrator's thoughts, Concordia College is associated with the history of the United States and with those "generations" who fought in its War of Independence and its Civil War. For Leacock, such associations elevate Concordia to "majesty" – historical associations that argue for the continuance and conservation of tradition. Humanistic, historical, and patriotic associations place Concordia in emphatic opposition to Boomer's ten-story *facultas* with its subversive and mechanistic elevators. Notice that Boomer's university is, like all Plutoria, closely associated with electrically powered machinery, with a "whirling machine," a "seismograph," and its "own presses" which send "out a shower of bulletins and monographs like driven snow from a rotary plough" (*AA*, 82). With his faith placed in machinery, Boomer cannot conceive that an order might exist beyond the present, the individual, and the destructively progressive.

The religious sketches of *Sunshine Sketches* deny the possibility of a return to the order of the old stone church. The Mariposans use their ill-gotten insurance money to build a bigger church. Concordia College persists tenaciously on the campus of Plutoria University, where "industrial science" is advancing with "increasing and gigantic strides" (*AA*, 90). Leacock conveys in both instances his regret at the mistaken progress that advances into a spiritual, ahistorical vacuum. And although Concordia still stands, Leacock suggests that he may soon have to apply to the college his poignant remark on Mariposa's old stone church, which, "like so much else in life, was forgotten" (*SS*, 105). Boomer's ambition is not simply to forget Concordia but to demolish it.

As has been shown, Tomlinson manages to escape from Boomer and Plutoria because he possesses that which Boomer denies: memory, a respect for the past and a reverence for the dead. Tomlinson's memory of home saves him. He persists, though, in his rustic naïvety. Ill-equipped intellectually to pierce the facade of plutorian hypocrisy, he *feels* himself to be unsuited to the Grand Palaver and an unworthy benefactor of Plutoria University. He contracts the services of Skinyer and Beatem (the literary descendants, perhaps, of the Dodson and Fogg of Dickens' *Pickwick Papers*), who arrange for Tomlinson to donate his fortune to Plutoria University. The one lesson that the Tomlinsons take with them from their adventure in the City is, as "Mother" tells Tomlinson, that "if you want to get a thing done you can always find people to do it for you if you pay them" (*AA*, 104). It is a lesson that is taught partially by the musing Boomer, who chants what could be a hymn to plutorian destructiveness: "'Money, money, money,' he repeated half-musingly. 'If I had the money I'd have [Concordia College] down and dismantled in a fortnight'" (*AA*, 83).

The first three chapters of *Arcadian Adventures* offer a scathing portrayal of plutorian business practices. Avarice and insatiable greed turn people such as Fyshe and Boulder into financial animals. When money is the sole standard of merit, art, literature, and the whole purpose of education are debased and vulgarized. The past is systematically destroyed; little is left but the individual and his progress into a vacuous future. Tomlinson's story argues further that wealth is gained not by the "dumb luck" of striking gold but by plutorian stealth. Revealingly, the plutorians cannot countenance the possibility that fortunes can be made by luck. Theirs is the myth of the self-made man (a man such as Mr Josh Smith). Although Tomlinson is patently the embodiment of dumb luck (in so far as his wealth is concerned), the plutorian press insists upon ascribing to him the less disconcerting virtues of "indomitable pluck and dogged industry" (AA, 62), and he is admired in "business circles" as "Devilish shrewd" (AA, 68) because the plutorians project cunning onto his simple reverence of the ground wherein his father is buried. In Carlylean terms, the plutorians are mistaken in their "hero-worship." Perhaps they fear that if a fortune can be gained by the whimsy of fate, it can as readily be lost. The more comfortable belief is that material success is achieved as it is by the Overend brothers, who came "up the business ladder hand over hand, landing later on in life on the platform of success like two corpulent acrobats, panting with the strain of it" (AA, 221).

In "Literature and Education in America," Leacock regrets what ensues when society allows such desecrating ignorance as Boomer's to flourish: "Hence all less tangible and provable forms of human merit, and less tangible aspirations of the human mind are rudely shouldered aside by business ability and commercial success. There follows the apotheosis of the business man. He is elevated to the post of national hero" (ELS, 77). Chapters four through eight of Arcadian Adventures trace the consequences of this "apotheosis of the business man," the "captain of industry," and the impact of such a development on romance, religion, and politics. But before Leacock again engages the emergent plutocracy, he offers an adventure that seems more anomalous in the ordered development of Arcadian Adventures than does the "Marine Excursion" in Sunshine Sketches. Chapter four, "The Yahi-Bahi Oriental Society of Mrs. Rasselyer-Brown," is a scathing portrayal of plutorian society in microcosm, but thematically it does not contribute directly to the development of an emergent plutocracy. It offers instead a collection of pretentious people, women mostly, who are gulled because of their vacuousness and affectations. "Oriental" in its interests, plutorian society is also foreign in its distance from the true meaning of society: a community of shared traditions and concerns.

In "The Devil and the Deep Sea," Leacock castigates the popular mentality that discards traditional religious beliefs for the fascination of the novel: "I suppose there never was an age more riddled with superstition, more credulous, more drunkenly addicted to thaumaturgy than the present. The Devil in his palmiest days was nothing to it. In despite of our vaunted material commonsense, there is a perfect craving abroad for belief in something beyond the compass of the believable" (*ELS*, 41–2). As might be expected from Leacock, he perceives that "material commonsense" does not satisfy the needs of the spirit. The obsession with materialism creates a spiritual vacuum; the rejection of older spiritual beliefs, which have served humanity well, allows for the entrance of all sorts of nonsensical mysticism into the spiritual vacuum. As the above quotation might suggest, chapter four of *Arcadian Adventures* is not simply another of Leacock's brilliant satires of mystical bunkum. Nor is it only gentle satire on the sham seer who accepts "six ten dollar pieces ... arranged in the form of a mystic serpent," and who then prophesies that "Many things are yet to happen before others begin" (*AA*, 132). A reading that appreciates only the satire on charlatanism is one that misapprehends the purpose chapter four does serve in the context of *Arcadian Adventures*. The first three chapters present a world that appears energized at least in its insatiable greed, a hypocritical world of idleness masquerading as busy-ness. Chapter four looks closely at the "society" and culture supported by this world of business, particularly at that society's pathetically vacuous, idle women.

The hub of plutorian society is the Rasselyer-Brown residence, where the husband sneaks about in a state of continual drunken tranquility. A successful plutorian, Mr Rasselyer-Brown also has a business life in which "a man has got to drink" (*AA*, 121). And he does drink, from morning till bedtime, dropping "down later in the night in his pajamas" to "compose his mind with a brandy and water ... suitable to the stillness of the hour (*AA*, 122). In fact, Mr Rasselyer-Brown is interested only in drinking and in his coal and wood business. Yet he, like the Duke of Dulham, is also partly a positive figure. He does not care for his affected wife, an attitude that certainly places him in a favourable light. He is hospitable and generous with his liquor (*AA*, 115, 119, 125), and his coal and wood business is, relative to the electro-chemical ventures of the other plutorians, concerned at least with natural products. (And it may be noted that Leacock, a founder and daily frequenter of McGill's University Club, would hardly frown upon Brown's drinking.) Even though Mr Rasselyer-Brown, whose "business name" is the unaffected and disavowing "Brown Limited" (*AA*, 118), partakes of Leacock's tory-humanist norm, he is, finally, a character who situates himself closer to the plutorian end of the "Mariposa-Plutoria" continuum.

Mrs Rasselyer-Brown, on the other hand, is a decidedly unpleasant character. She is the self-assertive grande dame of plutorian society. The opposite of a "helpmate" to her husband, she is ashamed of his business, though it provides the financial basis for her cultural pretensions; she is also ashamed of his drinking, though liquor appears to be what reconciles him to her and his plutorian life; and she is ashamed of his lack of interest in anything other than business, though her interests – collecting things – are an affected waste of money. For obvious reasons, husband and wife keep to themselves in the Rasselyer-Brown house that is not a home.

The narrator describes unequivocally the cultural "salons" Mrs Rasselyer-Brown holds. Hers is "the kind of cultivated home where people of education and taste are at liberty to talk about things they don't know, and to utter freely ideas that they haven't got" (*AA*, 125). These people who are "at liberty" to "utter freely ideas that they haven't got" could have been educated at Boomer's Plutoria University, where the liberal pluralist approach to education predominates. And yet, Leacock does not miss the opportunity to satirize simultaneously the professorial specialist who, armed presumably with (Gradgrindian) facts, "pulverizes" the humane, if inane, conversation of Mrs Rasselyer-Brown's *salons* (and notice that "booming" associates the professors with Boomer): "It was only now and again, when one of the professors from the college across the avenue came booming into the room, that the whole conversation was pulverized into dust under the hammer of accurate knowledge" (*AA*, 125). The opposition of overly warm conversationalist and cold academic specialist is characteristic of Leacock at his best: the conversation of the *salons* is inane and uninformed; the professors, armed with mere "knowledge," drop conversational bombs and wield weighty hammers; and the reader must seek for Leacock's humanistic position somewhere between the extremes of self-indulgence and impoliteness.

Leacock's narrator makes equally plain the reason for Yahi-Bahi's success with the women of Plutoria. They look restlessly for diversion during "a singularly slack moment in the social life of the City. … It was too warm to go south, and yet still too cold to go north. In fact, one was almost compelled to stay at home – which was dreadful" (*AA*, 126). From the point of view of Leacock's humanism, "one" should welcome the opportunity to stay at "home." The narrator continues: "As a result Mrs. Rasselyer-Brown and her three hundred friends moved backward and forward on Plutoria Avenue, seeking novelty in vain" (*AA*, 126). These female symbols of the plutorian businessmen's "conspicuous leisure,"[19] would elicit sympathy if they did not most fully represent the *idle rich* of the book's title. Idleness, restlessness, and sycophancy characterize the "business" of plutorian society. Moreover, pampered idleness seems to inculcate an almost masochistic desire for belittlement. Dulphemia

Rasselyer-Brown, the daughter, is attracted by the "splendid rudeness of the chauffeur's manner" (*AA*, 130). Her attraction to the rude chauffeur also illustrates the other extreme of Plutoria's idea of manners. On the one hand, there is the excessive, sycophantic deference of Mrs Rasselyer-Brown's "three hundred friends" – a vacuous chivalry with suggestions of effeminacy that Leacock associates also with the poet *manqué* Sikleigh Snoop (*AA*, 119, whose name also connotes a tendency to voyeurism).[20] On the other hand, Dulphemia's attraction to the curt chauffeur suggests the extreme of an atavistic rudeness that is considered to be masculine. The plutorians do not partake of the well-mannered aspect of Leacock's norm: social behaviour that is based on authentic respect and admiration for others, genuine manners that mediate between the members of a community.

If the satire on the idleness and sycophancy of the plutorian women does not succeed in forestalling the reader's sympathy for these female symbols of plutorian conspicuous leisure, the ironic implications of "Bahee" – sacrifice – does. As the narrator explains it,

The chief aim of Bahee itself was sacrifice: a true follower of the cult must be willing to sacrifice his friends, or his relatives, and even stangers, in order to reach Bahee. In this way one was able fully to realize oneself and enter into the Higher Indifference. Beyond this, further meditation and fasting – by which was meant living solely on fish, fruit, wine, and meat – one presently attained to complete Swaraj or Control of Self, and might in time pass into the absolute Nirvana, or the Negation of Emptiness, the supreme goal of Boohooism. (*AA*, 138)

This inversion and perversion of the ideal of Christian charity and tory community naturally finds an affinity in the hollow hearts of the plutorian women. In their vain attempts to negate the emptiness of their lives, they are expert at sacrificing their friends, their relatives, and even strangers. It is, in fact, their "Higher Indifference" to the poverty outside Plutoria Avenue that makes sympathy for these affected women difficult.

Mrs Rasselyer-Brown describes her first visit to Yahi-Bahi as follows: "It was *most* interesting. We drove away down to the queerest part of the city, and went to the strangest little house imaginable, up the narrowest stairs one ever saw – quite Eastern, in fact, just like a scene out of the Koran" (*AA*, 127). Her interlocutor, Miss Snagg, finds this description "fascinating." Leacock briefly dispenses with his ironic voice and offers an appraisal of Mrs Rasselyer-

Brown's reaction: "But as a matter of fact, if Mr. Yahi-Bahi's house had been inhabited, as it might have been, by a streetcar conductor or a railway brakeman, Mrs. Rasselyer-Brown wouldn't have thought it in any way peculiar or fascinating" (AA, 127). It is here chiefly that the reader's sympathies snag. The plutorian women live in a perpetual state of "Higher Indifference" to charity. They are, in the most literal sense of the word, and certainly in Leacock's opinion, *useless*. They are, in their self-serving pretensions to religious breadth, the sort of representative of "modern morality" whom Leacock vehemently denounces in "The Devil and the Deep Sea": "The whole of his virtue and his creed of conduct runs to a cheap and easy egomania in which his blind passion for himself causes him to use external people and things as mere reactions upon his own personality. The immoral little toad swells itself to the bursting point in its desire to be a moral ox" (ELS, 45).

The bubble bursts for Mrs Rasselyer-Brown and her coterie of affected acolytes in a manner that suggests parallels to the sinking of the *Mariposa Belle* in Lake Wissanotti. Although both episodes present a microcosmic portrait of their respective societies, there are critical differences between the conclusions that can be drawn from them. The Mariposans form an attractive, if somewhat foolish, society. They make their appearance in chapter three of *Sunshine Sketches* immediately following the chapter dealing with Jeff Thorpe's illusory fortune – a fortune which Jeff, like Tomlinson, intends partly for charitable purposes. The society of Mrs Rasselyer-Brown is unattractive for several reasons: for its pretensions to culture and intellectual curiosity; for its ennui and restlessness; for its sycophancy; and, most damagingly, for its "Higher Indifference" to the world of work and want outside Plutoria.

In the Plutoria of the first four chapters of *Arcadian Adventures*, appearances belie a reality wherein the give and take of deception feeds largely upon itself. No one is hurt: Fyshe and Boulder gull each other; the Duke of Dulham may not have borrowed any money, but he lost none to Boulder; the Tomlinson story resolves into "the most beautiful and complete cipher conceivable" (AA, 112); the women of the Yahi-Bahi Society suffer little. Even Yahi-Bahi and Ram Spudd accept their capture in a convivial spirit: "Mr. Spudd was heard to address the police as 'boys,' and to remark," in a demotic and characteristically plutorian perversion of moral language, "that they had 'got them good' that time" (AA, 155). In the fifth chapter, "The Love Story of Mr. Peter Spillikins," appearances triumph over (romantic) reality, with destructive consequences. Someone – "the Little Girl in Green" – is hurt. She, Norah, is a representative of those outside the plutorian Arcadia: those who work, those who are polite, those who acknowledge their familial responsibilities, those who are associated with the organic, and those who serve in the previous chapters as the understated moral norm of *Arcadian Adventures*. When the reader recalls the redemptive role that romance plays in *Sunshine Sketches*, the failure of romantic love in *Arcadian Adventures* assumes ominous proportions.

In *Sunshine Sketches* the love story follows the chapter dealing with religion; in *Arcadian Adventures* the love story precedes the two chapters dealing with religion. In the *Sketches* the realization of romantic love follows the dismal failure of Mariposa's Anglican church to curtail ostentation and to fulfill simply its religious function; in *Arcadian Adventures* a plutorian success in things religious follows a failure to realize romantic love. The love story in the *Sketches* is accorded three chapters, and the reader is never certain of the outcome; the love story in *Arcadian Adventures* occupies one chapter, and the reader knows from the outset that something has gone amiss. As the narrator remarks early in "The Love Story of Peter Spillikins," "The whole of this daily panorama [Spillikins' routine], to the eye that can read it, represents the outcome of the tangled love story of Mr. Spillikins" (*AA*, 158). When Spillikins and Norah are interrupted by Mrs Everleigh, the narrator reflects, "Now as this story began with the information that Mrs. Everleigh is at present Mrs. Everleigh-Spillikins, there is no need to pursue in detail the stages of Mr. Spillikins's wooing" (*AA*, 194). The relative space devoted to the love story in each book argues for the unimportance and improbability of meaningful romantic love in the City. In the *Sketches* the realization of romantic love is the focus of extended attention, with the narrator dwelling "in detail" on the "stages of Mr. [Pupkin's] wooing." The love story in *Arcadian Adventures* is, in contrast to the Pupkin-Pepperleigh romance, a tale that actually concerns the lost opportunity for romantic love, marriage, and a natural family.

Yet Leacock suggests that the potential for redemptive love is always present, even in Plutoria. (This suggestion is realized, though not without qualification, in the conclusion to the chapters on the rival churches.) Like the love story in the *Sketches*, "The Love Story of Mr. Peter Spillikins" occupies a central position in *Arcadian Adventures*. The successful realization of love's potential would have softened the savagery of the self-serving business community that is anatomized in the first four chapters; moreover, realized romantic love would have partially offset the depiction of stark avariciousness in the following three. Leacock could have utilized romantic love in a manner reminiscent of the way in which love in the *Sketches* sets to right the imbalance engendered by institutionalized religion. Instead, Leacock chose to reveal that love in the City, like all else potentially worthy, is debased by plutorian money-hunger.

Not only are the two protagonists of the love stories in the *Sketches* and the *Adventures* named Peter, but they possess similar surnames, Pupkin and Spillikins. In the preceding chapter of this study, the punning associated with Pupkin's name was discussed: the name suggests the hero's relation to a pup, which implies a relation between romantic love and "puppy love"; it suggests the "kin" or network of relatives who assist in the realization of romantic love; and it suggests Leacock's understanding of the relation between "kin," "kindliness," and the function of humour. In this light, the name Spillikins can be seen to suggest a kind of carelessness – a "spilling" – directed towards that which the word "kin" connotes. ("Spillikins" is also the former name of the game that has come to be called "pick-up-sticks," which reinforces the association with spilling and carelessness.) Part of the reason for Peter Spillikins' carelessness with the opportunity for love is innate: he is physically and mentally short-sighted (*AA*, 159). It becomes apparent, though, that the literal care-less attitude of Spillikins' Plutorian society is the true cause of the failure of romantic love. Otherwise, there is little difference between the two Peters. Both are similarly enthusiastic in their regard for women. Both are equally foolish. What saves Peter Pupkin and repeatedly redeems his Mariposan community is that which fails Peter Spillikins: a caring community that values the welfare of all above that of the individual, though not at the expense of the individual. In effect, as the love stories show, when the community is valued over the individual, the individual is best cared for.

Judge Pepperleigh and Pupkin Senior assist their children toward realizing an enchanted love and marriage. Recall further that Pupkin is allowed to attain the status of hero by that peculiarly self-aggrandizing and self-deluding Mariposan milieu that creates mystery and heroism where, unimaginatively speaking, neither exists. Because the community closes ranks around Pupkin, he is able to envision himself as the kind of hero who can propose outright to his heroine. The affected, self-aggrandizing and communal nature of Mariposa makes possible the enchanted marriage of Pupkin and Zena. Contrarily, the selfishness and avariciousness of the plutorian anti-community pervert the natural course of love between Spillikins and Norah. Whereas Pupkin is covertly entrusted by his father to the care of his old friend Judge Pepperleigh, Spillikins has for "his uncle and trustee" that busy financial animal, Mr Boulder (*AA*, 160).[21] Whereas Pupkin's father had the concerned foresight to see that his son, unsuited for business, was ideally suited to Mariposa, Boulder tries the equally incompetent Spillikins in a number of enterprises and then leaves him at loose ends (*AA*, 160-2). In a manner that suggests a debasement of the ideal of matrimony, Spillikins is dismissingly advised by everyone "to get married" (*AA*, 162). All of these factors support the contention that no one is truly concerned for Spillikins' welfare. He is abandoned, left vulnerable to the clutches of the "gold digger," Mrs Everleigh. For Mrs Everleigh, Spillikins is indeed an unguarded gold mine. For Spillikins, she appears to be the motherlode of love. The nearsighted Spillikins mistakes the fool's gold that is Mrs Everleigh for the true promise that is Norah. Unlike Tomlinson, Spillikins is a native plutorian and is therefore without the saving memory of a better place and way of living. He is deceived by himself and the "values" of his environment into believing that such salted charms as the dishonorable Mrs Everleigh possesses will stud the sordid scene of his dim plutorian existence.

In addition to the short-sightedness of Spillikins, the carelessness of his plutorian environment, and the blatancy of Mrs Everleigh's gold-digging, Leacock offers one further reason for Spillikins' failure to perceive Norah's authentic charms: "But of love Mr. Spillikins never thought. He had viewed it so eagerly and so often from a distance that when it stood there modestly at his very elbow he did not recognize its presence. *His mind had been fashioned*, as it were, to connect love with something stunning and sensational, with Easter hats and harem skirts and the luxurious consciousness of the unattainable" (*AA*, 191-2, emphasis added). But such a romantic-chivalric attitude to love is also Peter Pupkin's. Pupkin, too, suffers from "the luxurious consciousness of the unattainable." And Zena Pepperleigh, to accept Pupkin as a worthy mate, needed to forge an imaginative connection between the romantic-chivalric and the realistic: she envisions "a dim parallel" between Pupkin's fevered pedaling past her home and "the last ride of Tancred the Inconsolable along the banks of the Danube (*SS*, 183). Assisted by his realistic father and Judge Pepperleigh, Pupkin also manages to ground his romantic-chivalric ideal in the real world. Spillikins, who is short-sighted like Don Quixote and who at one point fancies himself in love with Dulphemia Rasselyer-Brown (the echo being of Quixote's Dulcinea), is the practitioner of a false chivalry which Leacock understood to be the sole target of Cervantes' ironic romance (*HH*, 129).

In short, there is in Leacock's view a true chivalry (Pupkin's and Zena's) and a false chivalry (Spillikins' and the "homage of such experts as Captain Cormorant and Lieutenant Hawk" [AA, 194]).

Nevertheless, for Leacock the possibility for true romantic love remains ever imminent, even in Plutoria. The innate human impulse to love almost overcomes Spillikins' plutocratically "fashioned" mind; human nature almost overcomes plutorian nurture. Following the explanation of Spillikins' romantic-chivalric turn of mind, Leacock's narrator stresses this latent potentiality: "Even at that, there is no knowing what might have happened" (AA, 192). But the arrival of Mrs Everleigh at castel Casteggio frustrates the emergence of love between Spillikins and Norah at two critical junctures: when he is holding Norah's hand on the tennis court and when Norah is departing (AA, 192, 196). As the diminutive suggests, Norah, as the "Little Girl in Green," embodies the potential for growth and for real family through romantic, that is, natural, love. She possesses the *green* promise that is opposed to the glitter of the plutorian Arcadia. The resolution of "The Love Story" inversely parallels that of the Tomlinson story. Whereas Tomlinson chooses the green of his farm in rejection of the falsely golden promise of mining riches and the City's Grand Palaver Hotel, Spillikins makes the wrong choice.

Further, the opposition between Mrs Everleigh and Norah is emblematic of the larger opposition between mechanistic Plutoria and the natural world. The plutorians appropriate land and turn it into "private property, as all nature ought to be" (AA, 169). They assail and at least temporarily dominate nature with their whole battery of electro-chemical mechanisms: thus "nature ... spread[s] her oiled motor roads"; thus the repeated mention in "The Love Story" of the "motor road," the "oiled road," the "motor boat parties," and the private "railway station" (AA, 166, 170–2). The plutorians have even raised the level of their lake, "stone-banked the sides, cleared out the brush, and put a motor road round it. Beyond that," concedes the ironic narrator, "it was pure nature" (AA, 170). Mr Newberry, with his dynamite, "steel girders," and "steel beams" (AA, 177), best personifies the plutorian electro-mechanical assault on nature.[22] In this Plutoria-nature opposition, Mrs Everleigh, with her dyed-blond, "perfectly wonderful golden hair" (AA, 193) and heavy make-up, exemplifies the tawdriness of Plutoria. Norah, on the other hand, is closely aligned with the natural world. When first mentioned, she is the lower-case "little girl in green" (AA, 180), but subsequently she becomes the naturally emblematic "Little Girl in Green" (AA, 181 ff.). And it is Norah's "littleness," like nature herself in the face of gigantically mechanized Plutoria, that makes her a victim: she is little in social and economic terms.

Norah "was only what is called a poor relation of Mrs. Newberry, and her father was a person of no account whatever, who didn't belong to the Mausoleum Club or to any other club, and who lived, with Norah, on a street that nobody who was anybody lived upon" (*AA*, 181–2). Norah lives in the kind of lower-middle-class dwelling that, when occupied by the charlatan Yahi-Bahi, is thought to be "quite Eastern, in fact, just like a scene out of a Koran" (*AA*, 127). But because her father is the kind of workingman mentioned sympathetically by the narrator in the Yahi-Bahi adventure, the Newberrys, like Mrs Rasselyer-Brown, would not think Norah's home "in any way peculiar or fascinating" (*AA*, 127). Rather than helping her "poor relations" with needed material assistance, Mrs Newberry condescendingly allows Norah to visit Castel Casteggio for a few days, "to give her air – which is the only thing that can be safely and freely given to poor relations" (*AA*, 182). Norah, like Tomlinson among the philistine plutorians, sojourns with the Newberrys in "fear and trembling" (*AA*, 182). It is understandable that the demure Norah lacks the nerve to reveal to Spillikins, as she could (*AA*, 193), the falsity of Mrs Everleigh's golden charms. As a result of plutorian socio-economic intimidation of "the Little Girl in Green," Norah's love for Spillikins is thwarted and Spillikins' one "shot" (*AA*, 199) at love in lost.

Norah's love for Spillikins is of a kind with Peter Pupkin's love for Zena Pepperleigh. It is a romantic love that transforms the beloved in the eyes of the lover: "She saw all at once such wonderful things about him as nobody had ever seen before. ... In short, she saw as she looked such a Peter Spillikins as truly never existed, or could exist – or at least such a Peter Spillikins as no one else in the world had ever suspected before" (*AA*, 181). Leacock believes that such romantic love contains the seed of a mature, realistic love. There are productive illusions, the useful fictions that people live by, and there are delusive, unproductive ones. There is the truly chivalric and there is the Quixotic. When Spillikins and Norah are left alone, the scene begins to suggest the potential for the kind of enchanted domesticity enjoyed by the Pepperleighs and the Pupkins: "During all of which time Mr. Spillikins sat with Norah on the piazza, he talked and she listened. He told her, for instance, all about his terrific experiences in the oil business, and about his exciting career at college; or presently they went indoors and Norah played the piano and Mr. Spillikins sat and smoked and listened" (*AA*, 190). The wasting of such a potential for marital harmony, the thwarting of such a sympathetic love as is evidenced by Norah – this is repugnant to Leacock. In the most pathetic scene of the book, he presents Norah departing "with tears brimming up into her eyes" (AA, 196). Though sentimental, the scene is not mawkish, at least not when the reader considers what has been lost. In fact, the use of pathos here is in accordance with Leacock's belief that "pathos keeps humour from breaking into guffaws" (HH, 233).

Leacock is satiric and sentimental in *Arcadian Adventures* when he considers the scene of Spillikins' and Everleigh's marriage. He satirically catalogues "all that goes to invest marriage on Plutoria Avenue with its peculiar sacredness" – ostentation, or what Veblen calls "conspicuous consumption" – and adds pathetically, "The whole town was there, or at least everybody that was anybody; and if there was one person absent, one who sat by herself in the darkened drawing-room of a dull little house on a shabby street, who knew or cared?" (AA, 197–8). Leacock's narrator knows of course that "the Little Girl in Green" lives in that "dull little house," and he would have his readers know and care about what has been done to her. The phrase "everybody that was anybody" echoes the earlier reference to Norah's father, her home, and the street on which she lives, "a street that nobody who was anybody lived upon" (AA, 181). The idle plutorians would have to climb up on the roof of St Asaph's to gain a charitable view of that "one person," "the Little Girl in Green, whose Christian name was Norah" (AA, 181). But like the Mausoleum clubbers who feel no inclination to view the slums from the roof of their club, the plutorians of the pagan Arcadia and the Greco-Roman names are not inclined towards such Christian-humanistic effort.

Norah departs from Castel Casteggio and goes home because, as she remarks, "Father's alone, you know" (AA, 196). Unlike Mrs Newberry, who has only air to give to her "poor relations," Norah thinks, even at the nadir of her adventure, of her familial responsibilities. What should be obvious is that Norah and her attributes – naturalness, politeness, tolerant kindliness, and familial loyalty – are, like the Tomlinsons, near the centre of Leacock's tory-humanist norm.

At the conclusion of "The Love Story," Mrs Everleigh-Spillikins, apparently impressed by the sheer doggedness of Spillikins' blind devotion to her, has reservations about her liaison with the gallant Captain Cormorant: "She moved her hand away from under Captain Cormorant's on the tea-table." Cormorant then cautions her: "'I say,' said the Captain, 'don't get sentimental over him'" (AA, 199). That such a one as Mrs Everleigh-Spillikins might "get sentimental" over such a one as Spillikins is a typically kindly Leacockian touch. Apparently, he could not dismiss this ultimately dismal adventure without suggesting the possibility that human love, however initiated, may achieve some good – a promising, if slight, transformation. Everleigh-Spillikins should indeed "get sentimental," for Leacock held that sympathy "improved [the] moral outlook" of mankind (*HH*, 26). As author, Leacock here enacts what he persistently recommends in his studies of humour: the need for "kindliness."

Nonetheless, the possibility of Mrs Everleigh-Spillikins' conversion is slight consolation for the truer romantic love that is thwarted and for the potential that is lost. The concluding words of "The Love Story," uttered by one of Spillikins' billiard-shooting sons – "Hold on, father, you had your shot" – would seem to suggest that romantic love offers itself but once. The game metaphor reinforces the implications of squander and game in the name Spillikins: Spillikins carelessly bungles his one shot. The fault is, however, only partly Spillikins'. In the person of Mrs Everleigh, the whole battery of plutorian guile and greed is ranged against him and Norah. Guile and greed come to prominence again in the closing sketches of *Arcadian Adventures*, where pecuniary passions completely determine the course of plutorian religion and politics.

CHAPTER SIX

Between a Vault and a Dark Place: Religion and Politics in Plutoria

Appropriately, the Spillikins-Everleigh marriage takes place in St Asaph's Church, for, as chapters six and seven of *Arcadian Adventures* – "The Rival Churches of St. Asaph and St. Osoph" and "The Ministrations of the Reverend Uttermust Dumfarthing" – demonstrate, religious matters in Plutoria are, like everything else plutorian, going business concerns. The similarly entitled chapters of *Sunshine Sketches* and *Arcadian Adventures*, "The Ministrations of the Rev. Mr Drone" and "The Ministrations of the Rev. Uttermust Dumfarthings," along with the similarity in the names Uttermost and Uttermust, initially invite comparison between religion in Mariposa and Plutoria.

Religious worship in *Sunshine Sketches'* Mariposa was once practised modestly in an old stone church, but it progressed toward the ostentation of Dean Drone's "beacon on the hill," a construction that landed the Anglican parish in financial straits. Recall also that the Mariposans were "saved" by the resourceful Mr Smith who, with the blessing of the church's trustees, decided to burn down the beacon for the insurance money. They then built a new church and contracted for the ministerial services of one "Mr Uttermost," who preached "the newer forms of doubt revealed by the higher criticism" (*SS*, 147). These events, it was argued in chapter four, must be judged a dismal failure of Mariposa's Anglican church to meet simply the spiritual needs of its community.

The churches of *Arcadian Adventures'* Plutoria Avenue also began in modest circumstances, in "the lower and poorer parts of the city" (*AA*, 203), St Asaph's in the west, St Osoph's in the east. In a plutorian magnification of Drone's mistaken ambitions, these two churches adhere brazenly to a creed of material success. By a kind of speculative leap-frogging, they move towards each other and land on Plutoria Avenue, following behind the "better" part of their upwardly mobile congregations. Competition between St Asaph's and St Osoph's prompts St Osoph's to hire the Rev. Uttermust Dumfarthing. Dumfarthing's sensationally abusive sermonizing steals St Asaph's congregation, thereby threatening the Episcopal (Anglican) church's financial profits. The solution to St Asaph's financial dilemma is a proposal for the union of the two churches. This proposal is, in its patently pecuniary, anti-spiritual aims, more morally horrendous than was the motive behind the burning of Drone's beacon.

In his introduction to the New Canadian Library edition of *Arcadian Adventures*, Ralph Curry writes that at the time of the *Adventures'* publication (1914), "the oecumenical movement was making progress throughout the Christian world and, while the story was written before church union in Canada [the 1925 union of the Presbyterian, Methodist, and Congregational Churches into the United Church of Canada] there can be little doubt that Leacock has in mind the preliminary discussions in Canada toward this end."[1] The ecumenical movement and, to be more specific, the compromising of traditional doctrinal distinctions that have arisen in response to genuine human needs, is one target of Leacock's satire in these chapters. But he has more "in mind" than that. Other targets of the satire are materialism and the business practice of monopoly. Anglicanism in Mariposa was slowly rising toward a High Anglicanism that Leacock associated with unnecessary ostentation; in Plutoria, St Asaph's is, as will be seen, already High Anglican. Although High Anglicanism remains a target of Leacock's humorous satire in the religious ventures of *Arcadian Adventures*, the specific target is ecumenism as a form of monopoly. As in the case of Drone, the satire on ecumenism-as-monopoly is multilayered but consistent: Leacock dislikes High Anglicanism because it seems to him to be materialistic; he dislikes ecumenism because it seems to him akin to monopoly capitalism. Since monopoly capitalism is rooted in materialism, all these targets are inter-connected. Moreover, the satire on self-serving monopolistic practices is in keeping with the one relentless theme of *Arcadian Adventures*: the moral, ethical, and spiritual bankruptcy of a plutocracy that debases both physical and spiritual aspects of life. Robertson Davies has observed of the church union that "Leacock detests this sort of flabbiness, where principle runs a bad second to financial or administrative expediency in every realm of life, and his disgust that it should invade religion is apparent."[2] When the reader of the *Adventures* realizes that business practices are now being applied to religious matters, the caricatured plutocrats of *Arcadian Adventures* attain their most ludicrous proportions. Furthermore, the plutorians demonstrate from chapter seven onward what concerted, as opposed to competitive, effort can achieve. Like Mr Smith in his progress from woodsman to saviour of the church, the plutorians who engineer the creation of the "United Church Limited" are prepared for their triumphant grab at political power.

The two churches begin, nevertheless, in rivalry. Of the two, the steadfast, old-fashioned, and somewhat regressive St Osoph's is favoured by Leacock, the tory humanist, over the changeable, modern, and progressive St Asaph's. The Episcopal St Asaph's began its journey towards Plutoria Avenue from "away in the west of the slums," whereas the Presbyterian St Osoph's began "away in the east" (*AA*, 203). The mock-biblical phrasing, "away in," suggests not only the two churches' original distance from Plutoria Avenue but also St Osoph's nearer proximity to the origins of Christianity, in the east. Leacock also favours St Osoph's minister, the Reverend McTeague, over St Asaph's Reverend Edward Fareforth Furlong. The frivolous Fareforth Furlong, whose name connotes an adventurous excursion (Fareforth) and a mere measurement (Furlong), plays the flute "as only the episcopal clergy can play it" and dances "the new episcopal tango" (*AA*, 205). He is something of a dandy in his dress, effeminate in his inability to shake a fist, and, in his concern for food, a man of indulged physical appetites (*AA*, 213, 238, 210). He views his church as a place for anything but prayer, wherein he preaches an historical-critical kind of sermon: "Hell itself was spoken of as She-ol, and it appeared that it was not a place of burning, but rather of what one might describe as moral torment. This settled She-ol once and for all: nobody minds moral torment" (*AA*, 206). Certainly the calloused plutorians do not mind "moral torment." Their Minister Furlong is not a spiritual leader. He shines instead as an organizer of activities for the distraction of those same plutorian women who seek novelty in the *spiritualism* of the Yahi-Bahi Oriental Society (*AA*, 216).

Furlong's theology, along with his espicopal flute-playing and tango-dancing, may constitute, as was the case with Drone and his beacon, an attack on the spiritual shortcomings of the nineteenth-century Anglican Church. At one point the narrator remarks that Furlong was "as broad-minded a man as an Anglican clergyman ought to be. He had no objection to any reasonable use of his church – for a thanksgiving festival or for musical recitals, for example – but when it came to opening up the church and using it to pray in, the thing was going a little too far" (*AA*, 212). In "The Love Story," Leacock's narrator remarks that Philippa Furlong's beauty "was of that peculiar and almost sacred kind found only in the immediate neighbourhood of the High Church clergy" (*AA*, 171). Flippant Philippa is implicated in the moral crime of "The Love Story," wherein her deceptive treatment of Spillikins is associated with "a standing principle of the Anglican Church" (*AA*, 174), this being secrecy or lack of communication. But Furlong best characterizes himself and his frivolous service with his remark to his sister: "I have a great deal of business – that is, of work in the parish – to see to" (*AA*, 200).

McTeague, on the other hand, is at once favoured and gently satirized for being too unworldly. In contrast to the progressively-bent Furlong, and in a manner at least partly congenial to the tory in Leacock, "Dr. McTeague slid quietly backwards with the centuries." For his concerned plutorian parishioners who are feeling the financial pinch of diminished congregations, his "crowning sin" is that "He is not up to date ... He don't go forward any" (*AA*, 207). There should be little doubt, given Leacock's reactionary attitude in "The Devil and the Deep Sea" (*ELS*, 37–52), that Leacock finds distasteful the opinion of the "business members of the congregation" who dismiss McTeague as follows: "That old man believes just exactly the same sort of stuff now that he did forty years ago. What's more, he *preaches* it. You can't run a church that way, can you?" (*AA*, 207). Such an attitude, which terms religious beliefs "stuff," is in accordance with the plutorian emphasis on *things* over such intangibles as the community, romantic love, charity, and the spirit. President Boomer's remark that McTeague indulges in "a rather dangerous attempt at moral teaching which is apt to contaminate our students" (*AA*, 105) is a view not condoned by Leacock, who ironically commended Concordia College for having had "no teaching of religion except lectures on the Bible" (*AA*, 81–2). Yet McTeague is not without fault. He, too, is guilty of a pride in material wealth, for he "loves to think that there are men among [his congregation] that could buy out half the congregation of St. Asaph's" (*AA*, 202). Moreover, McTeague is, in his theological-philosophical obsessions, guilty perhaps of spiritual pride.

Furlong and McTeague can be seen to embody the two sides of the *Sketches'* Dean Drone. Like Drone, Furlong is at fault for his busy-ness and for his practice of beautifying his Episcopal (Anglican) church with unnecessary adornment. McTeague, lost in his attempt to reconcile St Paul and Hegel, is akin to Drone wrestling with Greek and slumbering over his *Pastorals of Theocritus*. Like Drone, who suffers a stroke when he perceives his mistaken beacon in flames, McTeague suffers a stroke when his philosophic obsession is revealed to him in stark terms: Boomer reports that a student asks McTeague "how he could reconcile his theory of transcendental immaterialism with a scheme of rigid moral determinism" (*AA*, 230). And as he does with Drone, Leacock treats the enfeebled McTeague with a pathos that appears elsewhere in *Arcadian Adventures* only in reference to "the Little Girl in Green." In a typically penetrating and characteristically sympathetic passage, he notes that "there were more kind things said of [McTeague] in the three days during which he was taken for dead, than in thirty years of his life – which seemed a pity" (*AA*, 233). It is probably unnecessary to remark that the "three days during which" McTeague is taken for dead serve to parallel him with the crucified Christ.

McTeague's wrestling with Pauline dualism and dialectic materialism mirrors the movement of the two churches towards monopolistic union. To think that the two philosophies can be reconciled would be an indication of madness. Thus, at the conclusion of "The Ministrations," McTeague is reported to believe of St Paul and Hegel that "so far as he can see they both mean the same thing." His position is echoed six paragraphs later in the view of the plutorian trustees on the contractual matter of choice of attendance in either church – "it doesn't make the slightest difference" (*AA*, 270–1). As the vestige of an order that recognized the worthiness of pursuits beyond the material and the individual, however recondite those pursuits, McTeague represents what is lost when all is reduced to financial expediency. Like Tomlinson and "the Little Girl in Green," however, McTeague offers an ineffectual opposition to the powers of Plutoria. Plutoria reduces all forms of aspiration to the commonest denominator – money – and then subsumes them.

If religion is simply a matter of pecuniary profit and loss, it follows that the only sin in Plutoria is poverty:

Whatever sin there was in the City was shoved sideways into the roaring streets of commerce where the elevated railway ran, and below that again into the slums. Here there must have been any quantity of sin. The rector of St. Asaph's was certain of it. Many of the richer of his parishioners had been down in parties late at night to look at it, and the ladies of his congregation were joined together into all sorts of guilds and societies and bands of endeavour for stamping it out and driving it under or putting it into jail till it surrendered. (*AA*, 214)

Although Furlong considers that "his creed was one of works rather than of words" (*AA*, 205), apparently his works do not even extend to the fascinated tokenism of his "slumming" parishioners. Recalling the book's opening reference to the slums, which can be seen only if the Mausoleum clubbers were to climb up on the roof, the narrator remarks that "the slums lay outside the rector's parish. He had no right to interfere" (*AA*, 214). As has already been shown, both churches began in these "lower and poorer parts of the city," and both were initially nudged towards Plutoria Avenue because they were purchased by liquor interests (*AA*, 203). No doubt the distilleries remained in the poorer sections, malodorously dispensing what is the truer opiate of the masses. In any case, ministering to the poor is not the concern of either plutorian church.

Beyond the borders of the plutorian Arcadia, the poor in *Arcadian Adventures* provide, in Donald Cameron's expression, "the foci of values."[3] The reference to the slums with which the book begins is reiterated in the churches' origins in "the lower and poorer parts of the city," and this, in turn, is echoed in the closing sentence of *Arcadian Adventures*, in the reference to "the lower parts of the city" (*AA*, 11, 203, 310). In the chapters on plutorian religion, Leacock implicitly chastises both fashionable modernism (Furlong) and scholastic obsession (McTeague) for their failure to do anything in the way of "works" to alleviate the problem of a glaring discrepancy between plenty and poverty. By so doing, Leacock can be seen to engage in the nineteenth-century controversy over the failure of the Anglican Church to fulfill a meaningful social function. In *A Dream Of Order*, Alice Chandler summarizes the debate: "The modern Anglican church was attacked for neglecting its duties and becoming more a fashionable establishment than a meaningful social organization."[4] Such is Leacock's criticism of the churches and their ministers, as, indeed, was the point of the reference to the Salvation Army in *Sunshine Sketches* (*SS*, 110). Failing to fulfill a meaningful social function, the plutorian churches fall prey to the clutches of the plutocrats, who, like Darwinian nature itself, inevitably rush in to fill a vacuum with self-enriching abundance.[5]

The extent to which the plutorians travesty religious concerns is the extent to which *Arcadian Adventures* attains the heights of burlesque. In this context, however, travesty and burlesque may be too kind a verb and noun (*pace* Leacock). The plutorians blatantly vulgarize the essence of Christian charity and the purpose of communal worship. All is, of course, a matter (a *thing*) of money and profit. This vulgarization is personified by the Reverend Uttermust Dumfarthing, who is valued as "a first-class man" (*AA*, 235) and hired by St Osoph's trustees because of the exorbitant salary he demands.

Asmodeus Boulder is impressed after hearing Dumfarthing preach to the poor and tell them that they are "no good" (*AA*, 234), an evaluation that points up the plutorian debasement of moral language (an issue that will be addressed later in this chapter). Furlong Senior establishes the terms for the discussion of the merger of St Asaph's and St Osoph's: "I am not speaking now as a Christian, but as a businessman" (*AA*, 225). With an insistently ledger-like mind, he convinces his foolish son to accede to an inversion of Christian charity, to the businessman's golden rule: "Anything which we give out without return or reward we count as a debit; all that we take from others without giving in return we count as so much to our credit" (*AA*, 224). He impresses upon his son that "there is no higher power that can influence or control the holder of a first mortgage" on a church (*AA*, 252). And it is Furlong Senior who scoffs at the notion of comparing "the Standard Oil Company to a church" (*AA*, 257), a mere church.

Vulgarization follows incrementally upon vulgarization. The discussions of church merger take place under the guidance of the lawyer Skinyer of "Skinyer and Beatem." Skinyer is at a loss to convey to Edward Furlong his wish to ascertain the basis of St Asaph's in "the real sense" as opposed to "the religious sense" (*AA*, 259). Furlong's inability to satisfy Skinyer's legal mind may well reflect favourably on the naïve minister, but it constitutes an ineffectual opposition to the plutorian machine. It is Skinyer, representing the interests of the plutorians, who triumphs. It is the lawyer who designates as "minor points" the items concerning "doctrines or the religious belief of the new amalgamation" (*AA*, 264–5). The vulgarization of religion finds fulfilment here in Skinyer's legalese. Only the lawyer's jargon is enunciated, the articles of faith being stated as "such and such" (*AA*, 266). As Skinyer remarks earlier, "For the merger we need nothing – I state it very frankly – except general consent" (*AA*, 261). Where belief has been reduced to such terms, "removing all questions of religion" (*AA*, 263), it is indeed time to put "the churches once and for all on a business basis" (*AA*, 264).

Until they achieve the merger of the churches, the plutorians are characterized by their savage, competitive individualism. "General consent" is the one thing they have lacked in their capitalistic ventures. In economic terms, "general consent" becomes merely a euphemism for monopoly capitalism. The target of chapter seven's satire is merger that results in monopoly. Left to their own methods in an extremely *laissez-faire* economy, an economy that accords well with the philosophy of liberal individualism, businesses can form into conglomerates which eliminate competition and artifically manipulate the supply and demand for their products. In *The Unsolved Riddle of Social Justice*, Leacock dismisses the nineteenth-century economic practice of *laissez-faire* and regrets the capitalistic motive behind supply-and-demand economics: "The world's production is aimed at producing 'value,' not in producing plenty. ... When there is *enough* the wheels slacken and stop. This sounds at first hearing most admirable. But let it be noted that the *'enough'* here in question does not mean enough to satisfy human wants. In fact it means precisely the converse. It means enough *not* to satisfy them, and to leave the selling price of the things made at the point of profit" (*UR*, 74). When what constitutes "enough" is determined by a monopoly, the consumer is the loser, and none loses more than the poor consumer. The proposal for merging the rival churches comes from Mr Fyshe: "Certainly a head which had brought peace out of civil war in the hardware business by amalgamating ten rival stores and had saved the very lives of five hundred employees by reducing their wages fourteen percent, was capable of it." It is Fyshe who expresses the rationale for merger: "It's the one solution. The two churches can't live under the present conditions of competition. We have here practically the same situation as we had with the two rum distilleries, – the output is too large for the demand" (*AA*, 257). When Fyshe applies the rigors of profitable supply-and-demand to religious "competition," plutorian religion resolves into ludicrousness: "In fact it is one of the ideas of the day and everyone admits that what is needed is the application of the ordinary business principles of harmonious combination, with a proper – er – restriction of output and general economy of operation" (*AA*, 258).

Fittingly, Fyshe is suggested to be the prime mover in the effort toward church union. The rivalry of the two churches can also be seen as an extension of the business rivalry between Fyshe and Boulder, which was the concern of "A Little Dinner." Fyshe, a "prominent member" of St Asaph's (*AA*, 247), is the first to question openly the Rev. Furlong's "business" capacity (*AA*, 248). And it is Fyshe who takes the first step toward merger by inviting Boulder to lunch. Boulder, who is Peter Spillikins' trustee, is also one of the "managing trustees of St. Osoph's church" (*AA*, 234). It can be suggested, therefore, that the union of the churches is further degraded for being Boulder's revenge for the vengeance that Fyshe had enacted against him with the Duke of Dulham. Just as Fyshe had known that the Duke was in America not to invest but to borrow money, so Boulder knows that Osoph's Dumfarthing is leaving the City. The church union can thus be viewed as but a larger version of the competitive business practices of those financial animals, Fyshe and Boulder. It is, ironically, the culminating act of vengeful competitiveness between Fyshe and Boulder and the end of pluto-rian competitive individualism. From this point onward, the plu-torians work together.

In keeping with the animal imagery of "A Little Dinner," the birth of the "United Church Limited" (*AA*, 263) is presented as a sort of fowlish gestation, one that parodies the Spirit in *Paradise Lost* which "Dove-like satst brooding on the vast Abyss / And mad'st it preg-nant" (*PL*.I.22–3): the plutocrats sit around "a huge egg-shaped ta-ble," "brooding" and "murmuring" (*AA*, 264, 5). The first "minor" point of doctrine that they dismiss is "in regard to the creation" (*AA*, 265). (In *Too Much College*, Leacock compares economists who argue over the concepts of "cost" and "value" to "Milton's arguing devils, who 'found no end in wondering mazes lost.'"[6]) Filled with a pas-sionately pecuniary intensity, the plutocrats hatch their plot and easily give birth to the "United Church Limited," a cold-blooded beast which, disguised as anti-sectarianism, covertly incorporates their sole conviction, money-getting. When Alpha and Omega – St Asaph and St Osoph – are united, the result is indeed the parodic anti-Christ, the "beginning and the ending" (Rev.1:8).

Before closing this discussion of the religious adventures, I must add a word on the marriages that conclude the business of the rival churches, the marriage between Edward Furlong and Catherine Dumfarthing, and that between the Rev. Dumfarthing and Juliana Furlong. Those marriages can be understood favourably as examples of Leacock's belief in the need for kindliness in humour. The satiric humour on the plutorian churches has been harsh, much harsher than the satire on Drone's beacon, and Leacock may have felt the need for a kindly, hopeful touch. In its broad outline, this story of bitter rivalry leading to union and marriages parodically parallels the movement of a Shakespearean romantic comedy: from the "har-mony" of the two churches competing side-by-side, to the discord engendered when St Osoph's gains economic advantage, to a new order that is further solidified by marriages between the discordant parties.[7] In *Arcadian Adventures* the pattern assumes miscreant pro-portions, for the marriages further solidify the self-serving monopoly which lies behind the entire business of church merger. In *Sunshine Sketches*, the marriage of Pupkin and Zena is made possible by all that is best in Mariposa: community pride, concerned relatives and friends, and an older order of business (represented by Pupkin Se-nior). Because the marriages that conclude the chapters on religion in *Arcadian Adventures* solidify the plutorian monopoly of the religious product, it appears, as "The Love Story of Mr. Peter Spillikins" also suggested, that love in the City serves plutocratic greed. The reader of *Arcadian Adventures* might well wonder, If business, society, love and religion have fallen to the now-unified plutorians, can rule by plutocracy be far behind? The final adventure, "The Great Fight for Clean Government," answers this question with a resounding negative.

Glenn Clever has observed that the movement of *Arcadian Adventures* is one of incremental occurence of the characters until, in the final chapter, they join forces and rule; thus the apt title of his essay, "Leacock's Dunciad."[8] The divisive plutorians joined forces earlier, however, in the concerted effort to gain control of the rival churches. The inaugural meeting of the "Clean Government Association" (*AA*, 289) recalls the recently achieved truce: the first participants distinguished from the others present are Mr Lucullus Fyshe (St Asaph's) and Mr Asmodeus Boulder (St Osoph's), who are now the prime movers in "The Great Fight for Clean Government." Perhaps their successful venture with the churches has made Fyshe more cold-blooded and Boulder bolder; inspired perhaps by the ease with which their demonically concerted efforts set religion on a sound business footing, Boulder and Fyshe and their plutorian "anglers" cast forth now to become *political* fishers of men. Like Josh Smith at the helm of the *Mariposa Belle*, the plutorians demonstrate to the electorate that they are best suited to steer the ship of state. Unlike the "The Great Election" of the *Sketches*, the election that left Mariposa free of the outward – "Ottaway" – bound Smith, "The Great Fight" leaves the alarming impression that the plutocracy has dropped anchor.

The final sketch of *Arcadian Adventures* differs from *Sunshine Sketches'* concluding "L'Envoi: The Train to Mariposa" in ways other than the pessimism of the former and the qualified optimism of the latter. As with the final stories in the best short story cycles (James Joyce's "The Dead" and Alice Munro's "Who Do You Think You Are?" for example), *Arcadian Adventures* concludes with a forceful reiteration and amplification of its major theme: the irresistible push of the plutocrats toward complete control over the life of the City. "L'Envoi" concludes the *Sketches* with a meditation on the importance of "home." It reaffirms the *Sketches'* concern with the values of community and with the necessity for continuity between past and present. Although "The Great Election" offers *Sunshine Sketches'* readiest parallel to "The Great Fight," the chapters on failed religion, on the razing of Drone's beacon, present the *Sketches'* truer approximation of the ominous portents of "The Great Fight." Nonetheless, a comparison of the chapters on politics does reveal much.

As the chapter titles suggest, in Plutoria politics is merely a "Great Fight," whereas in Mariposa it remains, at least to some extent, a "Great Election": the difference is that between a spectator sport and parliamentary democracy. The issue of "The Great Election" is trade reciprocity with the United States; the issue of "The Great Fight" is "clean government"; which is to say, whereas the campaign in Mariposa grounds itself on a real issue, City politics flies off unencumbered by real issues. As with the rival churches' articles of faith, the true purpose of the municipal election is obfuscated by a smoke-screen of generalities. Connotatively charged jargon (debased language) such as "clean government" disguises the true purpose of plutorian politics – the desire for total power to satisfy insatiable money-hunger.

The leaders of the "Clean Government Association (AA, 289, the name of which is subsequently changed to the more diabolical "Clean Government League," 294, 295, 299, 300), become involved in politics only to become wealthier. Though he serves Mammon, "the least erected Spirit that fell" (PL.I.679), Lucullus Fyshe is the Lucifer-like leader of the true "cohorts of darkness" (AA, 295). He wants to extend his franchise for the invertedly named "Citizens' Light (AA, 284). One hundred years is too brief a period for Fyshe: "They expect us to install all our poles, string our wires, set up our transformers in their streets and then perhaps at the end of a hundred years find ourselves compelled to sell out at a beggarly valuation" (AA, 285). The motives of the other plutorians are equally reprehensible. Mr Furlong, Sr, wishes to capitalize on a piece of real estate which he feels is best suited for a cemetery. His "reward lay merely in the fact of selling it" (AA, 286), the "it" being land which Fyshe favourably assesses for its "loose sandy soil with no trees and very little grass to overcome" (AA, 287). (Their readiness to make money even off the dead recalls from the Tomlinson episode the plutorian vogue for claiming to have fathers buried in the speculator's sacred ground [AA, 69]. Furthermore, such opportunism, with its suggestions of desecration, can be understood as the sin that finds a parallel in the Mariposans' forgetfulness of their older graveyard.) Mr Rasselyer-Brown becomes a member of the League in order to secure the City's coal contract. He is reported by Fyshe to be self-righteous at the thought of the City buying its coal wholesale at "three-fifty" when he is prepared to sell it "at five, or at anything over that they like to name" (AA, 288). Mr Asmodeus Boulder, who is in "The Great Fight" Bëelzebub to Fyshe's Satan – "One next himself in power, and next in Crime" (*PL*.I.79) – wants the stone and asphalt contract, presumably to pave the City's streets cheaply, in reality to line his own pockets richly (*AA*, 288). Skinyer wants the legal department because the City needs "a good man ... at, say fifteen thousand"; the present head of the legal department draws "only six thousand dollars" (*AA*, 289). According to the plutorian scheme of evaluating worth, and the plutorian or satanic penchant for debasing moral language, the present head cannot he "a *good* man." And although the truer reason for changing the City's form of government from a "council" to a "board" (*AA*, 300) is to give the plutorians indefinite control, the first distinction that strikes Fyshe is that on a board "the *salary* is higher" (*AA*, 302). Every instance of motivation among the plutorians of the Clean Government League illustrates the movement from a council that is riddled with relatively acceptable (that is, humanly fallible) levels of graft to a plutorian board that is shot through with blatant self-seeking and unacceptably high levels of graft.

The figurehead of the League is the once-denounced, opportunely embraced, Mayor McGrath (whose name suggests "graft"). If Fyshe recalls Josh Smith as financial animal, McGrath resembles Smith both in size and as a politico. McGrath talks like Smith, and he oversees his "henchmen," his "boys," playing Smith's card game, "freeze-out poker" (*SS*, 79). "'Boys,' [McGrath] said to Alderman O'Hooligan and Alderman Gorfinkle, who were playing freeze-out poker in a corner behind the pool tables, 'you want to let the boys know to keep pretty dark and go easy. There's a lot of talk I don't like about the elections going round the town. Let the boys know that just for a while the darker they keep the better'" (*AA*, 281–2). In advising his boys to "keep pretty dark," "the darker ... the better," McGrath introduces one of the controlling imagistic patterns of "The Great Fight": the (again Miltonic) struggle between light and dark (which will be discussed shortly). Like Smith, who often inspires the *Sketches'* narrator to mock-heroic metaphors, and who is at one point described as "an overdressed pirate" (*SS*, 10), McGrath is eulogized in mock-heroic terms suggestive of the piratic: "The look which the mayor directed at his satellite was much the same glance that Morgan the buccaneer might have given to one of his lieutenants before throwing him overboard" (*AA*, 282). As the comparison suggests, McGrath is most like Smith in his readiness to use and discard people. After the mayor joins forces with the piratic plutocrats, Fyshe repeats the nautical metaphor, informing Boulder that McGrath "is willing to throw overboard Gorfinkle, Schwefeldamp and Undercutt" (*AA*, 299). The nautical metaphor may be intended to suggest, as it did in "The Marine Excursion" of the *Sketches*, that the culminating political adventure of *Arcadian Adventures* is to be viewed in terms of the "ship of state" trope and, consequently, as a paradigm ·for the emerging society that will be ruled by a plutocracy: there are pirates aboard the ship of state.

In keeping with *Arcadian Adventures'* understated sympathy for the workers and the poor, the favoured incumbents of the municipal government are members of the working middle class of merchants: "To tell the truth, the aldermen had been much the same persons for about fifteen or twenty years. Some were in the produce business, others were butchers, two were grocers, and all of them wore blue checkered waistcoats and red ties and got up at seven in the morning to attend the vegetable and other markets" (*AA*, 278). Such early risers and workers stand favourably in contrast to the plutorian "idle rich"; consistent with Leacock's practice elsewhere in *Arcadian Adventures* and *Sunshine Sketches*, their associations are with the natural world of animals and vegetables rather than with the artificial realm of machines and electricity. And in accordance with the book's subtle attack on the plutocratic perversion of the ideal of American liberal republicanism, the incumbents are associated with more populist clubs such as the "Thomas Jefferson" and the "George Washington" (*AA*, 282). In his unfinished autobiography, *The Boy I Left Behind Me*, Leacock writes that "the theory of a republic, and the theory of equality, and the condemnation of hereditary rights [seem] obvious and self-evident truths, as clear to me as they were to Thomas Jefferson."[9] The plutorians are the enemy of Jeffersonian democracy, of agrarianism (Tomlinson), of continuity with their own past (Concordia College and its associations with Washington and Lincoln), and, in short, of the ideals of the founders of the democratic republic. A political realist, Leacock is not suggesting that the incumbents are, as Tom Marshall argues, "poor but relatively honest"; nor is he presenting the plutocrats' triumph as a "victory of power and money over decency."[10] The incumbents are neither "poor" nor "decent." Leacock is simply suggesting that the merchant class with its small-scale graft is as a governing body at least a more acceptable alternative than are the plutorians of the Mausoleum Club with their large-scale graft. Appropriately, the Mausoleum clubbers are called "stiffs" by the president of the George Washington Club (*AA*, 282). A plutocracy heralds the death of republican idealism. Because only the wealthy plutocrats will be able to afford influence with the new rulers (*AA*, 302–3), they achieve in "The Great Fight" that towards which *Arcadian Adventures* resolutely moves – totalitarian rule by plutocracy. "The Great Fight" actually prefigures the great defeat of republicanism, democracy, and the ideals of liberty and equality set forth in *The Constitution of the United States*. The capping irony of *Arcadian Adventures* is that the victory of the plutocracy defeats competitive capitalism itself.

The debasement of the Constitutional ideals was anticipated in the Yahi-Bahi adventure, wherein Judge Longerstill serves as a sort of pathetic Uncle Sam. Longerstill is a specialist in "the Constitution of the United States" (*AA*, 134). He sits patiently at the inaugural meeting of the Yahi-Bahi Society, waiting for someone to ask him to address the self-indulgent initiates to Boohooism on the Constitution (that is, on the founding ideals of their country). The Constitution of the United States is ignored in favour of the "constitution" (*AA*, 135) of the Yahi-Bahi Society, until it appears that Yahi-Bahi is going to be late arriving. Mrs Fyshe then completes the debasement of the democratic-republican ideal by equating *the* Constitution with the constitution of the Yahi-Bahi Society. She does this by referring to Longerstill as "a most eminent gentleman who *probably* has thought more deeply about *constitutions* than – " (*AA*, 136, emphasis added). The repetition of "constitution" in these three pages (*AA*, 134–6), and the confusion of the kinds of constitutions, cleverly adumbrates *Arcadian Adventures'* concluding satire on the plutorian vulgarization of the democratic republic's founding ideals of liberty and equality.

In "The Great Fight" unbridled capitalism gives rise to plutocratic corruption, which breeds a form of totalitarianism, which issues in further rottenness. "Corruption" and "rottenness" are also dominant images of "The Great Fight." Such decadence is attributed to the incumbent government by the clique of plutocrats; it is also ascribed to the standing government by the patently ironic narrator. Because the plutocrats reveal their totalitarian ambitions and corruption by their own words, it will prove rewarding to consider the language of "The Great Fight" before turning to an examination of the imagery.

What Matthew Hodgart has observed of satirists in general aptly applies to Leacock's use of language in "The Great Fight." "The satirist," writes Hodgart, "puts elaborate and bombastic language in the mouths of his victims: they express their paranoic delusions of grandeur and their monomaniac greed by inflated rhetoric."[11] The plutorians' corruption of language in "The Great Fight" reveals the capitalist clique for the league of blatant hypocrites that it so obviously is. As Henry Fielding prescribes in his preface to *Joseph Andrews*, hypocrisy is the fittest object of ridicule; vanity, the Mariposan affectation, is the lesser evil: "For to discover anyone to be the exact reverse of what he affects, is more surprising, and consequently more ridiculous, than to find him a little deficient in the quality he desires the reputation of."[12] The corruption of language also engages that favourite of Leacock's themes: the incongruity between appearance and reality, between what is professed and what is intended. Even as it inadvertently reveals character and motive, language in "The Great Fight" relentlessly struggles to conceal behind a barrage of ethical generalities the raw hunger for total control that motivates the plutocratic politicos. In this way, the use of language in the final chapter anticipates George Orwell's insights into the debasing relation between rhetoric and totalitarianism.[13]

The hypocrisy of the plutorians need not be illustrated at length. In the opening scene of "The Great Fight," Mr Newberry establishes the loud tone of deceptiveness when he "whispers" that "the time has come to speak out about [graft] fearlessly" (*AA*, 274). Such cowardice, which betrays the hypocrite's fear of discovery, is evident again when Mayor McGrath passes the gossiping Newberry and Dick Overend: "Did he hear?' whispered Mr. Newberry as the mayor passed out of the club. … 'I don't care if he did,' whispered Mr. Dick Overend" (*AA*, 281). Mr Lucullus Fyshe is the epitome of blatant hypocrisy when he complains that the incumbents are crooked because they accept his bribes (*AA*, 283). Similarly, President Boomer wonders whether the Clean Government League "can best fight [the corruption of the press] by buying the paper itself or buying the staff" (*AA*, 294). Every time a member of the plutorian clique speaks, he exposes himself as a hypocrite and demonstrates that he, like the inner-circle of plutorians – Fyshe, Boulder, Furlong, Sr, and Skinyer – has entered politics only for what he will get out of it. This collective political subterfuge is epitomized by the sort of deception seen in the repetition for the public of the inaugural meeting of the League: "This first meeting was, of course, confidential. But all that it did was presently done over again, with wonderful freshness and spontaneity at a large public meeting open to all citizens. There was a splendid impromptu air about everything" (*AA*, 295). This is "back-room politics" with a vengeance. It is also a repetition, exactly, of what happens in the great consult of *Paradise Lost*, for there too the conclusion of the public debate is foreknown by Satan and Bëelzebub. Like Satan, the inner-circle of debasing plutocrats knows that their "*better* part remains – To work in close design, by fraud or guile" (I.645–6, emphasis added).

But what is most telling with regard to the hypocrisy of the plutorians is their encouraging acceptance of one another *as* hypocrites. For example, in the attempt to solicit Furlong's support for the League, Fyshe condemns the incumbents' price for the cemetery land. Fyshe senses, however, that Furlong does not think the price exorbitant because he (Furlong) has land of his own to sell at a higher price. Like a shark that smells blood, Fyshe slices about and seizes the opportunity: "'Certainly not [a high price],' said Mr. Fyshe, very quietly and decidedly, looking at Mr. Furlong in a searching way as he spoke" (AA, 285–6). The plutorians of the clique understand one another perfectly: "After this conversation Mr Fyshe and Mr. Furlong senior understood one another absolutely in regard to the new movement" (AA, 287). Their shared guile makes it unnecessary for the plutorians to voice their true motives; instead, they couch their hidden intentions in civic-sounding lies, in "high words, that [bear] / Semblance of worth, not substance" (PL.I.528–9), and they exchange looks which mean "volumes to those who would read them" (AA, 301). With caricature and hyperbole, and with his characteristic touches of litotes, Leacock makes of plutorian politics a primer in political rhetoric for "those who would read" it.

To succeed politically, the League's blatant private hyprocrisy requires an equal forthrightness of hypocritical language in the public domain. And it is in this regard that George Orwell's "Politics and the English Language" provides again an apt gloss on the rhetoric and sloganeering ot the "Clean Government League." Orwell writes that "the great enemy of clear language is insincerity."[14] At various points in "The Great Fight," plutorians such as Dick Overend and Newberry, Furlong, Sr, and Skinyer (AA, 275, 287, 289) are unable to express themselves. When their true intention collides with obfuscating jargon, they fumble words. Fear of clarity and specification leads Fyshe and Boulder to construct for the League a platform that is defined by its lack of definition: "As Mr. Fyshe and Mr. Boulder said there was no need to drag in specific questions or try to define the action to be taken towards this or that particular detail, such as the hundred-and-fifty-year franchise, beforehand. The platform was simply expressed as Honesty, Purity, Integrity" (AA, 294–5). "Honesty, Purity, Integrity" are, like Yahi-Bahi's "modesty, locquacity, and pomposity" (AA, 144), a typical plutorian parody of the Christian trinity, Faith, Hope, and Charity. The League's "great free voluntary movement of the people" (AA, 190) is, as has been remarked, a covert operation. The "Students' Fair Play League" (a product, of course, of Boomer's Plutoria University) terrorizes candidates who oppose the senior League (AA, 305–6). The Clean Government League plays dirty politics. But, as the narrator notes, "the word 'clean government' had been no sooner uttered than it turned out that every one of the papers in the city was in favour of it: in fact had been working for it for years" (AA, 296). In the conclusion of his essay on political rhetoric, Orwell observes that "political language – and with variations this is true of all political parties, from Conservatives to Anarchists – is designed to make lies sound truthful and murder respectable, and to give an appearance of solidity to pure wind."[15] The League's manipulative debasement of language also illustrates Leacock's observation that "there is more clap-trap, insincerity and humbug on the surface of politics than over any equal area on the face of any institution."[16]

The corruption of language is, of course, in itself cause for alarm, particularly so when language is manipulated and mangled to suggest the opposite of the speaker's true political intentions, as when, for instance, politicians talk of defence, deterrents, and peace while they prepare for war. But debased language in "The Great Fight" is also symtomatic of a general rottenness of the political process, particularly, *Arcadian Adventures* implies, in the United States of America. Although the raw and rampant avariciousness of big business characterizes the plutocrats of any nation, Leacock would have us keep in mind that politics in *Arcadian Adventures* is explicitly American. The narrator's first observations in "The Great Fight" reveal that Dick Overend's and Newberry's complaints about their municipal government are the vague outcome of a more general discussion. They had begun by lamenting "the present rottenness of the federal politics of the United States," proceeded to regret the composition of "the United States Senate" (a phrase that is immediately repeated twice [*AA*, 275]), and thence to talk of "the rottenness of the state legislature" (*AA*, 276). The narrator notes ironically that the "new wave of public morality ... was sweeping over the entire United States" (*AA*, 279); and as Fyshe proclaims, there will soon be restricted "Boards" rather than representative "councils" in "every city and town of the state" (*AA*, 300). Finally, when it becomes evident that the governor and the state legislature are as corrupt as Fyshe and Boulder, Fyshe describes the state's support of the League as a "thoroughly American support," (*AA*, 301). If it will be granted that Leacock could have made his language unspecific had plutocratic politics *per se* been his only target, then it may be argued that the repeated emphasis of the "American" setting and the repeated mention of the legislative bodies of the American republic are intended to indicate something essentially American in the drive toward a plutocracy.[17]

Thus Leacock offers in *Arcadian Adventures* a presentiment of encroaching plutocratic totalitarianism on the national scale *in the United States*. In contrast to this movement into an envisioned American future, the *Sketches'* "L'Envoi: The Train to Mariposa" offers an imaginative train that moves towards a northern, typically Canadian Mariposa. This is a symbolic movement towards the past, towards what was, with the implicit warning that *what was* must be selectively recovered if the future is to be saved from the issue of the *things that are*. As was stated at the beginning of chapter five, *Arcadian Adventures* depicts the sort of society that issues when the implicit warnings of "L'Envoi" are ignored. The *Adventures* begins with the words, "The Mausoleum Club" – a definite article, a deathly noun, and a destructive club – an alarming phrase that also partly comprises the closing sentence of "L'Envoi." Most important, the plutorian Arcadia is a vision of that America from which the Envoi narrator subtly cautions his Canadian auditor: "Perhaps you had come back now and again," regrets the Envoi narrator (*SS*, 263). Perhaps then there would have been less need for the horrifically humorous vision of "The City of the End of Things" that comprises *Arcadian Adventures*.

What is dying or dead in the Mausoleum Club, the City, and the liberally individualistic America of *Arcadian Adventures* are the values of community: genuine concern for the welfare of the community and its members, reverence for the dead and respect for continuity with the past that they honoured, pride other than in individual material wealth, and intimations of an order that transcends the pecking order of lucre. Because such tory-humanist values are dying or dead in the plutorian city, "The Great Fight" is appropriately rank with images of decay.

The first few pages of "The Great Fight" describe an atmosphere of sepulchral putrefaction. Beginning with Newberry's and Overend's conversation *in* the aptly named Mausoleum Club, the words "rotten" and "rottenness" are soon repeated no less than seven times (*AA*, 274–77), implying the organic decay – the decadence – of a once-viable society. The similarly repeated words "corrupt" and "corruption" suggest the particular application of this progressive rottenness to the "body politic." These images of decay culminate in the narrator's ironic observation that the names of the incumbents "were simply a byword throughout the United States for rank criminal corruption" (*AA*, 277). The grandiose extension of plutorian rottenness and corruption to include the whole country inversely parallels the way in which Newberry's and Overend's talk of rotten municipal politics derives from a discussion of the "rottenness of the federal politics of the United States" (*AA*, 275). In "The Great Fight," Leacock is suggesting that the plutocracy's "rank criminal corruption" portends the decadence and death of, in the least, America's founding ideal of democratic republicanism.

The crass individualism that values only money and power (for the purpose of acquiring more money) is the bacterium that, cultured liberally, has infected and is consuming the organic body of American society. In "L'Envoi: The Train to Mariposa," the repetition in the first few paragraphs of the word "home" is intended to suggest to the auditor a braking measure, as it were, on his tendency towards the southern plutocratic putrefaction. But because *Arcadian Adventures* is predicated upon the assumption that the values implied by the warnings of "L'Envoi" have either never pertained in the United States or have been debased and long ignored there (which latter possibility is, considering the events of the Tomlinson story, the more plausible suggestion), "The Great Fight" offers no such solution to the problems that *Arcadian Adventures* addresses. Only when the *Sketches* and the *Adventures* are considered together is Leacock's dark vision lightened. If Mariposa is not held in mind as the tory humanist's illuminating norm for Plutoria, the reader of *Arcadian Adventures* closes the book with the discomfitting impression that the reputedly kindly Leacock was chuckling cynically while the world was, in his view, going to hell in the hip pocket of the plutocracy.

The preceding image may seem extravagant, but it is Leacock who, by ironic implication, twice labels the clique of plutocrats "the cohorts of darkness" (*AA*, 295, 308). In a master stroke (one that is typically racist in its overtones), he notes that the *"Eureka Club (Coloured) endorses the League; Is done with Darkness"* (*AA*, 297). The remark begins to show the ironic manner in which the traditional (Miltonic) images of light and dark, and their associations with good and evil, are employed in "The Great Fight." The plutocracy, which contorts language to obscure its Machiavellian purposes, manipulates these key images to its princely advantage. For example, Fyshe, now the prime mover in Plutoria, virtually owns the "Citizens' Light," a name that is as misleading as Dean Drone's "beacon." The narrator plays ironically upon the misnomer of the "Citizens' Light" and on the way in which all kinds of *light* are assimilated to plutorian *dark*. As the darkness of plutorian totalitarianism creeps forth to cover the entire city, the narrator observes that "the light spread" (*AA*, 287), and that "the light broke and spread and illuminated in all directions (*AA*, 288). Here is the truly Miltonic "darkness visible" (*PL*.I.63).

The conclusion of "The Great Fight," which also concludes *Arcadian Adventures*, continues to depict the triumph of darkness over light. The victory of plutocratic totalitarianism is celebrated "as it fell dusk" (*AA*, 308); and appropriately so, for, as Milton writes of the lewd Sons of Belial, "when Night / Darkens the Streets, then wander forth the Sons / Of *Belial*, flown with insolence and wine (I.500–3).

The celebration at the Mausoleum Club continues "all night long" (*AA*, 309). Of all the self-enriching goals presumably attained by the plutocrats, the only one mentioned is "the franchise of the Citizens' Light" – Fyshe's interest – which is granted for "two centuries so as to give the company a fair chance to see what it could do" (*AA*, 309). The "artificial light" (*AA*, 309) of the illuminated Mausoleum Club will burn for two hundred years, turning night into day for the inhabitants and thus disrupting organic rhythms and natural cycles. This "artificial light," which once more recalls the artificial light of Milton's Pandemonium – fed by "*Naphtha* and *Asphaltus*" (I.729) – is compared favourably (and of course ironically) to the "cheap prosaic glare" of a natural daybreak (*AA*, 309).

Light, with its suggestion of fire, is but one of the four primordial elements. In his concluding depiction of the celebrants at the Mausoleum Club, Leacock refers imagistically to the other three (earth, air, and water) and has parting recourse to the governing metaphor of *Arcadian Adventures*, the plutorian false and pagan Arcadia. His description is subtly telling and portentous:

And through it all moved the shepherds and shepherdesses of the beautiful Arcadia – the shepherds in their tuxedo jackets, with vast white shirt-fronts broad as the map of Africa, with spotless white waistcoats girdling their equators, wearing heavy gold watch-chains and little patent shoes blacker than sin itself, – and the shepherdesses in foaming billows of silks of every colour of the kaleidoscope, their hair bound with glittering headbands or coiled with white feathers, the very symbol of municipal purity. One would search in vain the pages of pastoral literature to find the equal of it. (*AA*, 308–9)

The narrator's and Leacock's moral outrage is apparent in the comparison "blacker than sin itself." Not so obvious is the implication of the "heavy gold watch-chains." Instances of the debasing effects of the quest for gold are recurrent in *Arcadian Adventures*, in, for instance, the Tomlinson story and in the green/gold opposition of the Spillikins affair. Recall also that one of Josh Smith's prominent attributes is "a gold watch-chain in huge square links and ... a gold watch that weighed a pound and a half" (*SS*, 20). The reference to the "gold watch-chains" at the conclusion of *Arcadian Adventures* may suggest that time alone stands between the literary descendants of Smith and their ambition to bind all the world's gold to themselves. Even less obvious in the above passage is the suggestion that the plutocrats, having exerted their control over business, love, religion, and now politics, are an all-controlling force that will prove irresistible. As has been shown, they control the "light," with its suggestion of the element fire. They also embody earth itself: their shirt-fronts are "broad as the map of Africa"; their waists are "equators." Images of water and air – "foaming billows" and "white Feathers" – complete the elemental picture. Leacock has described the onset of totalitarian rule by plutocracy, a plutocratic rule that is not confined to the City or even the United States, but a capitalist totalitarianism that threatens to girdle the equator and control the land and the seas.

The only viable opposition to a plutocracy that values *things* at the expense of all else will be those who cherish what can simply be called *human* values. Leacock himself is scarcely more specific, describing such human values as "all less tangible and provable forms of human merit, and less tangible aspirations of the human mind" (*ELS*, 77). It is a simple solution, though one no less compelling for its simplicity. As Matthew Hodgart writes, "Satire aims at simplification, at a pretence of misunderstanding and at denunciation."[18] By suggesting the need for periodic returns to "Mariposa" through informed memory and imagination – "such a book as the present one" (*SS*, 225) – the *Sketches'* "L'Envoi" illustrates the only means of opposing the tendency towards a "Smithian" plutocracy. One satiric norm of *Arcadian Adventures* is that which the plutorians reject, defeat, subsume, or vulgarize: true manners (the Duke, the "Little Girl in Green") agrarian simplicity and virtuous action (Tomlinson and son), continuity with the past (Concordia College), romantic love, the spirit of religion, and the ideals of democracy. Implicitly, however, the satiric norm of *Arcadian Adventures* remains "Mariposa." The Envoi narrator suggests the simple need to reaffirm the values of "Mariposa," a community that, for all its acknowledged faults, symbolizes Leacock's, the tory humanist's, hope for re-routing the Canadian train that may careen southward. "L'Envoi: The Train to Mariposa" should be viewed as the pivotal chapter of an extended work of fiction that begins with the preface to *Sunshine Sketches* and concludes with the masterfully humorous closing scene of "The Great Fight for Clean Government": "So the night waxed and waned till the slow day broke, dimming with its cheap prosaic glare the shaded beauty of the artificial light, and the people of the city – the best of them, – drove home to their well-earned sleep, and the others, – in the lower parts of the city, – rose to their daily toil" (*AA*, 309–10).

CHAPTER SEVEN

Humour and Humanity

What can Stephen Leacock teach us?

This question is taken from one of Leacock's later essays, "What Can Izaak Walton Teach Us?" In Leacock's view, the rambling Walton, author of the seventeenth-century fisherman's bible *The Compleat Angler*, has much to teach twentieth-century man: "This, especially," writes Leacock, "if we can catch something of the leisurely procedure, the old-time courtesy and, so to speak, the charming tediousness of people with lots of time, now lost in our distracted world" (*LL*, 13). The same can be said in partial answer to the question, What can Stephen Leacock teach us? Yet I cannot resist the academic temptation to expand somewhat upon the kind of humane statement that Leacock always had the good sense to let speak for itself.

For many Canadians "Mariposa" still conjures up the ironic ideal of an interdependent community, of small-town Canada at its best; similarly, the American city of *Arcadian Adventures With the Idle Rich* still captures the materialistic, individualistic, mechanistic metropolis that we fear we are becoming. Leacock, Mariposa, JOSH SMITH, PROP., Plutoria – these are words as Canadian as *bluff, puck, rink rat, concession road*. Perhaps a tentative answer to the question – What can Stephen Leacock teach us? – is that we must learn to accommodate ourselves to living somewhere between "Mariposa" and "Plutoria," as Leacock made home between Montreal and Orillia, socialism and capitalism, satire and sentimentality, England and the United States. [1] In the midst of such contrarieties, Leacock lived and wrote in the spirit of the "kindly humour" that he earnestly re-commended, the humour that tempers extremes, suffers the fallible, and chastises the uncharitable. What can Stephen Leacock teach us? Patience, faith, simplicity: "You ask perhaps, I hope not with im-patience, what we can learn from Izaak Walton. Why, don't you see we've learned a lot already; that fishing is the Apostle's own calling; that fishing must be carried on in an atmosphere of good will and forebearance; that the longest story must never seem prosy; that a cup of ale beneath a tree is better than a civic banquet, and an old familiar song from a familiar singer outclasses grand opera" (*LL*, 16). Leacock, the inveterate teacher, can yet teach us what he knew to be the essence of Walton's teaching: "All that he can teach is the *spirit*; yet the performance in the long run rests on that" (*LL*, 17).

Although Leacock disliked the business of summing-up, in the conclusion of *Back to Prosperity* (1932) he produced an admirable justification for the conclusion to a book. *Prosperity's* "suggestions and proposals," he wrote, "may be summarized here for readers whose rapid intelligence renders it unnecessary for them to read the book." [2] While the first chapter of the present book introduced and generously illustrated the tory humanism that animated Leacock's work, a brief glance here at his last completed work, the "Message to the Graduating Class of 1944" (McGill University), written from a hospital bed, serves as a conclusive illustration of the subtlety of his technique in conveying the essentials of his tory-humanist atti-tudes. (Leacock composed this message thirty-seven days before he died, "under the most distressing physical conditions, and at a time when war raged in all parts of the globe." [3] In consideration of the circumstances in which it was written, Leacock's message might be expected to contain at least a note of despair. But the reverse is the case.)

In his "Message" Leacock exhorts the students to try to improve their world "in the best traditions of honour, courage and decency," and he continues:

A college is a queer place, full of freak characters and odd activities, with alternating aspects of drowsy inefficiency and alert effectiveness; a queer place, but it gets there just the same. If all the world did its work as well as the college does, then the world, in the words of the old song, "would do very well then." ... In the first eagerness of life's struggle the college seems left behind and but little thought of; but as the years pass and the foreground of life loses its color and its interest in favor of the deeper background, your memory of college will rise before your mind in an outline as deep and firm as that of some ageing picture which a garish illumination confuses and a softened light revives.[4]

More than a message to a graduating class, this passage written on Leacock's death-bed can be seen as his valedictory to "all the world." Looked at closely, it reveals once again Leacock's humanistic tolerance for human fallibility, for "freak characters and odd activities." It also suggests the tory in Leacock who disliked mechanical efficiency: the college "gets there just the same" as do the factory and the department store, but it gets there in a humanely tolerant manner. (And notice that Leacock prefers "college," with its connotation of "colleague," to "university," with its suggestion of "corporation.") "If all the world" were run on the principles of humane tolerance, it would "do very well then." Leacock did not expect perfection in an imperfectible world. "Getting there" in a leisurely manner, with spurts of "effectiveness," characterized Leacock's view of how life should be lived. In terms of one of his favourite pastimes and metaphors, it is the companionable quiet of leisurely fishing that the true fisherman values, not the counting of fish. And of course Leacock turns to an "old song" to put his point familiarly: a new song would have been heard from the radio; an old song would have been remembered in association with the voice that sang it – the human voice that still speaks so attractively to the reader from Leacock's writings.

The second part of the above passage provides an analogue for Leacock's view of humorous literature. The humour of sublimity (as Leacock termed the world's best humour, that of Charles Dickens, Mark Twain, and Alphonse Daudet) considers the disillusionments of life in retrospect and concentrates on the "deeper background." Humour at its highest reach reveals the general through the particular, the character type through the individual character, and flawed institutions through fallible man, with a view towards sympathetic comprehension as opposed to dismissal and dissociation. The "garish illumination" that "confuses" is a suggestive equivalent of Leacock's understanding of caustic satire; the "softened light" that "revives" suggests his conception of the purpose of "kindly humour." For Leacock, great humour literally revives what is worthwhile from the past and makes it live again for the present world of men. Furthermore, the contrast of "garish illumination" and "softened light," and the subtle difference between the connotations of "illumination" and "light," could be said to display the mirroring techniques and the ironic perspective that are the mainstays of Leacock's writings. Just as *Sunshine Sketches* provides the "softened light" of remembrance, so *Arcadian Adventures* offers a "garish illumination" of the present (*c.* 1914). Above all, Leacock's valedictory to the graduating class and "all the world" centres itself in memory – "your memory" – which, when informed by a sense of history and humanity, provides an "outline as deep and firm" as that which Leacock provided in the *Sketches* and the *Adventures*.

What can Stephen Leacock teach us? Always first and foremost – to laugh (and not simply at ourselves). But he can teach us also to value that which will forever seem, like what is "Canadian," to be on the brink of extinction: continuity in human affairs, the reasonable as opposed to the merely rational, the leisurely and tolerant, the organic in opposition to the mechanistic, and literature – imagination in the service of informed memory. When read carefully, Leacock's work can teach us what it meant to be Canadian during the first half of Canada's existence. Read imaginatively, his work can still teach us what it should mean to be Canadian.

Notes

PREFACE

1 Desmond Pacey, *Creative Writing in Canada* (1952; rev. Toronto: Ryerson 1961), 91.

CHAPTER ONE

1 Peter McArthur, *Stephen Leacock* (Toronto: Ryerson 1923), 133.
2 Charles Taylor, *Radical Tories* (Toronto: Anansi 1982), 110.
3 Ibid., 213.
4 Ibid., 214.
5 Erwin Panofsky, *Meaning in the Visual Arts* (Chicago: University of Chicago Press 1955), 2.
6 Stephen Leacock, *The Garden of Folly* (Toronto: S.B. Gundy 1924).
7 Desmond Pacey, "Leacock as a Satirist," *Queen's Quarterly* 58 (Summer 1951): 218; see Carl Berger, *The Sense of Power* (Toronto: University of Toronto Press 1970), 45.
8 See Ralph Curry, *Stephen Leacock: Humorist and Humanist* (Garden City, N.Y.: Doubleday 1959), 7.
9 The title of the present chapter was suggested by the similarly entitled fourth section of chapter seven in Desmond Bowen, *The Idea of the Victorian Church* (Montreal: McGill University Press 1968), 363, and by Harold Macmillan, *The Middle Way* (1938; rpt. with pref. London: Mac-

millan 1966).

10 Macmillan, *The Middle Way*, xviii–xix.

11 See Leacock, "What Is Left of Adam Smith?," *Canadian Journal of Economics and Political Science* 1 (Feb. 1935): 51: "This socialism, this communism, would work only in Heaven where they don't need it, or in Hell where they already have it."

12 G.G. Sedgewick, "Stephen Leacock as Man of Letters," *University of Toronto Quarterly* 15 (Oct. 1945): 19, 22. See further Alan Bowker, introd., *The Social Criticism of Stephen Leacock* (Toronto: The University of Toronto Press 1973).

13 Robertson Davies, *Stephen Leacock*, vol. 7, Canadian Writers Series, (Toronto: McClelland and Stewart 1970), 48, 51.

14 Taylor, *Radical Tories*, 73; see also 147.

15 Donald Cameron, *Faces of Leacock* (Toronto: Ryerson 1967), 25.

16 Maynard Mack, *The Garden and the City: Retirement and Politics in the Later Poetry of Pope, 1731–1743* (Toronto: University of Toronto Press 1969), 8, 11.

17 Matthew Hodgart, *Satire* (New York: McGraw-Hill 1969), 13. It may be observed that Leacock's humorous satire can only be described as Horatian; as Pacey notes in his early influential study, "Leacock as a Satirist," 212, Leacock is much closer to Addison than to Swift.

18 Gordon Roper, Rupert Schieder, and S. Ross Beharriell, "The Kinds of Fiction, 1880–1920," in *Literary History of Canada*, 3 vols., 2nd ed., eds. Carl F. Klinck et al. (Toronto: University of Toronto Press 1976), 1: 350.

19 See Pacey, "Leacock as a Satirist," 211, and Robertson Davies, "Stephen Leacock," in *Our Living Tradition*, First Series, ed. Claude T. Bissell (Toronto: University of Toronto Press 1957), 147.

20 Curry, *Stephen Leacock*, 88.

21 See David M. Legate, *Stephen Leacock* (Toronto: Doubleday 1970), 79, 81, 186, 247; see also Davies, *Stephen Leacock*, 28, who writes that "in his faith in progress Leacock was very much a Victorian – a surprisingly simple Victorian."

22 See Jerome H. Buckley, *The Victorian Temper* (London: Frank Cass 1952), 9; see also G.M. Young, *Portrait of an Age*, 2nd ed., ed. George Kitson Clark (London: Oxford 1977), 154.

23 Cameron, *Faces of Leacock*, 4–5; cf. Carl Berger, "Other Mr. Leacock," *Canadian Literature* 55 (Winter 1973): 38.

24 Stephen Leacock, *The Boy I Left Behind Me* (Garden City, N.Y.: Doubleday 1946), 9.

25 Cameron, *Faces of Leacock*, 15.

26 Ibid.

27 Stephen Leacock, *The Hohenzollerns in America* (Toronto: S.B. Gundy;

New York: John Lane 1919), 232.

28 Stephen Leacock, "Mariposa Moves On," in *Happy Stories – just to Laugh at* (New York: Dodd, Mead 1943; rpt. London: John Lane 1945), 197–202.

29 Stephen Leacock, "Greater Canada: An Appeal," *University Magazine* (McGill) 6 (April 1907): 136.

30 Stephen Leacock, *My Discovery of the West* (London: John Lane 1937), 306–7. The closing reference to "youth" seems to echo the sentiments of Benjamin Disraeli's "Young England" association, as does much of Leacock's toryism recall Disraeli's. B.N. Langdon-Davies (in his introduction to Benjamin Disraeli's *Coningsby* [1844; rpt. London: Everyman-Dent 1967], xiii) describes the Young England association as follows: "The power, the inspiration, the splendour of 'glittering youth' was its first belief, and perhaps this fundamental article of its creed has had the greatest influence of all as the years have gone on."

31 Cameron, *Faces of Leacock*, 16.

32 Ibid.

33 Leacock, "Greater Canada," 139.

34 See T.H. Huxley, *Evolution and Ethics* (1894; rpt. *Collected Essays*, New York: Verlag 1970), ix, 80–94.

35 Cf. William H. Magee, "Genial Humour in Stephen Leacock," *Dalhousie Review* 56 (Summer 1976): 269.

36 Stephen Leacock, *Elements of Political Science* (New York: Houghton-Mifflin 1906; rev. 1921); Stephen Leacock, *Baldwin, Lafontaine, Hincks: Responsible Government*, Makers of Canada no. 14 (Toronto: Morang 1907; rpt. 1910).

37 Leacock's use here of "abolition" with reference to poverty is interesting. In *Lincoln Frees the Slaves* (New York: Putnam 1934), 13, he argues that slavery was tolerated by nineteenth-century Americans of the South because "it was to them as poverty is to us."

38 For Leacock's laudatory opinion of Carlyle, see Leacock, *Elements of Political Science*, 368–9; see also Leacock, "What Is Left of Adam Smith?" 46.

39 Thomas Carlyle, *Past and Present*, in *The Works of Thomas Carlyle in Thirty Volumes* (New York: AMS 1969), x, 7; the two subsequent quotations are from 1 and 6 respectively.

40 Ibid., 23.

41 See ibid., 23–4.

42 Alice Chandler, *A Dream of Order* (Lincoln: University of Nebraska Press 1970), 140; interestingly, Chandler, 151, remarks Carlyle's "paradoxical Tory-radicalism."

43 Leacock, "Greater Canada," 132.

44 Cameron, *Faces of Leacock*, 2.

45 Leacock wrote a great deal on the question of "the Empire." In addition to the previously noted "Greater Canada: An Appeal," and "An Apology for the British Empire," see the following works by Leacock: "Britain and Canada: Old Phases and New" (*LL*, 61–70); *Economic Prosperity in the British Empire* (Toronto: Macmillan 1930); *Back to Prosperity: The Great Opportunity of the Empire Conference* (Toronto: Macmillan 1932); *The British Empire* (New York: Dodd, Mead 1940); *Canada: The Foundations Of Its Future* (Montreal: [Privately printed for the House of Seagram by the Gazette Printing Co.] 1941), 243–50; see also Carl Berger, *The Sense of Power: Studies in the Ideas of Canadian Imperialism, 1867–1914* (Toronto: University of Toronto Press 1970), and Berger's "Other Mr. Leacock," *Canadian Literature* 55 (Winter 1973): 23–40.

46 Carlyle, *Works*, x, 11.

47 See Desmond Bowen, *The Idea of the Victorian Church*, vii–ix.

48 Curry, *Stephen Leacock*, 87.

49 Leacock, an Arnoldian hero-worshipper of a kind, felt himself to be akin to John Stuart Mill (*RU*, 70). He considered Mill's *Liberty* (1859) to be "the best expression ever given to the reasoned idea of individual liberty, enjoyed in association with one's fellows" (*HL*, 48).

50 Elizabeth Kimball, *The Man in the Panama Hat* (Toronto: McClelland and Stewart 1970), 77; see further 66.

51 Stephen Leacock, *Hellements of Hickonomics* (New York: Dodd, Mead 1936), 79. The *Hellements* enacts what Leacock here espouses. The book is a collection of humorous verses which deal with serious economic theories. Moreover, the title is to some extent a burlesque of Leacock's first and financially most successful book, the workmanlike text, *Elements of Political Science*.

52 Cf. Matthew Arnold, "Doing As One Likes," in *Culture and Anarchy* (1869. rpt. in *Matthew Arnold*, ed. R.H. Super, Ann Arbor, Mich.: University of Michigan Press 1965), 115–36.

53 See George Grant, *Technology and Empire* (Toronto: Anansi 1969). Grant is the grandson of George Parkin, who was influential in the formation of Leacock's imperialist thinking. Moreover, Leacock was a friend of Grant's father, William Grant, the long-time principal of Queen's University. In Taylor's *Radical Tories*, 136, George Grant relates an amusing anecdote: "Mr. Leacock would come to our house and father would get him to swear – just to annoy mother. Once we were walking past an imposing building in Montreal [likely the University Club which Leacock was instrumental in founding] and my mother said with great disapproval: 'You know, Mr. Leacock spends his *life* in that club.'"

54 Samuel Taylor Coleridge, "*Conciones ad Populum*," in *The Friend*, 4th ed., ed. H.N. Coleridge (London: William Pickering 1844), ii, 192.

55 Carlyle, *Works*, x, 57.
56 Samuel Taylor Coleridge, *On the Constitution of the Church and State* (London: Hurst, Chance 1830), 17; see further 124, Coleridge's description of the "'State,' ... where the integral parts, classes, or orders are so balanced, or interdependent, as to constitute, more or less, a moral unit, an organic whole."
57 Stephen Leacock, *Funny Pieces* (1936; rpt. London: John Lane 1937), 295.
58 The paraphrase is of Coleridge, *"Conciones ad Populum,"* 196, wherein Coleridge turns "with pleasure" from considering radicals and "democrats" to "the contemplation of that small but glorious band, whom we may truly distinguish by the name of thinking and disinterested patriots."
59 Stephen Leacock, *Too Much College* (New York: Dodd, Mead 1941), 50–1; cf. Edmund Burke, *Reflections on the Revolution in France* (1790; rpt. London: Everyman-Dent 1967), 31: "People will not look forward to posterity, who never look backward to their ancestors."
60 See Stephen Leacock, "Come On Up," *McGill News* 22 (Summer 1941): 20, wherein Leacock writes of R.B. Bennett's departure to England following the resounding victory of Mackenzie King's Liberals in 1940: "There are only two Conservatives left, and one of them is in England."

CHAPTER TWO

1 Stephen Leacock, "Humour As I See It: And Something About Humour In Canada," *Maclean's*, May 1916, 113. See also *RU*, 146.
2 Matthew Arnold, *Culture and Anarchy* (1869; rpt. in *Matthew Arnold*, ed. R.H. Super, Ann Arbor, Mich.: University of Michigan Press 1965), 129.
3 See *ELS*, 155: "The half-truth is to me a kind of mellow moonlight in which I love to dwell. One sees better in it." See also Stephen Leacock, *The Garden of Folly* (Toronto: S.B. Gundy 1924), x: "A half truth, like half a brick, is always more forcible as an argument than a whole one. It carries further."
4 See Matthew Hodgart, *Satire* (New York: McGraw-Hill 1969) and Robert C. Elliott, *The Power of Satire: Magic, Ritual, Art* (Princeton N.J.: Princeton University Press 1960).
5 See, for instances, David M. Legate, *Stephen Leacock: A Biography* (Toronto: Doubleday 1970), 206; Robertson Davies, *Stephen Leacock*, vol. 7, Canadian Writers Series (Toronto: McClelland and Stewart 1970), 38–9; Donald Cameron, *Faces of Leacock* (Toronto: Ryerson 1967), 54–60; and William H. Magee, "Genial Humour in Stephen Leacock," *Dalhou-*

sie Review 56 (Summer 1976): 268–82.

6 To take examples from but one of Leacock's annual collections, see Stephen Leacock, *Short Circuits* (New York: Dodd, Mead 1923), 91, 95, 130, 149.

7 Leacock, *Short Circuits*, 149. Cf. *Hamlet*.I.ii.65: "A little more than kin and less than kind."

8 Malcolm Ross, pref., *Sunshine Sketches of a Little Town*, New Canadian Library, no. 15 (Toronto: McClelland and Stewart 1970), xi.

9 Aristotle, *Poetics*, ed. and trans. S.H. Butcher (London: Macmillan 1920), V.1.

10 Thomas Hobbes, *Leviathan* (1651; rpt. ed. C.B. MacPherson, Harmondsworth: Pelican-Penguin 1968), 125.

11 See Arthur Koestler, *Act of Creation* (London: Hutchinson 1964), 40–6.

12 William Hazlitt, *Lectures on the English Comic Writers* (1819; rpt. New York: Russell and Russell 1969), 6–7 The following quotation is from 1.

13 Ibid., 16.

14 Ibid.

15 Hazlitt, *Lectures on the English Comic Writers*, 38.

16 Ibid., 49–50.

17 Ibid., 48–9. For an instance of the same in Leacock, see Stephen Leacock, *Further Foolishness* (Toronto: S.B. Gundy; London: John Lane 1916), 308.

18 Hazlitt, *Lectures on the English Comic Writers*, 43.

19 The irony of Leacock's remark is that he was, as Ralph Curry, *Stephen Leacock: Humorist and Humanist* (Garden City, N.Y.: Doubleday 1959), 178, has observed, one of the *Encyclopaedia Britannica's* "important contributors" (beginning with the 1926 edition).

20 William Makepeace Thackeray, "Charity and Humour," in *The English Humorists, Charity and Humour, The Four Georges*, ed. M.R. Ridley (New York: Dutton 1968), 270. The following quotations are from 283, 285, and 280 respectively.

21 George Meredith, *An Essay On Comedy* (1897; rpt. in *Comedy*, ed. Wylie Sypher, Garden City, N.Y.: Doubleday 1956), 32. The following quotations are from 33, 37, 42, 48, and 44 respectively.

22 Northrop Frye, *Anatomy of Criticism* (1957; rpt. Princeton, N.J.: Princeton University Press 1971), 223.

23 Meredith, *An Essay on Comedy*, 44.

24 Jonathan Swift, preface to *Battle of the Books* (1770; rpt. in *The Writings of Jonathan Swift*, eds. Robert A. Greenberg and William Bowman Piper, New York: Norton 1973), 375.

25 Henri Bergson, *Le Rire* (1900; rpt. in *Comedy*, ed. and trans. Wylie Sypher), 84.

26 Ibid., 73. The following quotations are from 148 and 189 respectively.

27 Bergson's *Le Rire* is also listed in the bibliography of *Humour and Humanity* (*HH*, 249).

28 Bergson, *Le Rire*, 189–90.

29 Leacock's remark recalls Samuel Taylor Coleridge, *Table Talk*, 25 August 1833: "To resolve laughter into an expression of contempt is contrary to fact, and laughable enough," in *The Table Talk and Omniana*, ed. T. Ashe (London: George Belle 1888), 256.

30 Sigmund Freud, *Wit and Its Relation to the Unconscious*, trans. Dr. A.A. Brill (New York: The Modern Library 1938), 663. The following quotations and paraphrases are from and of 646, 693, 695, 773, 801, and 802 respectively.

31 An analogy can be drawn between Freud's three-party structure and the writer-characters-reader relationship, an analogy which can be understood in terms of the satirist humiliating his characters to give pleasure to the reader.

32 See, for instance, Leacock, *Further Foolishness*, 312.

33 See also *HH*, 22: "Our sense of humour, like so much else about us, sprang from lowly and even discreditable origins."

34 Cf. T.H. Huxley, *Evolution and Ethics* (1894; rpt. *Collected Essays*, New York: Verlag 1970), ix, 80–4.

35 Cameron, *Faces of Leacock*, 57; see 166–7 for a misapplication of Freudian psycho-sexual theory to Leacock's work; see also Davies, *Stephen Leacock*, 51.

36 Stephen Leacock, *Winnowed Wisdom* (New York: Dodd, Mead 1926; rpt. New Canadian Library no 74, Toronto: McClelland and Stewart 1971), vii–ix.

37 See Stephen Leacock, *The Hohenzollerns in America* (London: John Lane; Toronto: S.B. Gundy 1919), 9–72.

38 Charles Taylor, *Radical Tories* (Toronto: Anansi 1982), 106.

39 Frye, *Anatomy*, 223.

40 Ibid.

41 A scholarly study of the rise of the kindly humour that concerns Leacock can be read in Stuart M. Tave's *The Amiable Humorist: A Study in the Comic Theory and Criticism of the Eighteenth and Early Nineteenth Centuries* (Chicago: University of Chicago Press 1960). It is not the intent of the present chapter to cover ground that Tave has mapped so thoroughly; rather, my purpose is to analyze Leacock's relation to the tradition of "amiable humour" as that tradition extends (and as Leacock extended it) well into the twentieth century.

42 Leacock's dissertation, "The Doctrine of *Laissez-Faire*," is not available for examination.

43 Stephen Leacock, *Behind the Beyond* (1913; rpt. New Canadian Library no. 67, Toronto: McClelland and Stewart 1969), 124. The quotation

following is from 125.

44 Douglas Bush, "Stephen Leacock," in *The Canadian Imagination*, ed. David Staines (Cambridge: Harvard University Press 1977),150.

45 Interestingly, John Milton's assessment of "grim laughter," preface, *Animadversions*, in *The Works of John Milton* (New York: Columbia University Press 1931), iii, 108, anticipates Freud's analysis of wit and Leacock's of puns and epigrammatic verse. Milton justifies "grim laughter" as a "close and succinct manner of coping with the adversary," and as the "speediest way to see the truth vindicated."

46 Walter Allen, *The English Novel* (London: Phoenix House 1954), 71.

47 Henry Fielding, preface, *Joseph Andrews* (1742; rpt. in *Joseph Andrews and Shamela*, ed. Martin C. Battestin, Boston: Houghton Mifflin-Riverside 1961), 10.

48 The efficaciousness of Swift's "Drapier's Letters" would be a case in point. See Hodgart, *Satire*, 31: "The satirist appears in his noblest role when he accepts the challenge of oblivion, by taking on an ephemeral and unpleasant topic."

49 Samuel Taylor Coleridge, "Conciones ad Populum," in *The Friend*, 4th ed., ed. H.N. Coleridge (London: William Pickering 1844), ii, 189. See further ii, 190: "The ardor of undisciplined benevolence seduces us into malignity: and whenever our hearts are warm, and our objects great and excellent, intolerance is the sin that does most easily beset us."

50 See G.K. Chesterton, "Antichrist, Or the Reunion of Christendom: An Ode," in *Poems* (London: Burns and Oates 1915), 87–9.

51 In a similar defence of Dickens' method of characterization, Northrop Frye, *Anatomy*, 134, writes, "Some readers will complain that Dickens has relapsed into 'mere' caricature (as though caricature were easy): others, more sensibly, simply give up the criterion of lifelikeness and enjoy the creation for its own sake."

52 Leacock insists that Dickens could, when he chose, write as realistically as de Maupassant and Zola. Of Dickens' description of a guillotine execution in *Pictures From Italy*, Leacock advises, "Students of the literature of the nineteenth century who contrast the 'romanticism' of 1840 with the 'realism' of 1890 may mark these [quoted passages] with interest" (*CD*, 120).

53 See Eugene Current-Garcia and Walter R. Patrick, eds., *Realism and Romanticism in Fiction* (Chicago: Scott, Foresman 1962), 27–8. In his discussion of realism (*HTW*, 100), Leacock notes that "French writers and French critics have analyzed and discussed this aspect of fiction far more than we have in English, and have been far more self-conscious in regard to it."

54 See Jerome H. Buckley, *The Victorian Temper* (London: Frank Cass,

1952), 8–12.

55 Leacock, *Winnowed Wisdom*, 116.

56 Arnold, *Culture and Anarchy*, 135.

57 *Longinus on the Sublime*, ed. and trans. W.R. Roberts (Cambridge: Cambridge University Press 1907), 43.

58 In conversation with the author.

59 Elizabeth Kimball, *The Man in the Panama Hat* (Toronto: McClelland and Stewart 1970), 170, relates that Leacock's younger brother, Charlie, startled a few late-assembled commiserators after Leacock's funeral by remarking that Leacock "was a man, I tell you, of terrible despairs, ... a man beset with doubts."

60 Buckley, *The Victorian Temper*, 181. Leacock (*ELS*, 92) quotes Pater in support of his view that wit is subservient to humour.

CHAPTER THREE

1 See D.O. Spettigue, "A Partisan Reading of Leacock," *The Literary Half-Yearly* 13 (July 1972): 172.

2 Here, Leacock is contrasting "the new moral code, ... the simple worship of success" to "the morality which ... was essentially altruistic."

3 See Spettigue, "A Partisan Reading of Leacock," 172–3.

4 Ralph Curry, *Stephen Leacock* (Garden City, N.Y.: Doubleday 1959), 108.

5 See Forrest L. Ingram, *Representative Short Story Cycles of the Twentieth Century* (The Hague: Mouton 1971).

6 William H. Magee, "Stephen Leacock, Local Colourist," *Canadian Literature* 39 (Winter 1969): 38.

7 Northrop Frye, introd., *The Stepsure Letters*, by Thomas McCulloch, New Canadian Library no. 16 (Toronto: McClelland and Stewart 1960), ix.

8 Donald Cameron, *Faces of Leacock* (Toronto: Ryerson 1967), 134.

9 Northrop Frye, "Conclusion to a *Literary History of Canada*," in *The Bush Garden* (Toronto: Anansi 1971), 237.

10 See Desmond Pacey, "Leacock as a Satirist," *Queen's Quarterly* 58 (Summer 1951): 214: the "flaws in Mariposa life are chiefly things which ... arise from a misguided desire to ape the cities."

11 See Michael S. Cross, "A General Interpretation of Social Disorder on the Timber Frontier," in *The Frontier Thesis and the Canadas*, Issues in Canadian History, ed. Michael S. Cross (Toronto: Copp, Clark 1970), 100–3.

12 Leacock, who felt that he had no talent for contriving plots, revealed that the plots of his stories are always subordinated to characterization. Of *Sunshine Sketches* he remarked, "Such feeble plots as there are

in this book were invented by brute force, after the characters had been introduced." Quoted in Peter McArthur, *Stephen Leacock* (Toronto: Ryerson 1923), 136. Cf. *CD*, 109.

13 See, for instance, Stephen Leacock, *Economic Prosperity in the British Empire* (Toronto: Macmillan 1930), 149–70.

14 In his reduction of *Sunshine Sketches* to mean-spirited satire, Robertson Davies ("Stephen Leacock," in *Our Living Tradition*, First Series, ed. Claude T. Bissell [Toronto: University of Toronto Press 1957], 147), concludes that the Mariposans are a "self-important, gullible, only moderately honest collection of provincial folk; they cooked their election, they burned down a church." But it is Josh Smith who "cooks" the election and burns down the church.

15 See B.K. Sandwell, "Leacock Recalled: How the 'Sketches' Started," *Saturday Night*, Aug. 1952, 7.

16 The departure scene in "The Marine Excursion" bears a striking resemblance to the opening of chapter thirteen, "The Departure," in Alphonse Daudet's *Tartarin of Tarascon* (1872: rpt. in *Tartarin of Tarascon and Tartarin of the Alps*, trans. Jean-Pierre Richard, London: Everyman-Dent 1961), 27–9. Leacock greatly admired Daudet's *Tartarin* books (and it may be that Daudet's Christian name suggested the name for Josh Smith's "French Chief," Alphonse). He paid Daudet his highest literary compliment, observing that Tartarin "is Daudet's own, absolutely and triumphantly, but he is also a Dickens character, fit to sit beside the best of them" (*CD*, 189). It may be also that the oral quality of Leacock's fiction owes something to Daudet as well as to Mark Twain (the most obvious influence in this regard), and that Leacock's talent for caricature owes something to Daudet as well as to Dickens.

There are many noteworthy similarities between *Tartarin* and the *Sketches*. But it must suffice to consider the Mariposans in light of Leacock's appraisal of Daudet's *Midi*:

Reduced to a simple formula, as it often is, Daudet's picture of the "midi" is made to read that in Southern France all the people lie and exaggerate and bluff. That isn't it at all. Like all formulas it perverts truth by condensation. What Daudet meant was that in the South they live in a super-world, like children playing games: a world where they can believe anything they want to believe, and where emphasis lies not on actuality but on appearance: not on whether a thing is or is not so (a matter of no consequence), but on how it sounds (*HTT*, 149).

17 Cameron, *Faces of Leacock*, 128.

18 It is generally accepted that Orillia, Ontario, inspired the conception of Mariposa. Stephen Leacock, *Canada: The Foundations Of Its Future* (Montreal: [privately printed for the House of Seagram by the Gazette

Printing Co.] 1941), 36, writes that "foreign words were now and then dropped on to our map without trace of origin; as witness the Spanish 'Orillia' that fell mercifully out of the sky as an improvement over Champlain's 'Cahiagué.'" *Mariposa* is the Spanish word for "butterfly," which is a favourable image, suggesting, as it does, an organism that is colourful, beautiful, and delicate. *Sunshine Sketches* (as the second word of its title might suggest) at once partakes of, "explodes" the conventions of, and is the artistic fulfilment of the local-colour tradition of the turn of the century. Although not especially delicate, the organic integrity of Mariposa is, as has been shown, threatened by brutalities which are personified by Josh Smith. See David M. Legate, *Stephen Leacock* (Toronto: Doubleday 1970), 62, who has discovered that Leacock took the name "Mariposa" from "a little-known settlement, a stone's throw from Orillia, which had existed before he had come to Canada as a child."

CHAPTER FOUR

1 Edmund Burke, *Reflections on the Revolution in France* (1790; rpt. New York: Dutton 1967), 93; the following quotation is from 31.

2 Malcolm Ross, "A Strange Aesthetic Ferment," *Canadian Literature* 68–9 (Spring/Summer 1976): 17.

3 Stephen Leacock, *Sunshine Sketches of a Little Town*, New Canadian Library no. 15 (Toronto: McClelland and Stewart 1960), 60, misprints the comparative "larger" as "large."

4 Russell Brown and Donna Bennett, eds., *An Anthology of Canadian Literature in English* (Toronto: Oxford University Press 1982), i, 240, n. 3. The editors give the incorrect biblical reference, "I Kings 3:5."

5 Ibid., i, 243, n. 7.

6 In its original version in *The Montreal Star*, 30 March 1912, Sec. 2, 42, col. 8, "The Beacon on the Hill" was part of the installment entitled "Mariposa's Whirlwind Campaign." There, the sketch ended with the second-to-last paragraph of "The Beacon" (147), with the observation that Drone "can read with the greatest ease works in the Greek that seemed difficult before. Because his head is so clear now." The New Canadian Library edition of *Sunshine Sketches*, 86, mispunctuates the final sentence of this penultimate paragraph, replacing the second-to-last period with a comma, and thus turns the last sentence of the paragraph into a subordinate clause. The original version, by setting apart the "because" clause as the concluding sentence, emphasizes the questionable "clarity" of Drone's post-stroke mind.

7 See Dr C.H. Hale, *Orillia Packet and Times*, 12 March 1957, quoted in Robertson Davies, *Stephen Leacock*, vol. 7, Canadian Writers Series (To-

ronto: McClelland and Stewart 1970), 26–7. See also Elizabeth Kimball, *The Man in the Panama Hat* (Toronto: McClelland and Stewart 1970), 91.

8 Leacock's appraisal of the *Midi* of Alphonse Daudet's *Tartarin* books reads like a description of the Mariposans of the Whirlwind Campaign: "The Tartarin people live on delusions of greatness: on the least pretext they send delegations of congratulations, read addresses to one another, hold celebrations, fire off guns, and set up floral arches of welcome ... There is a contrast between the luxuriant beauty of their home, and the fact that they refuse to keep still in it. This riot of the mind, this exuberant fancy, this victory over truth finds its summation in Tartarin" (*HTT*, 150).

9 See *HH*, 39: "Exactly the converse to the Face Value form is found when words and phrases are rushed forward into a significance which they won't bear on closer inspection. ... The author of the present work ... has probably made more extended use of this than any other person who has written as copiously."

10 Northrop Frye, introd., *The Stepsure Letters*, by Thomas McCulloch, New Canadian Library no. 16 (Toronto: McClelland and Stewart 1960), vi.

11 Stephen Leacock, *Too Much College* (New York: Dodd, Mead 1941), 179, offers the following definitions: "GLADSTONE – a bag, travelling bag with a specially wide mouth"; and "BISMARCK – a specially fat German rump steak, not popular now." Leacock's opinion of President Taft can best be deduced from the fact that it was Taft who in 1911 initiated the discussion of a reciprocal trade agreement between Canada and the United States. Reciprocity became the central issue of the bitterly fought Canadian general election of 1911, during which Leacock spoke and wrote against reciprocity with the United States, thereby assisting the defeat of Prime Minister Laurier's Liberal government.

12 Thomas Carlyle, *Sartor Resartus, The Works of Thomas Carlyle in Thirty Volumes* (New York: AMS 1969), 1, 129.

13 John Milton, preface, *Animadversions*, in *The Works* (New York: Columbia University Press 1931), iii, 108.

14 Jerome H. Buckley, *The Victorian Temper* (London: Frank Cass 1952), 234.

15 See Gordon Roper, Rupert Schieder and S. Ross Beharriell, "The Kinds of Fiction, 1880–1920," in *Literary History of Canada*, 3 vols., 2nd ed., eds. Carl F. Klinck et al. (Toronto: University of Toronto Press 1976), 1, 352: "The feeling expressed with such fine modulation in 'L'Envoi: The Train to Mariposa' ... is much more prevalent than is the feeling 'You can't go home again.'"

16 See Al Purdy, "The Country North of Belleville," in *Selected Poems* (Toronto: McClelland and Stewart 1972), 118–19.

17 When the train carrying a weary Tartarin home from his mock-heroic adventures arrives in Tarascon, two words are shouted, "Tarascon! Tarascon!" I should also note here that my term "Maripocentric" owes something to Daudet's frequently used word for a similar manner of thought and action in Tarascon, the *"Tarasconnade,"* as well as owing something to Dickens' "in a Pickwickian sense."

18 The phrase "circle of affection" is Duncan Campbell Scott's, *The Circle of Affection* (Toronto: McClelland and Stewart 1947). To repeat, Leacock as prefacer claims that any "fault" of *Sunshine Sketches* "lies rather with an art that is deficient than in an affection that is wanting" (*SS*, xii).

19 "The Country of the Ought to be" was Archibald Lampman's intended subtitle to his poem, "The Land of Pallus"; see Richard Arnold, "The Clearer Self: Lampman's Transcendental-Visionary Development," *Canadian Poetry: Studies, Documents, Reviews* no. 8 (Spring/Summer 1981): 50; the second phrase is from Lampman's "The Land of Pallus," in *The Poems of Archibald Lampman*, ed. Margaret Coulby Whitridge, Literature of Canada, Series 12 (Toronto: University of Toronto Press 1974), 209.

20 Margaret Avison, "Snow," in *Winter Sun* (Toronto: University of Toronto Press 1960), 17.

CHAPTER FIVE

1 See the following: Desmond Pacey, "Leacock as a Satirist," *Queen's Quarterly* 58 (1951): 208–19; Donald Cameron, *Faces of Leacock* (Toronto: Ryerson 1967), 102–37; Ramsay Cook, "Stephen Leacock and the Age of Plutocracy, 1903–1921," in *Character and Circumstance*, ed. J. Moir (Toronto: University of Toronto Press 1970), 163–81; Douglas Spettigue, "A Partisan Reading of Leacock," *The Literary Half-Yearly* 13 (1972): 171–80; J. Kushner and R.D. Macdonald, "Leacock: Economist/Satirist in *Arcadian Adventures* and *Sunshine Sketches*," *Dalhousie Review* 56 (1976): 493–509; Tom Marshall, "False Pastoral: Stephen Leacock's Conflicting Worlds," *Journal of Canadian Fiction* no. 19 (1977): 86–94.

2 See, for examples, Leacock's prefaces to his *The Hohenzollerns in America* (Toronto: S.B. Gundy; New York: John Lane 1919), 9–10; *College Days* (Toronto: S.B. Gundy 1923), 7–8; *The Garden of Folly* (Toronto: S.B. Gundy 1924), v–x; *Hellements of Hickonomics* (New York: Dodd, Mead 1936), v–x; *Here Are My Lectures* (London: John Lane 1938), vii–x; *The British Empire* (New York: Dodd, Mead 1940), v–vi; *Too Much College* (New York: Dodd, Mead 1941), vii–ix; and *HTW*, v–vii.

3 Northrop Frye, *Anatomy of Criticism* (1957; rpt. Princeton N.J.: Prince-

ton University Press 1971), 223.

4 See Spettigue, "A Partisan Reading of Leacock," 173, who discusses some parallels between the *Sketches* and *Adventures*.

5 Claude Bissell, "Haliburton, Leacock and the American Humorous Tradition," *Canadian Literature* 39 (Winter 1969): 14. For Leacock's ambivalent appraisal of Veblen, see Stephen Leacock, *My Discovery of the West* (London: John Lane 1937), 171–4.

6 The compounds "money-getting" and "money-hunger," which will be used intermittently throughout this chapter, were suggested by Leacock's description of Shucksford College's President Snide, who is similar to *Arcadian Adventures'* President Boomer. "Alert, keen," writes Leacock of President Snide, "with every faculty awake – with a figure as erect at fifty as at twenty-five – the president's appearance was that of the ideal money-getter. There was something in the firmness of his face and in his keen intelligent eye which suggested the getting of money, while his long prehensile hand, with every finger joint working to perfection, suggested the keeping, or retention of it." Stephen Leacock, "RAH! RAH! COLLEGE," in *Afternoons in Utopia* (London: John Lane 1932), 153. See also *SS*, 263: "money-getting in the city."

7 Alexis de Tocqueville, *Democracy in America*, trans. George Lawrence, eds. J.-P. Mayer and Max Lerner (Garden City, N.Y.: Anchor-Doubleday 1969), 258.

8 Tomlinson's Creek is located in "Cahoga County" (56), "on a windy hillside beside Lake Erie" (113). In *The Hohenzollerns In America*, 158, Leacock writes of a "retired farmer of Cuyahoga, Ohio," which is a county of Ohio. Cleveland is the County Seat of Cuyahoga. Although the City of *Arcadian Adventures* has most often been taken for either Montreal or Toronto, it seems that Leacock would rather it be Cleveland.

9 Spettigue, "A Partisan Reading of Leacock," 178.

10 Stephen Leacock, "Democracy and Social Progress," in *The New Era in Canada*, ed. J.O. Miller (London: Dent 1957), 15–16.

11 Al Purdy, ed., *The New Romans* (Edmonton: Hurtig 1968).

12 See Stephen Leacock, *Lincoln Frees the Slaves* (New York: G.P. Putnam's Sons 1934), 51–83, and Stephen Leacock, "Forging the Fifteenth Amendment," in *Over the Footlights* (New York: Dodd, Mead 1923), 149–51.

13 Stephen Leacock, *Canada* (Montreal: [Privately printed] 1941), 245.

14 Cf. Leacock, *The Hohenzollerns in America*, 9: "The proper punishment for the Hohenzollerns, and the Hapsburgs, and the Mecklenburgs, and the Muckendorfs, and all such puppets and princelings, is that they should be made to work."

15 See Leacock, *Lincoln Frees the Slaves*, 54, 82, 96–7, 105, 108–9, 115–16,

123, 132, 145, 149–60.

16 Thorstein Veblen, *The Theory of the Leisure Class* (New York: Macmillan 1899), 68–101.

17 Leacock, *The Hohenzollerns in America*, 264–9.

18 See Leacock, *Too Much College*, vii; and Leacock, "Oxford As I See It," in *My Discovery of England* (1922; rpt. New Canadian Library no. 28, Toronto: McClelland and Stewart 1961), 71–96.

19 Veblen, *The Theory of the Leisure Class*, 22–67.

20 Tom Marshall, "False Pastoral," 89, suggests that Sikleigh Snoop, in his relation to Mrs Rasselyer-Brown, may be based upon Bliss Carman in his relation to Mary Perry King. Marshall writes that Leacock would have been satirizing the "popular image of Bliss Carman," though he does remark the parallel between King's role in Carman's adoption of "unitrinianism" and Snoop's conversion to "Boohooism." Marshall suggests further that Snoop may also be based on Swinburne. If Marshall had pursued his second suspicion, he would have found it more convincing than the Carman connection. Snoop "exquisitely" expresses the difference between Mrs Rasselyer-Brown and her daughter Dulphemia as "the difference between a Burne-Jones and a Dante Gabriel Rossetti" (123). Dulphemia is, in fact, described as a "Blessed Damozel" of a kind: she has "beautiful golden hair parted in thick bands on her forehead, and deep blue eyes soft as an Italian sky" (123). Rossetti was the founding spirit behind the "Pre-Raphaelite Brotherhood" and a friend of Swinburne. It is to be doubted, though, that Swinburne is the specific target of the satire on Snoop, or that Leacock had any specific target in mind. Leacock preferred a broader kind of satire. He may, however, have had the Pre-Raphaelites in mind as a compound target. The epithet "sex-poet" (119) does conjure up visions of a "fleshly school."

21 See Stephen Leacock, *Other People's Money* (Montreal: Royal Trust Co. 1947), 7, wherein Leacock observes that "a trustee, according to the old-fashioned Victorian novels, was a man to whom no one should ever have entrusted a shilling."

22 The satire on the Newberrys' manner of "roughing it" (166) at Castel Casteggio may contain a veiled attack upon Leacock's wife's uncle, Sir Henry Pellatt. David Legate, *Stephen Leacock* (Toronto: Doubleday 1970), 203–4, writes that Pellatt squandered his niece's inheritance on the construction of Toronto's famed "Casa Loma." Leacock was incensed at Pellatt's wasteful extravagance because his son, Stephen, Jr, became the legatee upon the death of Mrs Leacock in 1925.

CHAPTER SIX

1 Ralph Curry, introd., *Arcadian Adventures*, New Canadian Library no. 10 (Toronto: McClelland and Stewart 1969), x.

2 Robertson Davies, *Stephen Leacock*, vol. 7, Canadian Writers Series, (Toronto: McClelland and Stewart 1970), 30.

3 Donald Cameron, *Faces of Leacock* (Toronto: Ryerson 1967), 114.

4 Alice Chandler, *A Dream of Order* (Lincoln, Neb.: University of Nebraska Press 1970), 6. See T.J. Jackson Lears, *No Place of Grace: Antimodernism and the Transformation of American Culture, 1880–1920* (New York: Pantheon 1981), 198–215.

5 See Stephen Leacock, *My Discovery of the West* (London: John Lane 1937), 62: "There was created a sort of economic vacuum, and the air, an inblowing of men and goods, came rushing in."

6 Stephen Leacock, *Too Much College* (New York: Dodd, Mead 1939), 114. Leacock misquotes Milton's line, which should read, "found no end, in wand'ring mazes lost" (II.561).

7 See Northrop Frye, *The Anatomy of Criticism* (1957; rpt. Princeton, N.J.: Princeton University Press 1971), 182–3, for a succinct discussion of this pattern. Were this pattern to be faithfully followed, the lovers of *Arcadian Adventures* would have had to escape to what Frye calls the "green world." They would have to meet clandestinely in some such place as Tomlinson's farm and return to the court of Plutoria to revitalize its rigidly decadent society.

8 Glenn Clever, "Leacock's Dunciad," *Studies in Canadian Literature* 1 (Summer 1976): 238–41.

9 Stephen Leacock, *The Boy I Left Behind Me* (Garden City, N.Y.: Doubleday 1946), 84; Leacock proceeds, 85, to note his "underlying Jeffersonian republicanism."

10 Tom Marshall, "False Pastoral: Stephen Leacock's Conflicting Worlds," *Journal of Canadian Fiction* no. 19 (1977): 93.

11 Matthew Hodgart, *Satire* (New York: McGraw-Hill 1969), 126.

12 Henry Fielding, "Author's Preface," *Joseph Andrews*, in *Joseph Andrews and Shamela*, ed. Martin C. Battestin (Boston: Riverside-Houghton Mifflin 1961), 11.

13 See George Orwell, "Politics and the English Language," in *The Collected Essays, Journalism and Letters of George Orwell*, eds. Sonia Orwell and Ian Angus (London: Secker and Warburg 1968), iv, 127–40. In "Funny But Not Vulgar," in *The Collected*, iii, 283, Orwell considers Leacock in the company of P.G. Wodehouse, H.G. Wells ("in his lighter moments"), and Evelyn Waugh.

14 Orwell, "Politics and the English Language," iv, 137.

15 Ibid., 139.

16 Stephen Leacock, *The Hohenzollerns in America* (New York: John Lane; Toronto: S.B. Gundy 1919), 232.
17 See H.V. Nelles and Christopher Armstrong, "'The Great Fight for Clean Government,'" *Urban History Review* no. 2 (Oct. 1976): 50–66. Not a piece of literary criticism, Nelles' and Armstrong's well-documented study of the movement for municipal reform, 1880–1920, uses Leacock as a fictional gloss to show that the reform movement in Canada was not the plutocratic grab for power that it was in the United States. In short, *Arcadian Adventures* would not have been faithful to the facts had it been set in a Canadian city; moreover, Nelles' and Armstrong's study shows that Leacock was not overly exaggerating the situation as it existed in the US. Jackson Lear's, *No Place of Grace*, 198–215, shows similarly that Leacock's treatment of Fareforth Furlong's Episcopal (Anglican) dandyism is not as exaggerated as readers might have presumed.
18 Hodgart, *Satire*, 214.

CHAPTER SEVEN

1 Cf. J.B. Priestly, introd., *The Bodley Head Leacock* (1957; rpt. Toronto: McClelland and Stewart 1969).
2 Stephen Leacock, *Back to Prosperity: The Great Opportunity of the Empire Conference* (London: Constable 1932), 101.
3 David M. Legate, *Stephen Leacock: A Biography* (Toronto: Doubleday 1970), 248.
4 Stephen Leacock, "A Message to the Graduating Class of 1944," *McGill News* 25 (Summer 1944): 7–8; see Legate, *Stephen Leacock*, 248–9.

Index